A Financial **Survival Guide** for **Young Adults** on Their Own

Second Edition

DARA DUGUAY

Director of Citi's Office of Financial Education

This publication is designed to provide accurate and authoritative information in regard to the subject matter covered. It is sold with the understanding that the publisher is not engaged in rendering legal, accounting, or other professional service. If legal advice or other expert assistance is required, the services of a competent professional person should be sought.—*From a Declaration of Principles Jointly Adopted by a Committee of the American Bar Association and a Committee of Publishers and Associations*

Published by Sourcebooks, Inc.
P.O. Box 4410, Naperville, Illinois 60567-4410
(630) 961-3900
FAX: (630) 961-2168
www.sourcebooks.com

Originally published in 2001.

Previous edition cataloged as follows:

Duguay, Dara.
Please send money: a financial survival guide for young adults on their own / Dara Duguay
p. cm.
1. Young adults—Finance, Personal. 2. Finance, Personal. I. Title.

HG179 .D834 2001
332.024—dc21

00-066160

Printed and bound in the United States of America

POD 10 9 8 7 6 5 4 3 2

For Jean Duguay, may his memory never be forgotten; and for Alfonso Guida, who proves that life can go on

Contents

Preface

I learned about money the hard way. I was happily married, enjoying life to its fullest. We had lots of credit card debt and virtually no savings whatsoever. It didn't concern us since we were young. We had our whole lives ahead of us...or so we thought.

When my husband was diagnosed with a terminal illness, it was the beginning of the most trying time of my life. Not only was I distraught beyond belief over losing my husband, but I was also stressed over losing our house and cars. I kept picturing myself without a husband, a place to live, or transportation. My income and his disability payments were not enough to pay all our bills. Since we didn't have any savings in reserve, I was forced to get a second job at the worst possible time.

Somehow, through the grace of God, I made it through that time without having a nervous breakdown. I now believe that denial was a good thing for me at the time. Years later, I was eventually ready to confront the tragedy emotionally. I think back to that time and I regret that I couldn't spend more time with my husband before he died. If we had only been more financially savvy, I am certain I wouldn't have had to work two jobs. If we had saved some of our money and hadn't had so much debt, I wouldn't have had the added stress about our money troubles. Losing a loved one is enough stress for any one person to handle without also having to worry about how you will pay the bills.

I've always heard that everything happens for a reason. I couldn't fathom what reason could have been behind my husband's death at the age of thirty. I always thought it was a waste, a loss without reason. But if I am to make something good happen from something so bad, I hope it is through my passion for educating people about their finances. I firmly believe that through the understanding of money, a lot of unnecessary pain, anger, panic, blame, and other negative emotions can be avoided. Or, on the flip side, a host of positive experiences, wonderful adventures, and years of comfort can emerge. With knowledge comes peace and prosperity.

Dara Duguay

Introduction:
The Only Thing Most Understand about Money Matters Is That It Does

To be conscious that you are ignorant of the facts is a great step to knowledge.

—Benjamin Disraeli

For many people, money concerns are paramount in the list of anxieties that preoccupy their daily thoughts. The primacy that money plays in many peoples' lives is epitomized by the fact that money is the leading issue that couples fight about, with 37 percent of couples putting it on the top of their bickering list, according to a survey by PayPal. Most telling however is the fact that of the marriages that fail, approximately 57 percent cite arguments over money as the major contributing factor, according to a *USA Today* survey.

One of the best reasons to solve your money problems is that doing so can improve your relationships. This does not just refer to a relationship with a significant other, but also to your bonds with parents and friends. Why will your relationships improve? Because when we are stressed about our finances we become preoccupied with our troubles and find it hard to perform on the job or give attention to our loved ones.

A 2006 nationwide Pew Research Center telephone survey revealed that more than one in three Americans said that they have at some point in their lives felt their financial situation was out of control. The stress caused by these worries begins to show up in everyday life: phones remain unanswered to avoid bill collectors and a good night's sleep becomes a rarity as financial worries mount. You may become angry, irritable, or depressed, or feel defeated if you find yourself being managed by your money instead of the other way around. When your money has started to manage you, you give up your control. For example, you may believe in paying your bills on time, but if the due date has arrived and you don't have the money, you will be forced to pay your bills late or borrow money—situations that no one wants to encounter.

Getting control back is crucial to raising your self-esteem and making yourself the master of your own destiny. From very early on I was told that "Money doesn't buy happiness." This is true, but happiness cannot be assured through poverty either. An amazing thing happened to me when I got myself out of debt for the first time in my life. Since I was no longer worried about how I was going to pay my bills, I became happier! The joy that came from knowing that I was not constrained by debt and that I had savings to tide me over in case of an unexpected life event (one that causes a major expense) proved liberating.

Before I learned how to manage my money, I was always panic stricken when an unexpected expense or event came up. Learning how to stay out of debt and maintain a savings cushion has solved that problem. Unexpected expenses and life events now become temporary inconveniences instead of crises. For example, if you lose your job when finances are troubled, most likely you will be forced to take the first job offered and won't have the luxury of waiting for a job that you really want. This is exactly the type of scenario you want to avoid. By providing a secure financial foundation for yourself, you ensure that you have the time and resources to come through any situation with the best possible result.

Why does dealing with money seem so terrifying? The fear of the unknown is a very real fear and few of us have had the good fortune to be fully educated in financial matters. This is a major issue for young people, who are new to the world of personal finance—a world that grows increasingly difficult to handle.

When young adults are left to "figure it out themselves" this trial and error method proves costly and usually results in a pattern of poor financial management. As personal finance becomes more complex and people have access to more credit at a younger age, it becomes apparent that learning how to manage one's money has evolved into a life skill like reading and writing. By gaining an understanding of personal finance, you will have the tools necessary to avoid making costly mistakes.

For most young people, finance is learned at home. A 2007 survey by the Hartford Financial Services Group found that about 70 percent of college students cited their parents as their primary source of information. Unfortunately, parents are not always the best source for this information since many consider money to be a private matter and therefore a taboo topic for conversation or because they lack a proper understanding of finances themselves. This same study found that less than half of the students said their parents made a consistent and conscientious effort to teach them about money. So much of the learning happens through observation, which unaccompanied by explanation, can lead to confusion or misinterpretation.

Another unfortunate fact is that few of us learn about money at school. Before high school graduation, most students have the opportunity to enroll in an elective personal finance course. The most common electives are business or family and consumer science classes. In the end, only about 16 percent of students have had an entire course in money management or personal finance while in high school, according to a 2006 survey by the Jump$tart Coalition for Personal Financial Literacy.

In an effort to increase the number of students graduating with adequate money management skills, many states have introduced legislation in recent years to include personal finance instruction in classes that are required and not just optional. However, as of 2007, only fifteen states have personal finance as part of a class that students must take prior to graduation.

This lack of instruction in personal finance occurs in spite of the fact that most young adults are willing to learn. Several surveys have confirmed this point in addition to pointing out the low level of financial literacy:

- A 2005 survey by Visa of high school students' parents discovered that 76 percent believed that schools should be required to teach money management skills.
- The Hartford study found that less than one-quarter of students said that they felt very well prepared to deal with the financial challenges that awaited them after college graduation.
- A 2006 Key Bank poll found that nearly one-third of college students, when thinking about their freshman year, admitted that they were "not at all" or "not very well prepared" for managing their money on campus.
- A 2006 survey by the Jump$tart Coalition for Personal Financial Literacy showed the average score to be an F on a test of personal finance basics administered to high school seniors.

The good news is that education works! An often-quoted study ("The Long-Term Effects of High School Financial Curriculum Mandates" by Bernheim, Garrett, and Maki) found that students exposed to a financial education mandate maintained a net worth that was about one year's worth of earnings higher than the net worth of students not exposed to such a mandate. In addition, the National Endowment for Financial Education evaluated the curriculum it created for schools, called the High School Financial Planning Program, and discovered that as little as ten hours of classroom instruction can contribute to significant positive knowledge and behavioral changes in how teens handle their money. These findings provide strong evidence that education can reduce money mistakes and contribute to financial well-being.

This book chronicles common money mistakes many young adults make and provides instructions on how these mistakes can be avoided. Also included are real life stories gathered over my many years of working with people experiencing money problems. Their names have been changed in order to protect their identities. While not everyone who was profiled has changed his or her ways, with strength and courage you can break out of old habits and make your life more prosperous than it is now. Even though change is frightening to many, this book can help you gain control over your financial future.

1

The Ostrich Syndrome

Money ranks with love as man's greatest source of joy and with death as his greatest source of anxiety.

Many young adults behave like ostriches when they encounter financial problems, hiding their head in the sand. If they ignore the problem, then it doesn't exist. Sometimes the problem seems so overwhelming or insurmountable that denial becomes the most attractive solution. But avoidance of debt problems leads not only to blemishes on your credit report, but could also snowball into foreclosures, repossessions, and judgments.

In a 2004 Nellie Mae Study of undergraduates and credit card usage, approximately 37 percent said they felt very or extremely anxious about their ability to make their monthly credit card payments. Moreover, some university administrators routinely cite financial mismanagement as a crisis among college students.

Overwhelming debt combined with a lack of knowledge about how to manage it can easily lead to avoidance. Sixteen percent of students (ages sixteen to twenty-two) polled believed that avoiding money problems was mostly a matter of luck, according to ASEC's Youth and Money survey. It is easy to understand why students leave their financial problems to chance. If you feel you don't have any control over the situation, why bother?

A teenager, Kirk, once told me that after he stopped paying his gym club membership fees, he was harassed with bills for a while but then they stopped coming. Kirk was relieved that the problem had gone away. It wasn't until years later that he discovered an unpaid account on his credit report. Kirk was sure it was a mistake since he didn't recognize the company to whom he supposedly owed money. In fact, it was the collection agency that had received his account after the gym club gave up trying to collect from Kirk. His problem hadn't disappeared after all!

Problems ignored usually become larger problems. If a problem is dealt with early enough, many times the situation is easily resolved. But you can be assured that the longer you ignore it, the greater the probability that it will escalate into a confrontation with less favorable solutions. And if you avoid the situation for a long enough period of time, you may lose the privilege to negotiate or compromise at all. You may find that the final decision will be made unilaterally without your input and you will be stuck with the end result whether you like it or not.

This chapter will illustrate the actions and problems faced by young adults who choose to remain in denial of their money problems. The following subjects will be covered:

- Ignoring bills
- Avoiding collectors
- Contacting collectors
- Avoiding repossession and other losses
- Letting others control your finances
- Making only minimum payments
- Avoiding debt through gambling

What I Don't See Can't Hurt Me

We tend to believe that if we ignore unpleasant news, the problem will go away. That's what Beth fooled herself into believing. This strategy only works in the short run, as she soon discovered.

She fell behind on her bills shortly after she decided to live on her own for the first time at the age of twenty-two. Prior to that, her parents had paid her dorm and sorority housing expenses during college. Beth's first job out of college was a low paying entry-level position. She had a hard time finding another job that paid better since she didn't have any experience. Unfortunately for Beth, her company merged with a larger one about six months after she began working there. The most recently hired employees were laid off, including Beth.

After she lost her job, it took five months to find another one. She had fallen behind on her bills, and was trying to "catch up." Every day when the postman arrived, she separated the bills from the other mail. She couldn't bear to open the envelopes. She knew what she'd find—more late notices and demands to pay. Couldn't they just leave her alone? She'd pay them back as soon as she caught up.

Like Beth, when you fall behind on your debt payments, you will soon receive communication from the lender's collection department. When this happens, don't ignore the past-due notices or phone calls. If you do, your account may be turned over to an independent debt collector. Once that happens, the original creditor loses almost all control over what would be an acceptable payment plan to you. Collection agencies are usually more aggressive and less willing to compromise. In addition, since they frequently bring lawsuits against debtors to collect money and are more familiar with the legal system, they are probably more willing to go to court than the original creditor. You have a much better negotiating position with the original creditor. Don't wait until the debt is turned over to a collection agency to discuss your concerns.

Inexperienced, Beth preferred to ignore the collection attempts. Except for one creditor, her landlord, she had no physical contact with the rest of her creditors. They could be ignored, and were.

The strategy worked for a while. Her voice mail was full of messages from collectors, but she learned to not let it bother her. By deleting messages as soon as she realized it was a creditor, she never had to listen to their demands. She got in the habit of never answering her phone and letting it automatically go into voice mail. Her friends were told to call and let it ring once and then call back so Beth would know it wasn't a collector calling.

One day when Beth went to her car, which she normally parked on the street, she couldn't find it. In a panic she called the police to report it stolen. To her amazement, she was told that it had been repossessed. "What?" she exclaimed. "How could they repossess my car without telling me?" The police said she should have been notified.

Beth looked to the large stack of mail that had accumulated on her kitchen table. She took a deep breath and started opening the envelopes. Several of the letters were from her car lender. The last letter told of their intent to repossess her car if she didn't contact them. Without opening the letter, Beth had no way to know that soon her car would no longer be in her possession. And now it wasn't!

If Beth would have opened her mail daily and actually read it, she could have prevented the repossession. Her first step, as soon as she began having trouble making the payments, should have been to contact the creditor. It is advisable to contact the creditor in writing prior to discussing the situation over the phone. The following is a sample letter she could have written:

February 17, 2008

Payus First Corporation
426 Regency Lane
Anytown, CA 90800

Dear Creditor,

Due to a layoff, I am temporarily out of work and as a result, am experiencing financial difficulty. I have analyzed my current situation, and in order to provide for necessary household expenses plus credit payments, I am asking each creditor to accept a reduced payment for the next three months. By then, I anticipate being back to work.

I would appreciate your cooperation in making the payment plan work. In place of the regular payment of $80.00, I request that you accept payments of $30.00 per month during this emergency.

You can be sure that I will resume normal payments as soon as possible. If there are any changes in my situation, I will notify you of them as soon as possible.

Sincerely,

Name
Address
Account number

A formal letter such as this has certain advantages. You will have given yourself a chance to think through your circumstances and plan a budget for paying your bills, you won't get confused about details if the creditor tries verbal intimidation, and you both have a record of your proposal.

Before you write your letters, you should determine your net worth. A net worth sheet will summarize the assets that you have available:

Net Worth Sheet

Assets	Amounts ($)
Cash	
• Currency	________
• Checking Account	________
Savings Account	________
Investments	
• Real Estate	________
• Government Bonds	________
• Corporate Stock	________
• Mutual Funds	________
• Personal Property	________
—Automobiles	________
—Furniture	________
—Clothes	________
—Jewelry	________
—Collectibles	________

Continued

• Retirement Plans	______
—IRA	______
—401(k)	______
—Keogh	______
—403(b)	______
Other Assets	______
Total Assets	______

The liabilities portion of the net worth sheet will summarize your debts:

Liabilities	**Amounts ($)**
Unpaid Debts	
• Bank credit cards	______
• Other charge cards	______
• Personal loans	______
• Mortgage loans	______
• Home equity loan	______
• Automobile loan	______
• Student loan	______
• Other installment loans	______
Total Liabilities	______

Once the assets section and the liabilities section are completed, you can figure out whether your net worth is positive or negative:

Net Worth	Amounts ($)
Total Assets	
Minus Total Liabilities	
Net Worth	

You will also need to make a list of all your creditors. Each creditor will need to be contacted to work out payment arrangements. The secured creditors are the most important and should be contacted first. If you are not sure if a creditor is secured, ask yourself this question: "If I don't pay the bill, can they take the item away from me?" Common secured creditors are those who hold your auto loan and home mortgage.

Name of Creditor Owed	Total Balance Owed	Current Monthly Payment	Monthly Payment Goal
Totals			

From the information gleaned from both the net worth sheet and the creditors list, you now know whom you owe and whether you have any funds available to pay your obligations. You may discover that you do not have any assets that you can sell or borrow against. In this case, you are going to need to negotiate reduced payments with your creditors until your situation improves.

When you finally discuss your situation over the phone with the collector's agent, you should have all of your information handy. You need the letter to remember the payment arrangements you determined you could handle. The net worth sheet lists your assets that may be used to free up some cash. Some of these assets can be liquidated (savings account or stock), sold (real estate or motorcycle), or borrowed against (401(k) plan) in order to get access to money. This cash can be used to pay your bills until you catch up or find employment. Finally, the list of creditors will remind you of everyone you need to contact. By having a list of all your creditors in front of you, you won't be talked into paying any one creditor too much and then be left with no money to pay the others.

An important point to remember before you make your phone call is that a bill collector will almost always be friendlier if you call them *before* they call you. If you avoid the collector by never returning their calls or opening their mail, you are going to make them less willing to work something out when they finally catch up with you. Contacting the collector first lets them know that you are responsible and willing to work towards repaying your debt.

It is also important to realize that you do have protections under the Fair Debt Collection Practices Act (FDCPA). This act covers third party or outside collectors, not the original creditor with collection departments of their own. The FDCPA requires that debt collectors treat you fairly by prohibiting certain methods of debt collection. Collectors may not:

- Use obscene language or profanity
- Harass, oppress, abuse, or use threats against you or your reputation
- Require the debtor to accept collect telephone calls or telegrams
- Advertise the debtor's debts
- Imply they work as an attorney, work for a credit bureau, or Social Security (unless they do)
- Misrepresent how much a debtor owes
- Threaten legal action (which they do not intend to take or it is not legal for them to take)
- Threaten a debtor with arrest or imprisonment
- Tell a debtor their property will be repossessed (unless they plan to do this)
- Tell a debtor their wages will be garnished (unless they plan to do so)
- Contact a debtor at unreasonable hours (it must be between 8 A.M. and 9 P.M. your time)
- Talk to anyone but the debtor about the debt (not the debtor's neighbors, boss, or family)
- Contact you at work if you notify them in writing not to do so

If you feel you have been treated unfairly according to the law, you may report the collectors' agency to your state attorney general's office or the Federal Trade Commission that oversees your region.

Hopefully, you will never have to deal with debt collectors. However, if you do find yourself facing a debt collector, remember to approach them without reacting defensively or with anger. Yelling at the messenger does nothing to help alleviate the situation. In fact, it may serve to make the situation worse by making the collector less cooperative. Although it may be difficult (especially if the tone of the collector is less than friendly), try to stay rational, because in most cases you will be able to negotiate a reasonable settlement.

If Beth had explained her situation, her creditor might have been able to work out a payment plan for her car loan that Beth could have handled. Maybe her loan term could have been extended, thereby lowering the monthly payment, or she could have searched for alternate financing with a lower interest rate. These and other options (discussed in chapter 4) were never given a chance since Beth never even got to step one, opening her mail.

Since Beth was solely responsible for her own finances, when she chose to ignore her situation there was no one there to step in and take control. In the next case, Anne also ignored her finances by turning over control to her husband.

My Husband Handles the Finances

I am constantly amazed at how many people prefer to remain ignorant about their financial situation. They leave it up to their spouse or another manager to make all their money decisions. Unfortunately, this dependence on others can have negative consequences, as in the case of a very unhappy young woman named Anne.

Anne married young and started a family immediately. Her husband Bob seemed to control every aspect of her life. Although her two children were now in school full time, she still remained at home. She told me that she wanted to get a job, but that her husband would not let her. She had no education past high school and no job skills to put on a resume.

Not only did she feel trapped by her perceived inability to get a job, but also by the fact that she wouldn't know how to manage money, even if she had some to manage. Anne, now twenty-five, had no idea what the family financial situation was and had never even balanced a checkbook. In fact, she didn't even know where the checkbook was. Bob gave her money weekly, not unlike the allowance he doled out to the children.

Anne told me she felt more like one of the children than an equal partner in the marriage. This intelligent and competent woman came to believe that her abilities were no greater than those of her young children. She had not been allowed to make adult decisions without consulting her husband first, and in some cases, like the family finances, she knew to not even mention it. Whenever she did, Bob's favorite response was, "Don't worry. I'll take care of you." Anne interpreted this response as, "You can't take care of yourself."

This fear of living independently without her husband to rely on had so paralyzed Anne that she couldn't even entertain the thought. She didn't have the conviction that she was capable on her own so she was powerless to break out of a controlling marriage. She had become a "financial infant," with her husband the financial parent.The following statements are those of a financial infant:

1. My money situation is upsetting, but I feel I won't ever get into any real trouble because there's always someone to rescue me. I can count on my spouse, parents, brother, sister, or friends.
2. I want to be taken care of. It was nice when I was a child because everything was provided. I want it to remain that way.
3. I have a desire to remain dependent. I don't want to become self-reliant.

To many young adults, dependence on their parents is comforting. By not moving out, the financial decisions and worries can be delayed. If there are no financial obligations while living in the parent's house, life is simpler and not as frightening. Why complicate things by adding expenses and budgets to their lives? But there will always be a trade-off for financial dependence. It could be loss of knowledge, freedom, or, in the most psychologically complicated cases, control.

There are some positive steps that Anne could have taken to avoid becoming a financial infant.

First, she could have gained financial knowledge on her own. By reading personal finance books and magazines, or listening to financial reporters, Anne could have acquired the confidence that she was at least educated about financial matters. This confidence could have proven a determining factor if she ever found herself on her own.

Secondly, Anne could have volunteered to assist friends of hers who were put in charge of the family finances. By assisting in this capacity, she could have observed valuable skills like balancing a checkbook, constructing a budget, or making investment decisions.

But I Have Perfect Credit

Young adults often have a mistaken notion of what "perfect credit" means. It is true that by making the required minimum payment on your credit cards and never sending in the payment late, your credit report will not have any negative entries. Making payments on time should be rewarded since it shows that you are reliable. But timely payments are only part of the story.

In addition to timeliness, your debt level is also important to your credit rating. You could have never missed a payment and still be overextended. Since the minimum payments are often only 2–4 percent of the total that you owe (i.e., $20–$40 on a $1,000 balance), you can be heavily in debt and still manage to make all of the small, required monthly payments.

Teri believed she had perfect credit and was proud of her credit history. Her credit report was unblemished; not one late payment appeared. She felt she was a responsible twenty-two-year-old. Even though she only made the minimum payment on her credit cards every month, she still always paid on time. This perfect payment history allowed Teri to qualify for more and more credit and before she knew it, she had nine credit cards with a combined credit limit of $12,000. This amount equaled half of her yearly income as an administrative assistant. Even though all of the credit cards were at their limit, she was still able to make all her minimum payments each month without fail.

Teri often showed off her credit cards to her friends and wanted to impress them with how many she had. She was especially proud of her platinum and gold cards. She convinced herself that only valued customers could qualify for so much credit. Her memories of seeing adults with wallets full of credit cards confirmed the fact that she was finally an adult too.

Teri neglected to make the connection that her available credit line was now equal to her total debt since she had charged all her credit cards up to the limit. Her friend John tried to explain to her the cost of interest, but she didn't quite get it. To make his point, he showed her the last two statements from one of her credit cards. Even though she made a $10 payment, the balance did not go down correspondingly by $10 when she received the next month's bill. In fact, it went down by only $3. The rest went to pay the interest. That, John explained, was the cost of credit.

In fact, if Teri continued to make only the minimum payments of 2.5 percent on that one card's total debt of $2,500 without charging anything else, it would take her a total of fourteen years to pay off the debt at an interest rate of 15 percent. In addition, she would have paid an extra $2,377 in interest charges. The total amount to be repaid would be $4,877!

This big picture scenario was just too depressing to think about. Teri preferred to live in her fantasy world of having perfect credit and never missing a payment. Although she has not yet been forced to confront her debt, she will be forced to eventually do so if she continues to acquire more credit. One day, her minimum payments will surpass her ability to pay and then it may be too late!

The fact is that Teri should never have gotten more than two credit cards in the first place. Credit is a necessity in today's society, but how much is too much? Normally, several credit cards are sufficient. A walletful, as in Teri's case, is excessive. She needed to realize that having lots of credit cards did not necessarily signal that she was rich, but it could signal that she was in debt. Teri made several mistakes:

1. Getting too many credit cards
2. Not paying them off in full each month
3. Paying only the minimum payment in addition to continuing to charge more purchases

All these mistakes compounded with the result that Teri was accumulating more debt than she would soon be able to handle.

Fortunately for Teri, it is not yet too late. She is still able to handle her minimum payments. Her next step should be to get rid of all of her credit cards except for a few with the lowest interest rate. Then she should start paying more than the minimum payment each month. Soon she will actually start reducing her debt. Most importantly, she needs to curb her spending patterns. Cutting down on her spending will eventually make the biggest impact on her debt level.

Gambling with Your Life

Gambling may seem like an easy way to make a quick buck, but rarely are the consequences of not winning the bet considered. Once you fall into debt, you may find yourself gambling more money to try and recover your losses or even engaging in something illegal to pay your losses back. Take, for example, a player from the Arizona State basketball team who pleaded guilty to conspiracy to commit sports bribery. It started when Stevin "Hedake" Smith sunk himself more than $10,000 in debt to a student bookie. To wash the debt, Smith agreed to shave points off several games. Smith then enlisted the help of a teammate.

When more than $1 million in bets were placed on several games in Las Vegas, the FBI became suspicious. The setup was traced to organized crime in Chicago. Smith and his teammate were arrested and convicted of sports bribery.

Sports wagering is not the only type of gambling that young people are engaged in, but the pattern is consistent no matter what type of gambling is chosen. A recent study by the Annenberg Public Policy Center found that monthly card-game gambling among young people was up 20 percent from the year before, and 57 percent of the young men surveyed said they gambled at least once a month.

The popularity of gambling would lead one to believe that this is a highly profitable venture. However, the odds are that you will lose more than you will win. To recover your losses, you continue to gamble and a vicious cycle ensues. It is very difficult to break this cycle, as the case history of Felix reveals.

All of Felix's friends were envious of his success. Only two years out of medical school, it seemed that he had everything while they were still struggling. Felix had a loving wife, his own medical practice, a beautiful home, and a luxury car. On top of it all, he seemed content with his life. Whereas some people are never happy with what they have, Felix seemed perpetually happy.

Even to his family and friends, Felix always maintained his cheerful demeanor. When asked the common greeting, "How are you?" Felix always answered, "Wonderful." Felix's wife Lola developed a sense of assurance about the family's finances. She had no idea what their financial situation was, but she was quite confident that it, too, was under control.

Only Felix knew the real truth. His gambling addiction had gotten out of control years before. The losses had always been covered up first by his student loans and then his expanding medical practice. As long as he continued to grow his practice and make a lucrative living, he had nothing to worry about.

Unfortunately, Felix didn't count on his addiction becoming worse. He started gambling more often and placing larger bets to cover his increasing losses. He worked longer hours at his practice as his worry intensified. Even though Felix was scared to death, he hid his fears from everyone, including his wife.

Most gamblers, like Felix, are ignoring mathematical realities. You are eighty times more likely to die by flesh-eating bacteria than win the Powerball jackpot. On average, if you play $50 every month, you'll lose half of your investment the first month, leaving you with $25. The following month you add $50 to the $25 you put back in, and you again lose half. The pot is now down to $37.50.

Believe it or not, following this cycle for forty years, after pouring $24,000 into the lottery, the typical player will have just $50 left. While the average investor can grow that nest egg to $387,000, the average lottery player will be left only with enough for a nice dinner. This reality is ignored though, because many gamblers truly believe that they will eventually win the big one. Felix continued to believe this fallacy even as his losses continued to mount.

When it became apparent to Felix that he was going to lose his house, his car, and maybe his medical practice through bankruptcy, the thought of his lie being uncovered was more than he could bear. To admit the truth to his family and friends was not a possibility. He had been avoiding the problem until it became so insurmountable that he saw only one possibility. He solved his problem by taking his own life.

Felix felt his situation was hopeless because his debt was so high, but there are many other circumstances where people think their situation is just as impossible to resolve. They believe their financial situation is hopeless because they:

- Are not good with numbers
- Were never taught about money
- Are paid on commission, with no regular salary
- Are unskilled
- Have serious medical problems
- Are divorced and have to pay alimony and/or child support
- Are divorced and don't receive alimony and/or child support
- Are too old/too young

All of these situations present challenges, but no financial situation is ever hopeless. Even a bankruptcy allows for a relatively fresh start. Sitting back and doing nothing because you don't believe a solution exists is guaranteeing that your situation will never improve. Being willing to admit to yourself that there is a problem is the first step. Admitting the problem to others is the next step. Felix never got to the second step.

At first, Felix's death seemed incomprehensible. How

could a man with everything commit suicide? It was only when his financial affairs became known that people began to understand the truth. At Felix's funeral, people said they understood why he chose to stay silent. The pressure to be successful—or perhaps more to the point, not fail—was overwhelmingly echoed in that funeral parlor that day. Perhaps in Felix's death, he may have prevented another, as the room poured out their financial worries and problems to others for the first time.

If Felix's wife had been involved in the family finances, she would have noticed the irregular deposits and withdrawals due to his gambling habit. Then she could have taken steps to confront Felix on these transactions and hopefully uncover his gambling addiction. Once his addiction had come to light, she could have contacted Gamblers Anonymous groups who could have helped Felix, and by doing so saved his life.

It is noble to trust your spouse, but in Felix's wife's case, her blind trust enabled Felix to hide his addiction. Both partners should be actively involved in the family finances. One person might be assigned to do certain tasks, but full disclosure of the family's financial situation should be made known to all. Denying reality only makes the situation worse in the long run.

Words of Wisdom

Denial is only a temporary solution. Eventually you must confront the problem if it is ever to be resolved and go away. Denial of money problems is common if you don't feel in control of the situation. If you take the attitude that there is nothing that can be done, then your sense of futility prohibits you from working out a permanent solution.

People who feel powerless are in fact powerful if they confront the problem. The first step is to face the problem with total honesty and then, and only then, do solutions become apparent. Even if the solution is to lose everything and start over, it doesn't mean that your future must echo the past. By learning from your mistakes, the same mistakes will not be repeated. A clean slate can allow you to create a prosperous future if you have the right guidance.

When you have the urge to ignore the situation, remember the lessons learned in this chapter:

- Open your mail and answer your phone.
- Contact creditors before they contact you.
- Do your research before you agree to a repayment plan.
- Make all agreements in writing.
- You have rights that prohibit certain actions by collectors.
- Try to avoid the minimum payment trap.
- Gambling is not a solution, but a problem.

2

Do You Run Out of Money Before You Run Out of Month?

Just about the time you think you can make both ends meet, somebody moves the ends.

—Pansy Penner

There are only two legitimate ways to improve your financial status—increase your income or decrease your expenses. You usually don't have as much control over the former, especially if you are at your boss's mercy. And it's probably not a good idea to consistently ask for your paycheck in advance! You could choose to work more jobs, but then you will have relinquished control over your free time.

One area we do have more control over is where we spend our money, and spending money is something that young adults love to do. According to Teenage Research Unlimited, teens age twelve to nineteen spent $159 billion in 2005. Because young adults are such a large demographic group and combined have an enormous spending power, they are heavily marketed to by companies eager to capture some of this money. Evidence of this trend can be found in the emergence of a multitude of websites marketing items specifically to young adults. In addition, young adult versions of mainstream magazines, such as *Teen People*, line bookshelves.

Although young adults have more money than ever

nestling in their pockets, there is evidence that they are not spending this money wisely. A 2006 study by the Jump$tart Coalition for Personal Financial Literacy found that almost a quarter of the high school seniors polled classified themselves as seldom or hardly ever saving money. Only 16 percent of the students considered themselves "very thrifty," meaning they save money whenever they can. For many young adults, if there is money to burn, it does not stay in their possession for long.

When it comes to spending money there are, as we know, only three basic needs in life—food, shelter, and clothing. Anything else is a want. A credit counselor once told me a story about his wife, who was about to go shopping. She said, "Honey, I need a new dress for work." Her husband, in the habit of lecturing clients every day on the difference between a want and a need, started to give her the same lecture. She had heard these comments many times before and when he was finished she replied, "All right, I won't buy a new dress, but just remember you have *needs* too!" I asked him how he responded and he said, "I let her buy two dresses!"

There is no right or wrong way to allocate your money. We all have different financial goals that we are striving to achieve. I've met people who want to own a really expensive car and in exchange they are willing to live in a small shabby apartment to do so. I've known others who spend all their money on their house and therefore have no money to buy or do anything else. Some people love to travel, so they scrimp and scrape all year long in order to be able to afford that trip to Tahiti. The important thing is that however you decide to distribute your money, you should not spend more than you make.

This chapter will cover the most important concepts you need to know regarding money management:

- How to live within your means
- How to reduce expenses
- Common excuses to resisting cutting expenses
- Distinguishing between a want and a need
- Creating a budget and tracking where your money goes
- Identifying your spending priorities
- Keeping up with the Joneses
- It's not how much you make
- Establishing goals

Give Things Up? Never!

I remember reading an article about a popular television series. The characters in this show were young adults with jobs that ranged from bartender to lifeguard to aspiring actor. None of them were making great money but they somehow managed to share a large beach house in Malibu Beach, California. The article went on to show that taking into consideration a typical rent payment in this community, in addition to the furniture, clothes, and cars they drove, it would be impossible for the characters to pay for these things on their salaries.

Unfortunately, many viewers believed it was normal to live in this manner. Comparing our lives to those on television, or the lives of our coworkers or friends, can create unrealistic expectations. By first determining the lifestyle that you would like before finding out what lifestyle you can afford, you run the risk that the money you have will not match the vision. John and Sue White took that risk.

The Whites had a gorgeous view of the ocean from their penthouse apartment in Manhattan Beach, California. All it took was $2,500 a month in rent, plus some hefty payments for their leased luxury cars, to appear like they were living the high life. Their friends believed it too, since they could also afford to throw weekly catered dinner parties at their beachfront abode. No one would have suspected that this lifestyle was financed by credit cards!

They had recently graduated from the University of Southern California (USC) and many of their friends came from families with money. They were used to being around people who never looked at the price tag. John and Sue decided that if they wanted to continue to be included by their college friends, they would have to adopt their spending habits. It was all right to be a starving student, but now that they had entered the working world, they were expected to make money. Unfortunately, the money they needed to afford their lifestyle was not reflected in their paychecks.

By the time John and Sue had maxed out their credit cards and had raised their limits as high as they could, they were in way over their heads—$45,000 of debt between the two of them. For a long time they had been able to make the minimum payments, but now they couldn't even afford those amounts. Although they both had well-paying jobs, the magnitude of their debt had finally exceeded their capacity to pay. On the verge of being discovered as frauds by their friends, they became desperate and made an appointment to see a credit counselor.

Their reality was undeniable on paper. They were $400 short each month in what they needed to pay their bills. The counselor zeroed in on an expense that consumed the largest part of their earnings, their rent. Referencing the national average, financial experts advise that rent payments shouldn't exceed 25 percent of monthly net income.

That translates for a gross annual income of $25,000 (net income $21,250) into a rent payment of no more than $442 a month. According to this formula, John and Sue would have needed a combined net income of $120,000 in order to afford their $2,500 a month rent payment. Unfortunately, their combined income was not even close.

John and Sue's payment was dangerously high. It consumed 60 percent of their combined net income! The credit counselor suggested that if they moved inland, they could lower their rent and eliminate their financial problems. Sue responded to this suggestion by saying, "But we love to hear the ocean when we wake up in the morning." The counselor replied, "Tape it."

Being willing to settle for a taped version of the real thing seemed like a drastic solution to John and Sue White. But if you find that your expenses exceed your income, you need to start making some hard choices. What are you prepared to give up? You first need to know where your money is going before you can make that decision. Creating a budget is the best way to solve this problem.

Despite what you may have heard, a budget is a wonderful thing. Instead of being something that restricts how you live, a budget will empower you and allow you to have control over your life. A budget is just a mathematical confirmation of your financial situation. Once you know the bottom line of your finances, a plan can then be developed to increase the amount of money available to you.

Doing a budget for the first time can be confusing without guidance. If you follow these steps it will simplify the process:

1. Figure out how much you regularly contribute to any investments and fill in the blanks in the "savings" section. Your emergency fund should have as its target no less than three months of your total expenses.
2. Fill in the expenses that are regular and do not fluctuate each month, like rent, car payment, or student loans. Then continue to step #3.

Budget Form

Expenses	Monthly Amount
Savings	**$**
Emergency fund	
Investments	
Retirement fund	
Shelter	
Rent or mortgage payment	
Property tax	
Insurance	
Gas and electric	
Water, sewer, and garbage	
Association dues, space rent	
Gardening, pool care, repairs	
Food	
Groceries	
Meals out	
School lunches	
Transportation	
Car payment	
Gas and oil	
Insurance, license	
Auto repairs	
Parking	
Public transportation	
Health	
Life and health insurance	
Doctor and dentist	
Prescriptions and glasses	
Clothing	
Clothes	
Work clothes and uniforms	

Continued

Expenses	**Monthly Amount**
Laundry and dry cleaning	
Other (special events)	
Household	
Telephone, mobile phone	
Cable/Satellite TV	
Computer/internet fees	
Appliance repairs/replacement	
Cleaning supplies/maid service	
Personal Expenses	
Beauty care	
Recreation/entertainment	
Pets	
Gifts, charity	
Hobbies, lessons	
Miscellaneous	
Newspapers, magazines	
Church tithes	
Cigarettes and alcohol	
Vacation	
Christmas	
Childcare, counseling	
School tuition	
All credit payments	
Total monthly expenses (B)	
Total net monthly income (A)	
Difference: (A–B)	

3. Figure out the monthly cost for your periodic expenses. These expenses occur on a schedule other than monthly, such as every quarter, every other month, or once a year. These include car registration, school tuition, and insurance.

EXPENSE	YEARLY COST	MONTHLY COST
Car tax/registration fee	$	÷12=
Car insurance	$	÷12=
Car repair	$	÷12=
Christmas	$	÷12=
School expenses	$	÷12=
	$	÷12=
	$	÷12=
	$	÷12=
	$	÷12=
	$	÷12=
	$	÷12=
	$	÷12=
	$	÷12=
TOTAL	$	÷12=

The total is the amount to set aside each month in a separate account. If you do this every month, when your periodic expenses come up, you will have the money to pay for them. Go back and add the monthly amounts you have determined into the corresponding lines in your budget.

4. Figure out the monthly amount for those expenses that fluctuate.

Unfortunately, we don't usually receive any bills for expenses like "food" or "entertainment." It is difficult to know exactly how much you spend on these fluctuating items if you have never tracked your expenses. It's a waste of time doing a budget if you just guess. Guessing invariably results in figures that are far removed from reality and are usually on the lower side.

To track your expenses, you need to keep a daily tally of how much you spend in the different categories. One of the easiest ways to do so is to carry around a small notebook and write down the amount you spend on every single item. Include everything from coffee and soda to postage stamps and parking meters. Do this for two or three weeks (a month is better) to track where your cash has gone.

At the end of your tracking period, you can add the totals to your tracking form. You can then replace any estimates in your budget with accurate figures. Remember that it's the little things that add up. The first time I tracked my expenses, I discovered that I spent $100 that month on coffee. I had no idea that my morning cappuccino cost so much! After this discovery, I drank the office coffee and treated myself once a week to a cappuccino. If you can save $20 a week, that's $1,040 in one year!

Tracking Form

Item	Cost
Example: Lunch	$4.96

5. Go back to your budget form, total all expenses, and enter under "B."
6. Total your net (the amount you deposit) income and enter under "A."
7. Figure out the difference between "A" and "B" (you want "A" to be greater than "B").

Once John and Sue had completed their budget ("B" was greater than "A") they could begin the elimination process. This is not easy. No one likes to give things up. It is easy to go from economy to extravagance; it is hard to go from extravagance to economy. Go back to the wants vs. needs question, Do you really *need* this expense or is it more of a *want*? Giving things up also allows you to stop the endless worry about how you will pay your bills. Peace of mind is worth more than expensive dinners out.

Often, people like John and Sue get the homes and cars of their dreams first and then they try to figure out how they can afford them. If they had worked out a budget first, they would have realized that their income couldn't sustain both an expensive apartment and expensive cars at the same time. Then a decision could have been made between the cars and the apartment.

We all have different priorities in life. Take this quiz to see what your priorities are:

Read each pair of words. If you had $50.00, circle the item or activity you would prefer to spend your money on.

Savings OR Personal appearance

Social activities OR Savings

Clothes OR Social activities

Hobbies OR Clothes

Sports OR Eating out	Personal appearance OR Sports
Eating out OR Savings	Church/charity OR Eating out
Paying a debt OR Clothes	Savings OR Paying a debt
Social activities OR Church/charity	Clothes OR Social activities
Hobbies OR Paying a debt	Sports OR Hobbies
Personal appearance OR Sports	Eating out OR Personal appearance
Church/charity OR Hobbies	Paying a debt OR Church/charity

Count the number of times you circled each item or activity.

______Savings

______Eating out

______Hobbies

______Clothes

______Paying a debt_

______Personal appearance

______Sports

______Social activities

______Church/charity

List your item/activities in order from your highest number to your lowest number. (This will give you an idea of where you are more likely to spend your money).

1. ______________________________

2. ______________________________

3. ______________________________

4. ______________________________

5. ______________________________

6. ______________________________

7. ______________________________

8. ______________________________

9. ______________________________

*Source: National Endowment for Financial Education

What did you find your priorities to be? Were you surprised? Do you want to make any changes in the final order? Maybe you would like to spend less on eating out and more on savings, or you would like to increase the amount of money you give to your place of worship and cut down on social activities. Maybe you are content with your priorities.

When John and Sue completed this quiz, they discovered that personal appearance and clothes were their high priorities. They felt they needed to do some soul searching to figure

out why their priorities caused such a disaster. Did they feel pressured to live well by being around their wealthy friends? Did their impoverished childhood compel them to live a lifestyle they couldn't afford? The answer to this question is probably the most important factor in their successfully learning to live within their means.

What! Me Change Diapers?

As people make more money, they tend to spend more. Just when you think you have everything, something better or faster is developed. Your first used car that once thrilled you (even though it had no air conditioning and the radio didn't work) becomes replaceable once you can afford a better model. Your first furniture, a combination of garage sale purchases and hand-me-downs from your relatives, now becomes your garage sale items as you upgrade by shopping at a real furniture store. That cell phone that used to have the newest features now seems obsolete compared to the most recent model.

It is much easier to increase one's lifestyle than to decrease it. As soon as you become accustomed to a certain higher standard of living, it is very difficult to downscale. For many people, downscaling represents not only giving things up but also a sense of failure when the lifestyle that was attained cannot be maintained. This was true in the case of Tom and Anita March, who built their lifestyle up to a level they could afford when their income was high, but found themselves facing the dilemma of trying to maintain the same lifestyle when their income decreased.

When things were going well, Tom and Anita hired a nanny. They owned a large home in a wealthy neighborhood. Tom was a commercial real estate broker and Anita owned an art studio in a trendy beach community. The Marches were a very social couple; they entertained regularly at their home.

When the economy was booming, Tom made lots of money and was able to accumulate a small fortune. Unfortunately, the boom days didn't last forever, and Tom hadn't sold a property in over a year. At first they weren't worried since their nest egg was quite sizable and they were certain that he would sell a property before long. Even though their nest egg was large, so too were their monthly expenses. Before long their nest egg was down to $7,500. Considering the fact that their monthly personal and business expenses totaled $10,000, this was not a lot of money!

Anita decided she had to do something proactive, so she made an appointment for them to see a credit counselor. Their counselor started with recommendations of which expenses could be eliminated or reduced. Her suggestion was to close down Anita's art gallery, which was losing money each month. That would free up Anita to take care of the children and therefore, they wouldn't need the live-in nanny. This would result in savings in food costs, salary, and car payment and insurance for the nanny's leased car.

Well Anita wouldn't hear of it! She absolutely refused to change diapers and didn't know how to cook. Besides, she loved her art gallery regardless of the fact that it was losing money. Everyone in the neighborhood had a live-in nanny, even if the wife stayed home full-time. What would the neighbors whisper if they no longer had a nanny? They would be humiliated. No, these suggestions were totally unacceptable.

Many people, when asked to give things up, tend to resist and come up with all kinds of reasons that start with "yes, but":

- I'd give up my mobile phone, but what if my car breaks down?
- I'd give up my health club membership, but then I'll get fat.

- I'd give up my maid service, but I don't have time to clean.
- I'd give up smoking, but then I'll gain weight.
- I'd give up manicures, but I need to look professional for my job.
- I'd give up the nanny, but what would the neighbors think?

These excuses and a million more can justify almost any expense remaining intact.

At the end of the session the counselor looked at the couple and said, "If you leave here today and do not change anything in your lifestyle, you will be broke in three weeks." This shocking realization silenced Anita and Tom. The counselor was convinced she would never hear from them again since they were so steadfast in their beliefs. She was surprised when they called her about a month later.

After they were forced to confront the reality of their situation, they started to make some very difficult adjustments. Anita closed down her gallery temporarily and sub-leased it to another business, the nanny was referred to one of their neighbors, and Anita actually enjoyed playing mom! Their neighbors were envious that Anita was raising her kids without needing any help. Tom even had a property in escrow, and for the first time in a year they saw their financial situation improving.

Tom and Anita were stuck in the "keeping up with the Joneses" trap. All their neighbors seemed to have a nanny, drive expensive cars, own beautiful homes, and send their children to private schools. It takes courage to break out of this mold.

Tom and Anita made the discovery that the downsizing of their lifestyle didn't result in any lost friendships. All of their fears were never realized as their friendships survived their lifestyle changes. In fact, their friendships became stronger as their friends rallied to give them emotional support through this transitional period in their lives.

Realizing that nothing in life is a certainty is a great philosophy to maintain when confronted with income and expense fluctuations. Your reality now is the reality for the moment. This reality may change as events in your life change. How you respond to this change is your biggest challenge.

Shop 'Til You Drop

At the beginning of this chapter, I said there were only two ways to improve your financial situation—increase your income or decrease your expenses. For the greatest improvement, do both. The following story showed me that for some people there is a third way.

A young woman named Veronique asked me for advice as to how she could make her financial situation better. She had graduated from Florida State University the previous year and had moved to Miami. She was now employed as an assistant to the director of sales for a large hotel. This position required working long hours and weekends, but unfortunately she never received overtime pay because she was paid straight salary. She once calculated what she made per hour and it was shockingly close to minimum wage ($5.85 in summer 2007) after considering her average work week was sixty to seventy hours.

It is important to understand how much you actually earn after Federal taxes.

Hourly	Annual Gross	Taxes	Annual Net	Monthly Net	Bi-weekly
$5.85	$12,168	$1,825	$10,343	$862	$398
$6.55	$13,624	$2,043	$11,581	$965	$445
$7.25	$15,080	$2,262	$12,818	$1068	$493
$7.69	$16,000	$2,400	$13,600	$1,133	$523
$8.17	$17,000	$2,550	$14,450	$1,204	$555
$8.65	$18,000	$2,700	$15,300	$1,275	$588
$9.13	$19,000	$2,850	$16,150	$1,345	$621
$9.62	$20,000	$3,000	$17,000	$1,416	$653
$10.10	$21,000	$3,150	$17,850	$1,487	$686
$10.58	$22,000	$3,300	$18,700	$1,558	$719
$11.06	$23,000	$3,450	$19,550	$1,629	$751
$11.54	$24,000	$3,600	$20,400	$1,700	$784
$12.02	$25,000	$3,750	$21,250	$1,770	$817
$12.50	$26,000	$7,280	$18,720	$1,560	$780
$12.98	$27,000	$7,560	$19,440	$1,620	$810
$13.46	$28,000	$7,840	$20,160	$1,680	$840
$13.94	$29,000	$8,120	$20,880	$1,740	$870
$14.42	$30,000	$8,400	$21,600	$1,800	$900

*Based on 15 percent tax rate for incomes from $7,500 to $30,650. Above that amount, the next tax rate of 25 percent is applicable.
**In 2007, the minimum wage increased $2.10 from $5.15.
This increase was phased in through a three stage process: $5.85 in the summer of 2007; $6.55 in the summer of 2008; and $7.25 in the summer of 2009.

If you calculate your lifestyle based on your gross salary without taking into consideration the actual amount you'll receive from your paycheck after taxes (both Federal and State) and other deductions (401k, medical), you'll be "grossly" overstating the income you have available to pay bills and save.

The first thing I had Veronique do was figure out her financial situation. After she filled in as many blanks in her budget form as she could, I had her keep a record of her expenses for a month. In Veronique's case, this was a very important exercise since she had no clue how much she spent for certain categories like food or entertainment.

Veronique is not alone; most people don't know where their money goes. If you've ever left your home in the morning with $20 and by the end of the day it is gone and you have absolutely no idea where it went, you know what I mean. In fact, *USA Weekend* found that 19 percent of teens had no money in their wallet at the moment that their survey was conducted.

After Veronique completed her budget as accurately as possible without guessing, we sat down to analyze her options. Even though her income was not very high, Veronique was still making a decent income considering she had no children or husband to support. But when I saw her expenses, I understood why she was struggling financially. She took advantage of every possible service that others do for you. Veronique had someone wash her car and her dog; clean her house; give her a manicure, a pedicure, a facial, and a massage; do her laundry; give her personal training at the gym; mow her yard; and so on.

The obvious solution for Veronique was to do these things herself and eliminate the expenses from her budget. That wasn't possible. Veronique said nothing could or would be eliminated! All kinds of excuses abounded. She couldn't wash her car herself because she didn't have the time. Veronique needed weekly massages because her job was so stressful. The facials and personal trainer were essential, and so on. The normal solutions, which include increasing income and/or decreasing expenses, weren't an option for Veronique.

I finally gave up and asked her what she planned to do to make her financial situation better. Veronique replied with a very serious expression, "I'm going to go to bars in West Palm Beach and find a rich man to marry me." I thought she was kidding, but I saw Veronique a year later at a bar in West Palm Beach flirting with a man. I couldn't help but wonder if she was still looking.

Veronique had closed herself to all solutions to her financial problems except for the "shining knight" scenario. Unfortunately, this solution has a low success rate. She may find her shining knight, but is his money the only shining thing about him? Veronique could end up in a loveless relationship just to pay her bills.

If Veronique had been willing to try to cut back on some of her expenses, she might actually have solved her dilemma herself. Not having to rely on a man for his money could open up many more possibilities in her choice of a mate.

While Waiting to Win the Lottery

Being unwilling to try and increase the income available is just as self-defeating as being averse to making cuts in expenses. Increasing your income can sometimes be the solution to a budget imbalance, especially if you have already made as many reductions in your expenses as possible.

A young nineteen-year-old single mother named Nora came in for credit counseling. She had charged her credit cards to the max and, combined with her other expenses, was having a hard time making all her payments. Nora wasn't trying to collect child support, which would have helped her situation. She figured that it was a waste of time since the father wasn't employed; he was a student. He had graduated and went on to college like she had planned to do prior to becoming pregnant. Because of her child, she had dropped out of high school and was living on welfare.

The counselor discussed with Nora the various options she had to increase her income. She could look into free childcare programs, which would enable her to work. Another option was to continue her schooling at night and get her high school equivalency diploma. With a diploma, Nora could get a better job. Finally, a case could be started with the District Attorney's office to try and collect the child support owed her.

For one reason or another, Nora turned down every option. In exasperation, the counselor finally asked how she intended to make her financial situation better. Nora told her about an inheritance that she would collect after her grandmother died. This inheritance would solve all her financial worries. The counselor asked about her grandmother's health. Nora replied, "Great." The counselor then asked how old her grandmother was? She replied, "Sixty-three." The counselor thought to herself, "Either Nora's going to be waiting a long time or she's planning something I don't want to know about!"

Like Veronique, Nora was also looking for someone else to save her. In her case, it was her grandmother. Considering her grandmother's health and age, it was not likely that Nora would be receiving any inheritance soon. A better solution would have been for Nora to attempt to collect child support. This income could have significantly improved her situation. Many women don't try to collect support that is due to them. Consequently, their financial situation suffers as they try and support a child on their own. If they are young and haven't finished school, the financial demands are almost impossible to meet.

The Boss and the Mechanic

The question of what you do for a living usually surfaces within the first few minutes of meeting someone new. When I told people I worked for Consumer Credit Counseling Service, I was always amazed that they then proceeded to share with me the most intimate details of their financial lives. In fact, it was rare when I met someone who didn't have a problem. I started to think everyone had financial difficulties—even those who were wealthy. As long as you spend more than you make, everyone is a candidate. As I recount the story of Phil and Jose, keep in mind their salaries in relation to their financial situation.

One day when I dropped my car off for its maintenance checkup, the dealership gave me a ride to the convention center where I was scheduled to speak at a conference. On the way to the convention center I was driven by Phil, the owner of the dealership. On the way back, I was picked up by Jose, one of the dealership's mechanics. The two men were approximately the same age, but with very different salary levels.

I found out that the owner had an expensive home with a large mortgage. Phil also had a second mortgage, used to help pay his credit cards bills. He now owed almost $80,000. Since Phil was the owner, he was not being harassed by the dealership's collection department for the missed payments on his automobile lease.

At home, Phil's two teenage sons continually asked him for money. They didn't have part-time jobs and expected their father to pay for their college education. Phil didn't know how he was going to be able to pay their tuition since his savings had been depleted by his debt obligations.

The mechanic, on the other hand, earned only one-third of what the owner did. Jose had a modest house with no mortgage. He had paid it off ten years early by making an extra payment each year. Jose had no credit card debt, following the principle that he wouldn't buy something if he didn't have the money for it. Even his new car was paid for in cash. Jose also had two teenage sons, but his sons had part-time jobs and were saving to help pay for their college education. Jose agreed to pay half their tuition if they paid the remainder. He was able to help out since he had been systematically saving 10 percent of his net income for the past twenty years. Jose now had a substantial amount accumulated in the bank.

Who was in a better position financially? Judging only by their incomes, you would suspect that Phil, the owner, would be better off. Actually, Jose, the mechanic, had a much greater net worth position! Even though Jose's salary was much lower, he followed sound money management principles that over time demonstrated their effectiveness. He was able to set goals and develop a plan to achieve them.

Knowing your goals will keep you motivated to save and control your spending.

Goals	**Steps I Need to Take to Reach My Goal**
____________________	1.____________________
	2.____________________
	3.____________________
____________________	1.____________________
	2.____________________
	3.____________________

Total cost of goal ÷12 = Dollar amount I need to save each month.

$____________________ ÷12 = $____________________

$____________________ ÷12 = $____________________

$____________________ ÷12 = $____________________

TOTAL $______________ ÷12 = $______________

If this monthly amount is consistently put away in savings, by the end of a year you will have the money your goal

requires. If this monthly amount is too high for your budget, you may have to lengthen the time period needed to save the total amount. Almost any goal is possible if you are willing to adjust the monthly amount saved or the time period required to purchase your goal.

The moral of the story of Phil and Jose is that your income doesn't predetermine your financial situation. It doesn't matter how much you make if you spend more than you earn. Jose already mastered this concept, which allowed him to have a happy ending. If Phil had applied this philosophy, he could have improved his situation.

Phil could have taught his sons good money management habits by requiring them to contribute some of their own earnings to their college education. Phil's debt level was way too high, illustrated by the fact that he had to get a second mortgage just to help pay his credit card debt. Ironically, Phil's high income actually contributed to his sense of security, which allowed him to keep getting deeper and deeper in debt. He knew he would receive special treatment with his auto loan and that he could qualify to borrow large sums of money because of his high income. Unfortunately, for every income level there are limits. Eventually, Phil reached his.

Words of Wisdom

Getting in control of your finances and managing your money is fairly simple if you follow the steps detailed in this chapter:

- Create a budget.
- Track where your money goes.
- Determine goals and a plan to achieve them.
- Realize your spending priorities.
- Be willing to give things up.
- Don't spend more than you make.

3

Credit: It's Not Your Money

Most people would have fatter wallets
if they removed all the credit cards.
—*Ann Landers*

A father once told me a story about when he gave his daughter her first credit card as she left for college. He said, "Honey, use this only if it is an emergency." She then asked what he considered an emergency. He replied, "If you can eat it, drink it, wear it, or listen to it, it's not an emergency!"

In 2006, credit card issuers mailed out nearly 8 billion U.S. solicitations, according to CardWatch. That's a 30 percent increase over the prior year. Unfortunately, these solicitations are not all thrown in the garbage or the average American wouldn't have nine credit card accounts, as reported by MyFICO. This accumulation starts young as evidenced by the fact that 50 percent of the high school seniors surveyed by the Jump$tart Coalition in 2006 already had a credit card in their name.

How many credit cards do we need? At the most, two major credit cards. Major credit cards are now accepted almost everywhere and it's no longer necessary to have a gas card to pay for gas or a retail card to buy from a department store. By limiting the number of credit cards that you have, you'll also limit the amount that you ultimately charge. The more you have, the more you tend to use. It just doesn't seem like you owe a lot if you charge $10 on one card and $25 on another, and so on. Most people do not know the total that they owe on all their debt obligations combined; they are too scared to add it up.

When people find they have accumulated more debt than they can handle, many times they shift the blame to the credit card company. If only they had not sent me the application in the mail or made me sign up for the card at their booth at the student union. Instead of viewing credit as being the cause of your financial problems, you must realize that credit is not inherently evil. It is a wonderful tool to help you get things that are expensive or that you need right away. Credit used wisely is powerful; credit used in ignorance is very dangerous.

In this chapter, credit will be demystified and simple guidelines to its wise use will be provided. You will learn:

- What APR is and the reason to compare interest rates
- The cost of credit (time and money)
- When to buy on credit
- If it is ever smart to pay one debt with another
- How to figure out your safe debt level
- How to get out of debt
- What a debt consolidation loan is
- If you should ever rent-to-own
- The power of a credit report
- How to legitimately turn a credit rating from bad to good

Since a large percentage of bankruptcies are linked to excessive debt, this chapter will lay the foundation to understanding how to avoid becoming another statistic. Once you master how to use credit wisely, it can become a powerful financial tool to help you get the things you both want and need.

Appearances Can Be Deceiving

The first thing to understand about credit is that it is not your money. If you look at your credit cards as an extension of your salary, you may be setting yourself up for more debt than you can handle. Credit allows you to purchase things that you cannot afford and consequently live beyond your means. As long as the merchants accept your credit cards, you can keep buying. But if the merchant required you to pay cash, would you still have made your purchases?

To observe Chuck you would assume he was wealthy. He definitely looked and acted the part. Chuck drove a luxury car, had a Beverly Hills address, always wore designer suits, ate out frequently at expensive restaurants, and regularly went on weekend excursions. But the reality was a well-kept secret.

Chuck grew up in a very poor family. There was never enough food, clothes, or money for routine bills. There was never money for traveling, entertainment, or nonessential purchases. Chuck's goal was to escape a life of deprivation.

By the age of twenty-four, he had spent two years working hard as an investment broker and saved virtually all of his money. He now had enough money to leave his neighborhood. He moved to the one place that was synonymous with wealth, Beverly Hills. Chuck was able to rent a small apartment with a fancy address. But he soon wanted more. He wanted the cars his neighbors drove, the clothes they wore, and the vacations they went on. Chuck's answer arrived one day in the form of a credit card application in the mail.

With this newfound source of money, he was able to buy the things he coveted. Chuck used this new tool in earnest. It was the answer to his desires and only required a small payment each month. Over time, this small payment became larger, and Chuck had trouble making even the minimum payment. Eventually, he had reached the limit on all of his credit cards and couldn't qualify for any more, although he kept trying.

With fifteen credit cards and $50,000 in credit card debt, the precariousness of Chuck's lavish lifestyle came crashing down on him. For Chuck, this reality took four years to become evident—a short time compared to how long it would take him to get out of the debt that he had accumulated! You can run into debt, but you have to crawl out.

How long will it take to pay off balances on a credit card—and how much interest will be paid—if the cardholder pays only the minimum payment each month? The following information assumes a required minimum monthly payment of 2.5 percent at an annual percentage rate (APR) of 15 percent:

Amount Owed	Time Required	Interest Paid	True Cost
$500	2.4 years	$100	$600
$1,000	6.3 years	$552	$1,552
$2,500	13.9 years	$2,337	$4,877

This table shows what would happen if you paid more than the minimum payment on a $2,500 balance. It is obvious that as the amount of the monthly payment increases, you would significantly decrease the total interest paid and you would appreciably reduce the time required to pay off the balance.

Amount Owed	Monthly Payment	Time Required	Interest Paid	True Costs
$2,500	$55 (minimum)	13.9 years	$2,377	$4,877
$2,500	$80	5.1 years	$944	$3,444
$2,500	$105	3.1 years	$584	$3,084
$2,500	$130	2.3 years	$476	$2,976
$2,500	$155	1.8 years	$394	$2,894
$2,500	$180	1.4 years	$323	$2,823
$2,500	$205	1.2 years	$242	$2,742

However, if the amount of the initial debt were invested for the same amount of time earning 10 percent per year, the results would be as follows:

Amount Invested	Time Invested	Balance
$500	2.4 years	$624
$1,000	6.3 years	$1,814
$2,500	13.9 years	$9,270

This is a telling example of how interest and money can work for us, instead of against us. The magic of compound interest is magnified as the amount to be invested increases.

If Chuck had learned the value of waiting until he could make the purchase with his own money, maybe he wouldn't have gotten so deeply in debt. There is a West African saying, "Borrowing is the first-born of poverty."

It is a good idea to get into the habit of asking yourself ten questions every time you consider purchasing something on credit:

1. Do I really need this item right now or can I wait?
2. Can I qualify for credit?
3. What is the interest rate (APR)?
4. Are there additional fees?
5. How much is the monthly payment and when is it due?
6. Can I afford to pay the monthly payments?
7. What will happen if I don't make the payments on time?
8. What will be the extra cost of using credit?
9. What will I have to give up to pay for it?
10. All things considered, is using credit worth it?

Your answer to these questions will help you determine whether your decision to use credit is a wise one. Unfortunately, the thought of purchasing something for cash and never receiving a bill was a foreign concept to Chuck. He was still paying on items that he no longer owned, like a financed couch that his dog destroyed, a stereo that no longer worked, and clothing that stayed in his closet since it was out of style. The knowledge that the things you own can be yours and not the bank's is a valuable lesson that Chuck will hopefully learn someday.

Robbing Peter to Pay Paul

A common tactic that many people use when they cannot pay their debts with their own income is to pay these bills with other forms of credit. While this may temporarily keep your money troubles at bay, ultimately, it is just a form of procrastination. Paying a credit card bill with another credit card just delays the inevitable and makes the situation worse. If you already have too much debt, why would you choose a solution that involves getting yourself even more in debt? Unfortunately, Perla chose this way out.

Perla was an expert juggler of debt. She had developed this skill to a fine art throughout college. Now that she was in the working world, she was juggling more and more bills at the same time. Perla didn't expect things to be like this forever. Since she was twenty-two years old, she had just started working full time. Her salary was low, but she knew that in time, when she got raises and work experience, things would be different. In the meantime, each month her juggling skills assured her that all of her bills would be paid.

Of course, it helped that many companies now accept credit cards as a form of payment. As long as she had available credit on her cards, she didn't have to worry about her bills being paid. In the past, she got into the habit of running to the offices to pay her bills on the day they were due. But now, her electricity and phone would never be cut off again. She was elated when the IRS started to accept credit cards to pay her tax obligations.

Many of her credit cards made payment easier by sending her blank checks in the mail. These checks were tied to her account and made payment for other bills very easy. From time to time, Perla was forced to go to her bank and get a cash advance from her credit card to get accessible money.

Perla never analyzed her credit card statements to realize that cash advances were normally assessed at a higher rate of interest than straight purchases. In fact, she barely looked at anything other than the minimum payment that was due. Opening her statements became painful as the balances grew larger and larger along with the size of the stack of bills. In fact, on the day that she paid bills, Perla usually became very depressed. It didn't help that she used shopping as a way to combat depression. This ultimately just ended up fueling her depression even more by increasing her debt.

Eventually a day came when Perla had maxed out her credit cards and couldn't obtain any more, even though she had filled out numerous credit card applications. They all came back unapproved after the credit companies ran a credit check. When Perla requested a free copy of her credit report to find out why she had been turned down, she was horrified to discover the true extent of her debt. With such a high debt-to-income ratio, she now understood why she no longer was a good candidate.

If you don't know how much debt you can handle, it is easy to get in over your head. Experts say the secret to a healthy home balance sheet is to keep your monthly consumer debt payments down to around 10 to 15 percent of your total net income. The absolute maximum is 20 to 25 percent. This includes payments on credit cards, school, car, and other personal loans—but not first mortgages.

List Debts (don't include mortgage payments)	**Average Monthly Payments**
______________________	$______________
______________________	$______________
______________________	$______________
______________________	$______________
______________________	$______________
______________________	$______________
______________________	$______________
______________________	$______________
______________________	$______________
1. Total your monthly debt payments	$______________
2. Enter your monthly net income	$______________
3. To calculate your debt percentage, divide #1 by #2	______________%

If the debt percentage is:

Under 10 to 15 percent	Relax—Your debt to income percentage is well within acceptable guidelines.
15 to 20 percent	Be cautious—You may want to reduce your current debt loan. Do not take on new debt.
Over 20 percent	Danger—You are heavily in debt and should not under any circumstances take on additional debt!

Without the option of using her credit cards as a crutch, Perla panicked. For the first time, she was forced to confront the fact that her income was all the money she had available

to pay her bills. No longer able to use credit as an extra source of income, she decided to get a part-time job in the evening to replace the money that was no longer available from lines of credit.

The extra hours she now worked each week were exhausting on top of her full-time job. She felt trapped and unable to escape this world of constant work. After about a year of working two jobs, Perla had succeeded in paying down her credit cards enough so that one job could now handle the payments. Perla learned the hard lesson that credit is not something to be handled recklessly.

Perla could have avoided her world of constant work. First, she needed to get into the habit of paying her bills with her own money and not with the false income obtained from her credit cards. Having to rely on her credit cards to pay the basic necessities in life (groceries, gas for her car, utilities, and tax obligations) should have been a warning sign that she was overextended. An even bigger warning sign became evident when Perla had to resort to cash advances from other credit cards in order to pay off her original credit card debt.

To get out of the vicious cycle that continual borrowing had gotten her into, Perla should have constructed a budget as a first step. A budget will show you how much your expenses exceed your income. This information will give you a strategy to start living within your means. You can then follow these steps to get out of debt:

1. Immediately stop charging anything additional on credit cards.
2. Find out how much is owed.
3. Pay more than the minimum payment.
4. Send in payments as soon as the bill is received (every extra day you carry a balance, your interest charges may accumulate).

5. When one card is paid off, make the same payments on another (resist seeing the extra money as spending money).
6. Refuse the credit card issuer's offer of a minimum payment of zero or to skip a payment for a month.
7. Consolidate cards (make sure to cut up the cards whose balances are now zero).
8. Refinance high-rate credit cards (shop around for the best interest rate).
9. Consider using savings to pay off high-rate credit card balances (only if you already had a three- to six-month emergency savings fund).

Some people, who lack the discipline, need to actually cut up their credit cards so they aren't tempted to continue to use them. A second step is to close the accounts after the cards have been destroyed. Just because the physical card doesn't exist does not mean the account can no longer be used. For example, you can still access your credit card by giving the number over the phone or on the Internet to purchase an item. By closing the accounts, you can no longer use the account regardless of whether the card exists or not.

One Easy Payment

Perla kept getting more and more credit cards to pay her existing accounts. Another option that works along the same principle is to get one large loan and use this money to pay off the other smaller debts. This loan works in theory to "consolidate" debts. The smaller debts are now lumped into one payment instead of spread out among numerous smaller accounts. For Stacey, this approach was viewed as a huge time saver each month when she paid her bills.

Stacey allotted at least two hours monthly to paying her

twenty-five credit card bills plus her other living expenses. By the time she finished, Stacey had writer's cramp from filling out and signing so many checks in addition to a general feeling of nausea over giving away almost her entire paycheck.

When she had bought her first townhouse two years ago, she knew she could afford the mortgage, but never considered the other expenses that a homeowner encounters. She was so excited that, at the age of twenty-four, she actually qualified for such a purchase that she rushed into it before the bank changed its mind. So when she didn't have the cash and needed furniture, she charged it. Stacey charged her property taxes and the repairs on a leaky roof. Before Stacey realized it, she had accumulated twenty-five credit cards.

One evening, Stacey was watching television and saw a commercial that promised to consolidate existing debts into one easy monthly payment. The thought of not having to write out twenty-five checks each month was very tempting to her so she called for further information. Stacey was sent an application form for a debt consolidation loan.

The lender, ABC Consolidation Company, ended up approving her, but explained that since her credit rating was not very good, due to being overextended and making numerous late payments, the company could only offer her a secured loan. Stacey didn't know what a secured loan was so ABC explained that she needed to guarantee this loan with an asset like a car or home. ABC went on to explain that with a home equity loan, the interest would be tax deductible.

This sounded like a good deal to Stacey so she decided to accept their home equity loan. Besides, the interest rate was much lower than the average rate on her credit cards. It seemed like a smart money move to use a lower interest rate loan to pay off her higher interest rate credit cards. Stacey deposited this large check and promptly paid off all of her credit cards the following month.

Her feeling of relief was soon replaced by panic when her car needed new tires. Stacey rarely saved any money each month; she habitually spent every dime that she made. This left no money for emergencies and her credit cards became her emergency fund. Even though Stacey had promised herself that she would no longer use her credit cards, she found herself with no other option. Since she had paid off her credit cards, she now had access to open lines of credit again.

Within a year her credit card debt was approaching the same level it had reached before she got her debt consolidation loan. In trying to make her situation better, she had actually succeeded in making it worse. She now had her old credit card debt back again in addition to a home equity loan of an equal amount. She had ended up with double the debt that she originally had started with.

A debt consolidation approach can be smart if you move your debt to a lower interest loan and don't incur additional debt. Consider this example:

Family A and Family B both have $20,000 in total credit card debt at an interest rate of 18 percent. They are trying to become debt free. By getting a debt consolidation loan at 10 percent, they can lower their interest payment from $300 per month at 18 percent to $167 per month at 10 percent interest. Family A borrows only the amount needed to pay off the credit card debt and then cuts up all the credit cards and closes the accounts. Family B gets a loan for $5,000 more than they need and then they continue to charge on their credit cards, eventually charging them up to their initial level of $20,000. Notice the difference in ending debt levels.

	Family A	**Family B**
Debt Consolidation Loan	$20,000 (10%)	$25,000 (10%)
New credit card debt	0	$20,000 (18%)
Ending debt	$20,000 (10%)	$45,000 (14%*)

* 14% computed based on the average interest rate of both loans combined

Debt consolidation loans can be a good idea if, like Family A, you only borrow the amount equal to the existing debt and then cut up and close the credit card accounts in order to avoid the temptation to continue charging. By making the wrong choices, Family B has made their debt situation worse than when they started.

When Stacey started falling behind on her home equity loan payments, she realized another important difference between an unsecured and a secured loan. Since her home equity loan was secured to her house, if she couldn't make the payments, they could take her house. She could end up in foreclosure with her property seized and then sold. This was never a possibility with her unsecured credit card debt. No collector was ever going to repossess the clothes that she had purchased with her credit card.

By not closing her accounts and cutting up the credit cards she had paid off, she fell into the trap of using her open lines of credit again. Stacey learned that trying to get out of debt by acquiring more debt had actually succeeded in getting herself deeper in debt!

If Stacey had closed her credit accounts after having paid them off with her home equity loan, she wouldn't have had access to these additional lines of credit. Stacey had not been forced to live within a budget or save money because whenever an unexpected expense came up, she turned to her credit cards to cover that expense.

By starting to commit a certain percentage of her income to savings, Stacey could start to build an emergency fund that would be there for the unexpected expenses that are just part of life. Another possible solution to Stacey's money problems would be to analyze whether her mortgage was too much for her to handle. Usually prior to house hunting, a prepurchase home loan counseling with a loan officer or a credit counselor helps to ascertain the price range of a home that one can afford. Unfortunately, in Stacey's case, she didn't figure this out. Consequently, she ended up in a home that she qualified for, but which left her "house poor" with little money to pay for other expenses. Her possible solutions after the fact could include renting out a room, raising her income, or selling the house. All these choices are not necessarily pain free, but are a lot less painful than eventually losing the house to a foreclosure.

Surviving the Holidays

In contrast to Stacey, Melinda tried to avoid debt as much as possible. She did not believe in owing money and attempted to pay cash for everything she purchased. Melinda's philosophy was that if she did not have the money, she did not need the item. For this reason, Melinda dreaded Christmas. Her obligation to buy presents for her entire family forced her to purchase the gifts on credit. Melinda, at nineteen years old, was the youngest in a large family that each year grew in numbers as her brothers and sisters married and started to have children. This year she had to buy gifts for thirteen people.

How was it possible to enjoy the holidays when each purchase meant adding to her already overwhelming debt burden? But what choice did she have? She couldn't show up at her family's house on Christmas empty-handed. Melinda wondered how all the other relatives did it? Weren't they struggling too? Several of her sisters were stay-at-home moms and their husbands had entry-level jobs. In fact, her brother was a college student just like her. They both were relying on their student loans to support them until graduation. Melinda thought she must have failed as a money manager since everyone else obviously had no problems affording Christmas presents.

Every year Melinda charged her presents on her credit cards. Last year when her credit card bills arrived, she bravely added up her Christmas expenditures. They came to $900! She had read in the newspaper that the average family spent $900 for all things related to Christmas (presents, travel, tree, ornaments, food, entertaining, and alcohol). She remembered wondering, when she read that statistic, how anyone could spend so much money for that Yuletide holiday, and here she found herself reconfirming that statistic!

The article had gone on to explain that if only minimum payments of 2.5 percent were made on a $900 balance at 17 percent interest, it would take eleven years to pay off the balance. The total cost after this time, including interest charges, would be approaching almost double the original amount charged, $1,748. The most sobering fact was that she would be paying off this Christmas for eight Christmases to come. In fact, Melinda was probably already consecutively paying for many past Christmases since she had always paid by credit from the time she got her first credit card.

The actual cost of borrowing can be quite astounding in the long run, but the true cost of credit is something that few people calculate. As long as they keep making those minimum payments, everything seems under control. In fact, more than half of Americans revolve their credit card balances each month, meaning they do not pay them in full. The Federal Reserve reported that at the end of 2006 Americans owed $2.4 trillion in total outstanding consumer credit debt (excluding mortgages and home equity loans). These payments equaled 18 percent of their net income.

Equally remarkable is the impact that different interest rates have on credit payments. Lower interest rates equal lower payments when compared over the same time frame. Take a look at this example with different mortgage interest rates (thirty-year-term). See how just one percentage point makes a difference in the monthly payment:

Adjustable Rate Mortgages

Mortgage:	$200,000
Interest rate	8%
Monthly payment	$1,467

If rates increase:		**If rates decrease:**	
Interest rate	9%	Interest rate	7%
Monthly payment	$1,609	Monthly payment	$1,330
OR		OR	
Interest rate	10%	Interest rate	6%
Monthly payment	$1,755	Monthly payment	$1,199

Melinda decided to swallow her pride and suggest to her relatives that for next Christmas they draw names out of a hat and buy gifts only for that person. She felt embarrassed and ashamed when she made this suggestion. To her amazement, her relatives thought it was a great idea. In fact, many of them had been thinking about suggesting this idea for years, but they decided not to because they didn't want to appear cheap.

It turned out that her relatives only appeared to be in control financially. They too had been contributing to the national average debt for the holidays primarily through purchasing with plastic. In fact, consumers spent a whopping $438 billion during the holiday season of 2006 (Thanksgiving, Christmas, Hanukkah, and Kwanzaa). With the pressure to spend, spend, and spend greatly lessened, Melinda's family looked forward to the next holiday season for the first time that they could remember.

Only $9.99 a Week

Although credit cards may seem like they are available to anyone who can sign the application, in reality there are people who will be turned down for credit when they apply. The reasons given may be lack of a credit history or having a negative credit history. Lack of a credit history is easier to overcome than a negative history since certain credit cards target young adults and make it easier to qualify.

Unfortunately, a negative credit history signals that you are not a good customer. In the late 1800s, some bankers did drive-by credit checks to determine if someone would be a good customer. Before they funded a loan, they would ride their horse past the applicant's home around dawn. If the light was on, they'd make the loan. They figured if someone was up that early, they were industrious and would pay them back.

Now in the twenty-first century, credit reports have taken the place of drive-by credit checks. If your credit report shows that you have paid late or not at all, the creditor assumes this pattern will continue. For those with negative credit reports, traditional channels of credit may not be available and many people are forced to look to other options for credit.

Jerome learned the meaning of a credit report the hard way. Neither his parents nor his school had explained to him the importance of paying his bills on time or at all. So, he frequently skipped paying some months and just caught up the next month with a double payment. Since he eventually paid, what did consistency matter? He was now twenty-one years old and had been following this pattern ever since he had gotten his first bill at the age of eighteen. With this haphazard approach to bill paying, it was no surprise that Jerome's credit report had negative entries (late payments) for almost every account.

Now Jerome wanted a television set but wasn't willing to wait until he had saved up enough money to purchase one. In order to get it immediately, he had to buy one on credit. This was proving difficult because his credit report was not portraying him as a good risk to the stores who decided whether to approve his application. After five stores had turned him down, Jerome saw an advertisement in a rent-to-own store window promising not to turn down anyone for credit. The lure of low weekly payments was also very tempting. Jerome went in and left shortly afterwards with his brand new television.

Jerome felt he had made a wise decision. He got his television set without waiting and he only had to make a small payment of $9.99 each week. Ironically, the next week Jerome had a lesson in his college finance class that illustrated the total cost of his purchase. If Jerome's repayment terms were extended to 18 months, by the time he paid off his $220 television, he would have spent $800 with the additional interest charges. In fact, if he had read the small print on his contract, he would have discovered that the interest rate was 300 percent!

Jerome learned the lesson that his need for immediate gratification cost him a lot of money. He also learned that his poor credit record disenfranchised him from the traditional credit market and left only rent-to-own type stores as an alternative. He promised himself that in the future he would save before he made expensive purchases and he would learn to be patient. He also would make an effort to pay his bills on time and start turning around his credit history from a primarily negative to a positive one.

With the passage of time along with making consistent payments that are never late, you can improve your credit report. Most late payments will drop off after two years, with the exceptions of major blemishes like write-offs, repossessions, judgments, or foreclosures which stay on for up to seven years. In the case of Chapter 7 bankruptcy, the negative mark stays on your credit report for ten years.

It is a good idea to check your credit report at least once a year, or right before a major purchase is planned, for any inaccuracies. You can easily order credit reports online through www.annualcreditreport.com or by calling (877) 322-8228. You are entitled to one free credit report annually. The three major credit bureaus that compile your credit information are:

- Experian: (888) 397-3742; http://www.experian.com
- Equifax: (800) 685-1111; http://www.equifax.com
- Transunion: (800) 888-4213; http://www.transunion.com

Any time you are turned down for credit, you are supposed to be notified of the reason your request was rejected. There have been situations reported where information was merged for people that had the same name, or stolen credit card numbers were being used by another individual. For these reasons, it is a good idea to check regularly and make sure the information that is being reported is accurate.

A Fresh Start

Once negative information is reported to a credit bureau, it may take up to seven years until it is purged from the system. This is a long time for such powerful data to remain a part of your records. Since only negative information that was reported in error can be removed, people may become impatient and look for a faster solution. Unfortunately, many times the answer they find is not legal.

Trent didn't think it was fair that the mistakes he had made when he was young would follow him around for seven long years. He was a college student now and felt much wiser than when he was a teenager. Trent had many late payments, nonpayment of a few accounts, and a repossession of his car all listed on his credit report. He had just gotten off the phone with one of the major credit reporting companies that had explained to Trent that you couldn't just erase negative credit history if it is true.

Although you can't remove information which is correct, you can fix any inaccuracies. Contact the major credit reporting agencies to fix the inaccuracy. If your understanding of the disputed information is different from the creditors and they refuse to remove the entry in dispute, you may include up to a one hundred–word statement in your credit report explaining your side. Thereafter, any creditor checking your credit report will at least see both sides of the story.

Unfortunately for Trent, all of the negatives on his credit report were legitimate. But he believed he had learned his lesson and shouldn't have to be penalized for mistakes of the past. Besides, how could he replace his repossessed car if he couldn't qualify for a loan? He worked the night shift at a health club and public transportation wasn't available at that hour. How was he supposed to get to work?

The solution appeared to him in a radio ad promising to repair bad credit. The advertisement guaranteed that for an upfront fee, negative credit entries would disappear. After Trent contacted the "fix-it" company and paid his upfront fee, he was instructed to obtain a tax identification number as if he was going to start a small business. He was to use this number in place of his social security number whenever he applied for credit. Therefore, he would eventually create a brand new credit history in his name.

This tactic succeeded in getting him several credit cards, and soon he was even successful in getting a loan for a used car. Trent would have probably continued on with this new identity if the Federal Trade Commission (FTC), who had been compiling evidence against the credit repair firm, had not discovered Trent as one of its customers.

Trent thought that he had found the perfect solution, but had no idea it was illegal. He was falsifying his social security number and living under an assumed number. In fact, Trent learned all this when the FTC and the Attorney General's office contacted him after they closed down the fraudulent credit repair company. Trent lost the money he had paid to repair his credit in addition to being a party to an illegal enterprise. Now not only did he have credit problems, but legal ones as well.

If Trent had learned the art of patience, he would have eventually recovered from his negative credit history. True, seven years is a long time for negative credit to stay on a credit report, but many creditors look closely only at the most recent two years. Trent should have concentrated on improving his credit history. As the chart below illustrates, the most heavily weighted factor in determining a credit score is one's payment history (comprising 35 percent of the score).

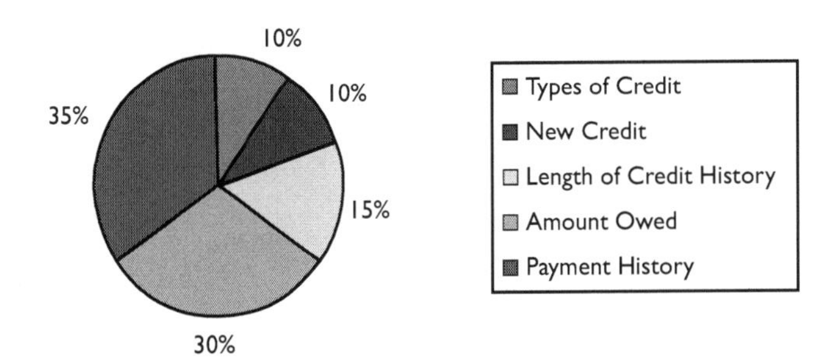

Source: "Your Credit Scores," Consumer Federation of America and Fair Isaac®

He needed to start paying his bills on time, keep his debt at a manageable level (the second most heavily weighted factor), and possibly get loans at a higher interest rate until his record improved.

Unfortunately, this is a slow process and can't be accomplished overnight. Trent had wanted an improved record immediately and hadn't been willing to wait. This impatience lead to a solution that seemed too good to be true, and it was.

Remember that it is illegal to lie about any identifying information such as your social security number. It is also illegal for any company promising to clean your credit to take payment in advance. Normally, what the credit repair clinics promise to do, you can do yourself for free.

Words of Wisdom

Credit handled wisely is a wonderful thing. The benefits of having access to credit and a positive credit report are numerous. Conversely, not understanding credit and making unwise decisions can affect you for years to come. Remember the advice from this chapter and you will become credit smart:

- Try not to charge more each month than you can hope to pay when the bill arrives.
- Know your safe debt level.
- Maintain only two credit cards maximum. The more you have, the more you'll charge.
- Don't fall into the trap where you pay off your credit cards with a debt consolidation loan and then continue to charge on your credit cards.
- Stop using your credit cards after you have paid them off if you're trying to reduce your number of accounts. Cut them up and close the accounts.
- Pay your bills on time and don't pay less than the monthly amount due.

- Check your credit report regularly or before a major purchase.
- Make the choice to receive interest and not pay it. When you run a balance, you are paying an average of 13 percent interest, according to Consumer Action (or a higher rate if you have bad credit), and losing out on any interest you could be receiving from saving or investing this same money.
- The journey to becoming debt-free requires patience.

I Need Wheels

Certainly there are lots of things in life that money won't buy, but it's funny — have you ever tried to buy them without money?

—Ogden Nash

Buying a car is usually the first major purchase for a young adult and it is often the second largest monthly expense after your housing payment (unless you live with your parents). In Merrill Lynch's third annual teen survey, 30 percent of the teens polled said that they were saving money in order to buy a car. Among the top plans for money being saved by teens, a car was second only to a college education.

To a teen, a car is more than just a set of wheels, an engine, and a metal body; it is a sign of freedom. It is the chance to be free from parental supervision and avoid having to be chauffeured around anymore. Once a teen begins working, the car becomes a necessity, a way to get to and from a job. And for a young adult, a car can be a sign of success. It can send a message to their friends, colleagues, and dates, "The nicer the car, the more successful the owner."

However, purchasing a car is often confusing for an experienced adult. Imagine how difficult it is for a first-time car buyer. Many decisions must be made on the spot, such as: should I buy a new car or a used one; should I lease the car or buy it outright; what type of insurance should I buy; should I purchase a service contract; and what can I afford?

Without research prior to visiting the dealer, the buyer may end up with a car that is not suited for his or her needs or is too expensive for his or her budget. Unfortunately, the minute the buyer leaves the car lot with their "new" car, it automatically becomes "used." If you should feel buyer's remorse a few blocks away (that sinking feeling that you shouldn't have made the purchase), there is not much you can do about it.

Some dealers may have a three-day return policy, which allows the buyer to return the car in exchange for another one of equal or greater value. However, if it is not specifically mentioned in the contract, don't assume a three-day cancellation policy exists.

Before being stuck with a car you don't want or can't afford, you need to become educated about the costs of ownership. Being armed with all the facts when you meet with the car salesman will give you an advantage. You will be in control of the negotiations instead of the other way around.

This chapter will help you to navigate the road to getting and keeping your first and subsequent automobiles. If you follow these directions, you will arrive at your destination without getting lost. You will learn how to:

- Do a car budget
- Conduct research
- Decide on service contracts
- Avoid impulse purchases
- Compare between interest rates and terms
- Compare various insurance companies
- Negotiate with your creditors
- Avoid repossession
- Choose between leasing or buying

The actual buying of your car should be thought of as the last step of an in-depth research project. The project's conclusions should never be determined without first conducting diligent analyses. You should be able to walk into the car dealer with an accurate idea of how much you can afford. Without this knowledge, you may end up a repossession statistic. The sticker price is just a starting point and may end up being significantly different than the price you end up paying. The amount listed on your final contract is what you will be responsible for. It is important that this amount is within your ability to pay.

The following case history chronicles Jack's first car purchase. You are about to learn the steps that should accompany not only your first, but all of your car purchases. If you skip a step, you may find yourself in trouble, just like Jack did.

Did You Do Your Homework?

Jack pulled into his parents' driveway with a new Mustang convertible. This was his first car purchase and he had insisted that he could buy it on his own. Jack had worked at a video store for over two years and had saved a large part of his salary. Now as a senior in high school, he finally had enough money saved for a down payment and he couldn't wait any longer. He was proud of his new car and could hardly wait to show it to his parents.

As they looked over Jack's Mustang, he noticed a worried expression appear on their faces. He asked what was wrong, and they replied that they weren't expecting such an expensive car. Jack hadn't planned on getting such an expensive car, but the dealer had convinced him that this Mustang was the perfect automobile for him.

Jack justified this purchase—after all, he lived in Los Angeles and needed this type of car. Jack felt he had to take full advantage of the beautiful weather and buy a convertible.

It was a crime to not have a convertible when it was sunny so often. He then focused on deciding which features to add. To begin with, he needed air conditioning. With the constant heat, it was simply not an option he could live without. Of course, he felt he also needed a leather interior and top of the line rims for his tires. A good sound system was a necessity, so he made sure they installed a top of the line CD player. Without these features, it would be embarrassing to drive around with the women whom he was dating.

As features were added or upgraded, the sticker price that Jack had initially seen was slowly being increased. Of course, the increase in price was not so apparent since the only figure Jack paid attention to was the monthly payment. He didn't realize that his loan had been stretched out to seven years or that his first year's payments were only covering the interest on his loan. None of this was important to Jack; only the fact that he knew he could afford the monthly payment.

As Jack drove away from his parents' house, leaving them in the driveway with worried looks on their faces, he told himself that they were just cheap. They were still driving a car that was built before he was born. He could afford his new car and that was all that mattered. Unfortunately, Jack soon came to realize that he only thought he could afford the convertible—reality said otherwise.

True, he could afford the car payment, but he didn't calculate the other expenses that went into car ownership. In addition to the car payment, there are four other major expenses involved in owning an automobile: gas, insurance, maintenance, and annual registration or car tax. Other minor expenses include traffic tickets, parking, tolls, and storage. Since Jack didn't plan for these expenses in advance, whenever he needed maintenance or repair work or had to buy gas, he ended up charging them on his credit card.

Jack soon got behind on his car payment. He didn't believe it was his fault. Because he had started to attend community college, he had been forced to cut down on his hours at work. He had stopped making his payment over two months ago, but was sure he would catch up this month since he had begun working extra hours at his job. He ignored the letters from his car lender. He wasn't concerned; soon he would be on track again.

When Jack came home one night after work, his father was waiting for him. It turned out that the collection department had called the house looking for Jack earlier that evening and his father had answered the phone. Jack could no longer ignore his problem. His father had scheduled an appointment for the next day to go the dealership and see what solutions were available to Jack.

Jack could have avoided this situation altogether if he had done a budget prior to shopping for a car. The total car budget (bottom line) should be an amount that he could realistically afford. Each line needs to be filled in so that the total is accurate. Leaving out substantial expenses like "insurance" will not reflect the total expense of his new purchase, especially because insurance for young males on sports cars can sometimes be more expensive than the monthly loan payment.

Car Budget (monthly)

Fixed Expenses:

Car payment	____________
Car insurance	____________
Car registration (annual expense)	____________

Flexible Expenses:

Gas/Oil	____________
Parking/Tolls	____________
Repairs	____________

Fun Expenses:

Car wash/wax	____________
Gas for special trips	____________
Hands-free phone capability	____________
CDs/Satellite radio	____________
Other	____________
Total Monthly Car Budget:	____________

In order to be able to fill in the blanks that related to his "fixed" expenses, Jack needed to do research to find out the sticker price of new and used cars. By knowing the price ranges of various cars, he could then find one within his budget. By knowing the total price minus his down payment, he could then figure out his monthly payment (the dealer or lender can assist in this calculation). Similar quotes for insurance can also be given once the type of car is determined. Finally, the annual registration fee or car tax can be found by contacting the state Department of Motor Vehicles. The following are sample prices for different 2007 model automobiles:

Compact

Volkswagen Beetle: $16,490
BMW Mini Cooper S: $18,700

SUV/ Trucks

Mercedes Benz GL 450: $54,900
Chevy Silverado Classic SS: $34,180

Luxury/Sports

Porsche Boxster S: $55,700
Lotus Exige S: $59,890

Hybrid

Toyota Prius: $22,175
Saturn VUE Green Line: $24,172

*Source: Motor Trend.com

It is important not to fall in love with any particular vehicle. The salesman will be able to sense your infatuation and you will be less able to act rationally and objectively.

During your research phase, realize that our nation spends as much on advertising as it does on elementary education in public schools. Advertisements may be very persuasive and awaken interest in a particular car, but don't stop there. Check out magazines like *Consumer Reports*, which objectively rate automobiles in their annual "Car Guide." The Internet is also a wonderful place to comparison shop. Most car companies and large dealers have websites where you can find out prices and features. As you find cars you are interested in, add them to your comparison list.

You'll also need to decide whether you want a new or used car. There are advantages and disadvantages to both. New automobiles lose their value more quickly, but you'll probably be covered under a limited-time warranty if you need to do repairs; whereas, a used car may not be covered by a warranty and you do not know how the previous owner cared for the car. An obvious advantage of used cars is that they require less money and will free up your money for other things. For example, instead of buying a $30,000 sport utility vehicle, you buy a $10,000 used compact car and invest the remaining $20,000. At a 10 percent interest rate, that money becomes $1 million over the course of forty years! And think of the money you'll be saving in gas!

A final decision to be made by the purchaser is whether to purchase a service contract. Every new vehicle comes with a factory warranty (covering repairs for an initial period of time after the purchase), but an optional extended service contract is usually available at an additional cost. The price of the service contract should be negotiable. Keep in mind that less than 20 percent of service contracts are ever used. The price range could stretch from several hundred dollars to over $1,000, depending on how much the car costs and the length of the contract. Because car repairs can prove costly, some people consider this expense the price you pay for peace of mind. Before deciding whether to purchase the service contract, you should ask your salesman the following questions:

1. What is the difference between the warranty and the service contract being offered?
2. Is the warranty with the dealership directly or with an outside firm that has been contracted to provide this service?
3. What problems are seen most often on this model?
4. Should the dealer or service go out of business, what protection is there for the purchaser?
5. What repairs are covered?
6. What costs of repair labor and parts are you responsible for?
7. Must all repair work be done at the dealer? Will repairs made elsewhere be covered?
8. What is the cancellation and refund policy?

After all the research is completed, you need to match your budget with the cars (and their corresponding expenses) that interest you. This is a very important step. Without being realistic about what you can actually afford, you may end up getting in over your head, like Jack. By knowing all the costs of ownership (not just figuring out the monthly payment he could afford) and by knowing which cars were within his price range, Jack could have made a wiser decision. As he rode his bike to work, his parents' old car suddenly didn't look so bad!

Congratulations! You've Won a Shopping Spree

Contrary to Jack, Jessica knew that she was in trouble. She was opening her mail and taking the collectors' phone calls, but there just wasn't anything she could do. Jessica wondered how she had gotten herself into the mess she was in. She thought back to that day at the car dealership.

She knew she needed another car. Her old car had finally died after her parents had handed it down to her sister, then her brother, and finally to Jessica. Her parents were very conservative, having been raised in rural Kansas, and never bought anything new. They felt it was a waste of money. Jessica was used to getting things that had been preowned.

Jessica had no intention of buying a new car, she fully intended on getting a used one. But once she was at the dealership, the salesman showed her how she could afford a new automobile with 100 percent financing. This meant that she didn't have to put any money down and she could leave with a new car. Jessica thought this was a great deal and the added perk of finally having something that was brand new was too much to resist. She promptly signed all the paperwork and left with her new Toyota Camry.

Jessica made her first mistake. She made a major purchase on impulse and on the first day of shopping! Always let the salesman know that you will be shopping several dealerships. Don't fall for the line, "Special price for today only." If you make an impulse purchase you may regret it for several reasons:

1. Your payment may be higher than you had planned to spend.
2. Your insurance payment is outrageous.
3. You could have gotten a better deal at a dealer across town.

4. The contract interest rate will be higher than the rate negotiated verbally (only the written contract counts).

Jessica was able to make the payments without difficulty for the first year, and then her monthly payment increased substantially. She thought it was a mistake and called her lender. Unfortunately, it wasn't a mistake. If Jessica had read her loan paperwork before signing it, she would have realized that she was borrowing money with a loan that had an adjustable interest rate. After the first year, the interest rate increased dramatically. Now her monthly payments were more than she could afford. She never compared auto loan terms to see which loan would be the best one for her; she just signed the paperwork that the salesman suggested.

Take a look at the differences between a loan with a thirty-six-month term and one with a sixty-month term. Also, see how the different interest rates affect the total to be repaid. As a general rule:

- The shorter the loan term, the lower the total to be repaid vs. the longer the loan term, the higher the total to be repaid
- The lower the interest rate, the lower the total to be repaid vs. the higher the interest rate, the higher the total to be repaid.

Combining a low interest rate with a short loan term is the best scenario. Unfortunately, the lure of a low monthly payment causes many people to choose the worst-case scenario, which is to stretch out the loan as long as possible. Take a look at the below example for an initial loan amount of $5,850.

Thirty-Six-Month Term

Credit Grantor	No.1	No.2	No.3
APR	10%	12%	13%
Length of Loan	36	36	36
Monthly Payment	$188.78	$195.01	$197.12
Total Finance Charge	$946.08	$1170.36	$1246.32
Total To be Repaid	$6796.08	$7020.36	$7096.32

Sixty-Month Term

Credit Grantor	No.1	No.2	No.3
APR	10%	12%	13%
Length of Loan	60	60	60
Monthly Payment	$124.36	$130.88	$133.12
Total Finance Charge	$1608.60	$2002.80	$2137.02
Total To be Repaid	$7458.60	$7852.80	$7987.20

*Source: National Endowment for Financial Education

As she tried to figure out what to do, Jessica started hiding her Camry to avoid repossession. She worked in a building with a secured parking lot so she wasn't worried that they could repossess her vehicle while she was at work. But she didn't have a garage at home and had to park her car on the street. She started parking her vehicle far away from her apartment and sometimes had to walk over a mile to her home so that the repossessor wouldn't be able to find her Camry.

One Saturday, Jessica received a call from the local grocery store telling her that she had won a shopping spree. They told her to come right away and look for the man with the red jacket who would be holding a parking space for her. She was to park her car there and enter the store, where she would have thirty minutes to get all the groceries she could for free. Jessica was ecstatic. She took her car away from its hiding place and raced to the store. Just like they had said, there was a man with a red jacket holding a parking space for her. Her encouraged her to run into the store and start her shopping spree.

Jessica began to pull items off the shelves until her cart was overflowing. After her thirty minutes were up she went to the cashier and exclaimed that she was the winner! The cashier asked with a perplexed look, "Winner of what?" Jessica then had a panic attack as she realized what happened. She ran outside to the parking lot to find her Camry was gone. Repossession can be a very creative profession.

Jessica should have known that 100 percent financing is to be avoided. You start out with a problem because you owe more than the car is worth. This situation is what is referred to as buying "upside down." It will end up costing you money to get rid of the car. Jessica discovered this unpleasant fact when she tried to sell the car to get rid of her obligation. She found that she couldn't sell her vehicle for the amount she owed. She didn't have the money to pay the difference so this wasn't an option for her.

Ironically, after her car was repossessed, Jessica received a bill in the mail. This bill was for the deficiency balance. The lender was billing her for the difference between what the car was worth and what she still owed. Remember that a car is a "secured" loan, and when you can't make the payments the lender can and will take back the car. You'll be left in most cases paying on a car that you no longer have.

The second lesson that Jessica learned was that if a repossessor really wants your car, they will probably get it. Most people will never actually see their car being repossessed. The repossessor will try to take your car when you are not around and will employ creative ways to do so. Jessica's experience in the supermarket was an unusual, but pointed example of these tactics.

By keeping the lines of communication open, Jessica could have probably prevented her car's eventual repossession. Her options could have included:

1. Interest only—which would have allowed her to make interest only payments over a short period of time
2. Refinance of the loan terms—which would have resulted in the monthly payments being reduced but the repayment period being extended
3. Extension—which would have allowed the addition of the delinquent month(s) onto the end of the loan
4. Loan assumption—which would have allowed someone else to have taken over the loan and the car would then technically become their property
5. Sale—which, if the dealer would agree to this, the car could be sold and the proceeds would help to pay off the loan. Usually the amount the car is sold for is lower than the amount owed the dealer, causing a deficiency balance.

These options were not available to Jessica since she chose to avoid the situation altogether. Avoidance of the problem, as you learned in Chapter 1, will almost never lead to a resolution of the problem that is the most favorable for you.

Insurance: A Want or a Need?

Youth often feel they are invincible. They will never get sick, injured, or have a car accident. If you do not believe that these things will happen to you, then why would it be necessary to have insurance? Even though it is required by law, many young people choose to have no coverage or not enough coverage. Instead of insurance being a "need" it is regarded as a "want," a luxury that will be included if there is money left over in the budget.

Regrettably, when incidents happen and you do not have car insurance, the costs are high. If your car gets stolen, you must fully replace the car yourself; if your car gets damaged, you must pay for the repairs yourself; or if you injure another person or yourself in an accident, you must pay the medical bills yourself. So why then do so many young people choose to have no coverage or not enough coverage? The following example shows why Carlos made the decision to omit car insurance from his budget.

Carlos recently filed a Chapter 7 bankruptcy at the age of twenty-five. He got his first credit card as a senior in high school from a retail store where he worked. After this first credit card, he steadily acquired more cards until he owned over thirty of them. He finally realized his debt was out of control. Unfortunately, this realization came too late and his only option was bankruptcy. His lawyer told him that his Chapter 7 bankruptcy would remain on his credit report for ten years and that it would be difficult to be approved for credit with a bankruptcy listed.

This warning didn't stop Carlos from trying to get financing a year later for a car. He lived in a suburb of San Francisco and transportation proved difficult unless he wanted to go directly to the city. Unfortunately, his job was outside of San Francisco and was not even remotely close to any public transportation stop. His coworker with whom he had been carpooling for the past year was leaving the company. Carlos was now without a ride.

Carlos was surprised when the car dealer approved him for the loan, but not surprised when they explained the price of bad credit, a 30 percent interest rate. Carlos knew the interest rate they were offering was extremely high, but he didn't feel he had a choice. He signed the paperwork and left with his new Ford pickup.

Carlos' payments were quite steep. He needed to cut out some other expenses so that he could handle this hefty car payment. He decided, since he was a good driver and hadn't ever been in an accident, he would let his car insurance lapse. This decision turned out to be disastrous. Less than a week after he had stopped making his insurance payments, Carlos got into a collision. The damage to his pickup was extensive and, since he no longer had insurance, he couldn't afford to repair it.

Carlos then stopped making his car payment since he couldn't use his pickup and it was just sitting in his driveway. This didn't stop the repossessor from towing away his vehicle one evening. After the dealer sold his car in an auction, Carlos got stuck with the loan balance minus the auction value received on the Ford. Since the car was almost new, the balance owed was almost the full amount, $20,000. Since Carlos had just filed for bankruptcy, he wasn't allowed under law to file another bankruptcy for eight more years. This meant that he couldn't get out of paying what he owed on the car.

Carlos wasn't worried. "How," he thought, "can they squeeze blood out of a turnip? I don't have any assets so what can they possibly take away from me?" His answer came the next month when his paycheck was reduced by 25 percent. The auto lender had filed a garnishment against his wages. They legally were able to take away up to one quarter of his paycheck to cover the money owed them. Carlos now realized an important lesson that his bankruptcy hadn't taught him, "Not all money problems will go away."

If Carlos had realized that insurance is a "need " and not a "want," then he never would have stopped paying his insurance premiums. If he had shopped around for car insurance, he might have been able to reduce his monthly expense. Use this chart to help you compare companies:

Keep in mind that many factors go into the price of auto insurance. If you are a young adult, your insurance rates will probably be higher than any other demographic group, because young, inexperienced drivers have more accidents. To insurance companies, a young age often reflects a lack of skill, maturity, and judgment behind the wheel. In addition, males up to twenty-five years of age cause significantly more accidents than females in the same age group. These statistics account

Kinds of Coverage	Limits You Want	Company #1	Company #2	Company #3
Liability Bodily Injury Property Damage	$___per person $___per accident $___per accident			
Medical Payments Uninsured Motorists	$___per person $___amount	$ $	$ $	$ $
Collision Comprehensive	$___deductible $___deductible	$ $	$ $	$ $
Annual Total of Premium		$	$	$
Installment Payments		$	$	$

*Source: National Endowment for Financial Education

for the higher cost of insurance for young males.

Your driving record can help to lower your rates once you've had time to prove you are a good driver. Many companies give discounts if you drive for an extended period with no claims on your record. Learn to be patient and demonstrate your driving skills over time.

The major coverages offered through an automobile insurance policy include:

1. Liability—pays for injuries, sickness, or death of other people and damage to their property when the insured has caused an accident. All states require liability insurance.
2. Medical payments—covers "reasonable" medical and funeral expenses for the insured or anyone riding in the covered automobile, whether or not the accident was the insured's fault (i.e., the concept of no-fault insurance). Medical payments also cover members as pedestrians if an auto strikes them.
3. Uninsured/underinsured motorists—provides immediate payment for whatever bodily injury the insured is legally entitled to receive from a driver who carries no insurance or from a hit-and-run accident.
4. Collision—pays for repair of the covered automobile if not paid by the insurance of someone else causing the damage. Most lenders require all owners to have this coverage because they want the car to be in good shape if the "owner" defaults on payments and the lender repossesses the car.
5. Other—covers theft and damage to the covered automobile from projectiles (such as water damage or windstorms) or from vandalism or fire.

The huge expenses that can result from car accidents are a

compelling reason to always have insurance coverage. Auto insurance is designed to reimburse you for damages to your property (the car and its contents) and for liability claims that other people make against you. Just because Carlos considered himself to be a good driver doesn't mean that other drivers are "good" drivers. It usually takes at least two to get into an accident.

Remember Murphy's Law—what can go wrong probably will. Your car can be stolen, another driver may back their car into yours, or a driver you hit may be injured. These events aren't planned; they just happen. Some unfortunate incidents are minor. If your car radio gets stolen, it can be replaced without a huge expense. But other events can be disastrous. If you cause a car accident and injure other people, for example, you could face significant financial and legal problems for years.

After Carlos filed his bankruptcy, he should have minimized his accumulation of additional expenses and debt since, as noted earlier, he would not be able to file another Chapter 7 bankruptcy for eight more years. By getting a car loan, he was making a very risky decision. He should have scaled down his choice. That way he could have saved his money and paid cash for a used pickup instead of needing a loan. It might not have been as nice of a pickup as the one he got, but at least he wouldn't have lost one quarter of his paycheck!

You Could Always Live in Your Car

The type of car that you drive is viewed by many as a status symbol. The more expensive the car, the more successful the driver. This correlation may not be the case at all, but on first glance many make that assumption. If the image that you project is important to you, then the type of automobile that you drive can be influenced by your need to fit this image.

As long as you can afford the particular car that will portray the image that is important to you, you will not face a financial dilemma. The problem results when your finances and your image of what you would like to drive do not match. A struggle then ensues and whichever has the greater pull will win. If your desire to stay within your budget is stronger, then you will settle for a less expensive car. If your need to have a certain auto for status reasons is more important than affordability, then you may end up with a car that is too expensive for your budget. The next couple found the image pull to be the stronger one.

Bill and Heather Jones both drove expensive cars. Heather was a real estate agent and had to drive clients around in her car to show them properties. If she didn't drive a nice car (she drove a BMW), they wouldn't think that she was successful. Since she was only twenty-five years old, she felt she needed to try even harder to prove herself than someone who was older and was therefore assumed to have more experience. It was important that her clients have faith in her abilities. Without a luxury car, it would be obvious to them that she was not a success, even though her track record proved otherwise.

Bill also justified his need for a luxury car (he drove a Lexus). He worked for a large corporation and was climbing his way up the corporate ladder. Bill was the same age as Heather and this was his first job after receiving an MBA. He definitely wanted to look the part. By driving an old car, he wouldn't be considered top management material.

They weren't sure whether they wanted to get a loan or lease their cars. This decision can be a confusing one. An important reason for the popularity of leases is the price of purchasing a car. With a new vehicle price of over $30,000 for many vehicles, for instance, buyers have found it increasingly difficult to afford the down payment. Furthermore, the monthly payments for leasing are often lower than those for buying.

However, the out-of-pocket expenses are not necessarily the primary consideration in the lease or buy decision. The important issue is whether the buyer is prepared to live by the unique rules of leasing. Leasing is primarily a lifestyle decision, not an economic one. Some simple questions to ask yourself before deciding to lease or buy are:

- Do you want to make a large down payment before driving off the car lot or do you have another use for the money? If you think your money could be more profitably invested in something other than a car (the stock market, for example), then a lease might make more sense.
- Are you comfortable with having to make a car payment every month or do you live for the day when your vehicle is paid for? Consumers accustomed to car payments are ideal candidates for leasing because most experts believe that the best way to lease is to turn a car in at the end of the contract and to start all over again.
- Do you do a lot of driving? Leases are not the right choice for people who put many miles on their cars. Most contracts impose limits of ten thousand to fifteen thousand miles per year. Any mileage over that amount is usually subject to a ten-cent to twenty-five-cent mile charge at the end of the lease.
- How long do you want to keep the automobile? If you plan to drive your car until it dies in your driveway, then you are better off purchasing it. Even if you know how to negotiate a lease that protects your interests, you will face a second round of talks when the lease expires, either to finance the remaining cost or to reduce it. It is simpler and the outcome is probably the same if you do all the negotiations at the time of the initial purchase.
- Are you prepared to stick with the lease for its entire term? Penalties for breaking a lease before it expires can be substantial. Remember that you are guaranteeing a payment, you are not buying a car. Consider it more like renting.

- Are you self-employed? In general, leases are more attractive if your business is responsible for making the payments.
- Are you a tough negotiator? Lease agreements are hard to understand and many consumers find it especially difficult to calculate exactly what their agreements require them to pay for a car.

Experts recommend that before you decide to lease, you learn to perform present-value calculations, whereby you determine how much a payment plan will ultimately cost. Be sure to take your calculator with you to the auto showroom and run the numbers as talks progress. If you do not have an understanding of how to calculate present-value, make sure you insist the dealer perform these computations for you. You need to know the total costs of the various payment plan options in order to be able to make an informed decision.

In the case of Bill and Heather Jones, who were shopping for luxury cars, they really didn't know the difference between leasing and purchasing, so they randomly chose to lease them. These luxury cars did not come cheaply. The Jones' combined lease payments totaled $900. Full insurance coverage on both cars totaled about $300. Bill's insurance was almost double that of Heather's since he had a DUI/DWI (Driving While Under the Influence of Alcohol) on his record and his rates shot up after that incident. Heather's gas purchases were about triple Bill's since she drove around continuously because of the nature of her job. This led to more frequent maintenance and oil changes. Factoring in their annual car registration, their combined monthly automobile costs totaled $1,500.

Bill and Heather's rent payment came to $1,200. They lived in Dallas, Texas, and it was difficult to rent an apartment for two persons for less than what they were paying. They joked that they should start living out of their cars and save money on rent. Since Heather was having a slow year due to the slump in the real estate market, that would not have been a bad idea. Unfortunately, all good ideas are not always practical.

Their combined average net income per month was only $3,500. After they paid their BMW and Lexus payments and their rent, they had barely enough money to take care of their credit card bills, make student loan payments, and buy groceries. In fact, their car expenses by themselves were almost 50 percent of their income. Following the 20 percent debt rule (see Chapter 3), the Jones were extremely overextended.

Bill decided to turn his Lexus in after his lease expired and have Heather do the driving. Not having Bill's expensive car insurance or car payment reduced their car expenses by more than half. Of course, it was not as convenient to drop Bill off at work or pick him up afterwards, but it was possible since Bill didn't need his car during the day. He spent all his time in his office building and didn't have to travel. Heather had to arrange her client appointments around Bill's schedule, which sometimes caused a conflict. But all in all, the conflicts caused by carpooling were quite minor compared to the arguments they used to get into when it came time to pay bills each month.

They are now concentrating on saving the money that otherwise would have gone to pay Bill's automobile expenses. After two years of a clean driving record, Bill's insurance company has promised to give Bill a reduction on his car insurance premiums. By that time, they should have saved enough money to buy Bill a car. This car will have much lower payments than his previous one since they will put a large percentage of the total price into the down payment.

They have also realized an unexpected side benefit. They find they actually talk more to each other. The time they spent in the car together was time that they used to spend

apart. In addition to improving their financial situation, they also improved their marriage.

Words of Wisdom

If you are prepared and knowledgeable about buying a car, the experience can be pleasant and rewarding. All that it requires is research and calculation. The more educated you are, the less chance you will end up with a "bad deal."

It is important to remember that the minute you drive that car off the dealer's lot, it is "used" and "yours." You can't return it like that department store purchase that you changed your mind about as soon as you arrived home. Getting rid of your car obligation is definitely not as easy as showing a receipt and getting a refund.

To recap this chapter's advice:

- Create a car budget.
- Comparison shop.
- Don't buy on impulse.
- Decide whether to lease or buy.
- Don't forget insurance.
- Don't let your car be repossessed (reread Chapter 1).

5

The Semester of Living Dangerously

For the parents of today's college students, a Visa was more likely to be needed for entering a country than for paying your way through college.

This chapter covers the most common ways that college students get into debt. It is a fact that today's collegians and new graduates are accumulating more debt than ever before. In the past, a college student who attempted to acquire a credit card would have been turned down. That situation is not true for college students today. There are now two requirements for most students to obtain a credit card—a college ID and a pulse! In fact, being wooed by credit card companies from the moment you step foot on a college campus has become a rite of passage.

Take a look at when most students are acquiring their first credit card:

Class Standing	
During High School	14%
After High School/Before College	20%
Freshman Year	46%
Sophomore Year	14%
After Sophomore Year	5%

*Source: Student Monitor 2000

The average credit card balance of a college student is $2,169, and nearly 56 percent of students have four or more credit cards, according to a 2004 survey by Sallie Mae (a major national handler of student loans). The trend among graduate students is much worse, with an average credit card balance of $7,831 per student, a significant increase of 59 percent over 1998's average of debt of $4,925. A significant percentage owe even more—15 percent owed more than $15,000.

Credit card debt has become the norm, and students are graduating with student loans in addition to the heavy debt they have accumulated from credit cards. Your parents probably do not understand this trend since they graduated from college with much less debt. But their college experience was not as expensive. Costs to attend a four-year public institution more than tripled between 1985 and 2005, topping $5,000 (including tuition and fees) a year. Four-year private institutions are considerably more expensive, coming close to $20,000 a year. Your parents probably also had more personal savings in relation to the cost, there were more federal grants available to them, and high inflation existed to help their repayment.

Considering all these factors, it is not surprising that college students today have chosen to finance their college education more and more through the borrowing of money. The result has been a huge increase in college-related debt. In the 1990s, college students borrowed more than $100 billion, as much as was borrowed in the 1960s, 1970s, and 1980s combined, according to the report "College Debt and the American Family." On top of the debt burden, there are other costs that you, as the student, must face.

In the cases where families bail out their children's debts, the cost is embarrassment and family tensions. If your family either chooses not to pay off your debts or doesn't have the financial capacity to pay off this debt, the result may be that you are forced to cut back on your course work in order to increase your time on paid jobs. In the worst-case scenario, you may have to drop out of college and work full-time. A University of Indiana administrator was reputed to have said, "We lose more students to credit card debt than to academic failure."

Since credit reports are becoming a standard hiring practice for many firms, bad credit may even hinder your employability after graduation. Finally, the psychological problems can leave a lasting legacy. If you have filed bankruptcy, you may consider yourself a failure and have a difficult time rebuilding your self-esteem. Dealing with debt collectors can, at the minimum, be anxiety provoking. The accompanying stress can make it difficult to concentrate on studying and your grades may suffer.

The consequences of accumulating excessive debt are not inevitable. Even though easy access to credit may be very tempting, it still is possible to learn how to manage debt while in college or after graduation.

This chapter will illustrate the following common money management situations experienced by college students:

- Easy access to credit
- Becoming overextended on credit cards
- Dealing with parental reaction to money problems
- Using student loans and scholarships to finance non-school expenses
- Peer pressure to spend
- Risky stock trading
- Online gambling
- Dropping out of school

The Three R's of College: Reading, 'Riting and Revolving Debt

The college years are probably the first time in your life where your parents will not constantly monitor you. The hour you go to sleep or wake up, your activities, what you eat, whom you hang out with, and how you spend your money become your decisions, not theirs. This newfound independence can be quite liberating, as your parents' rules and guidance are no longer controlling your life to the extent they used to. However, this may cause you to make decisions that you are not truly knowledgeable about, just because you can.

Decisions involving credit cards will be yours as long as you are at least eighteen years old. Prior to this age, any credit cards you may have had were in your parents' name. Even though you were able to use the card, it still was your parents' account. Once you reach a legal age though, the card becomes yours and so does the liability.

You are free to have as many credit cards as you can obtain with a credit limit as high as you can qualify for. But being responsible for making spending decisions on your own also means being responsible for repaying the debt you've accumulated. You'll find that your freedom in choosing how to spend your available credit does not apply to your freedom in choosing how and when to repay it. There are payment deadlines and set amounts that you are required to repay. With some studies showing that as many as one third of college graduates have experienced problems with credit card debt, your credit obligations should be carefully considered prior to getting that first card.

Jane came from a small Midwestern town to attend Ohio State University, a school whose student body totals over 50,000 undergraduates. Jane knew almost everyone in her hometown and now she found herself living in a dorm with more people than her entire town's population. This "new world" was overwhelming and liberating at the same time. Jane was finally free from her strict parental rule. Now all she needed was money.

Her parents were very conservative, especially in regards to financial matters. They always paid cash for everything and put themselves and Jane on a strict budget. In addition to monitoring Jane's allowance, they had always paid close attention to her friends and activities. Now that she was away from their watchful eye, she planned on asserting her newfound independence.

As a freshman, she signed up for her first credit card when an application caught her eye. It said, "Finally, a credit card that gives you something you really want, fun." She had to admit that the free cell phone also made the offer irresistible. Jane filled out the application immediately.

Armed with her first credit card, Jane made sure that she did not deny herself anything. Her credit cards were always there for her when she needed financial help. They did not ask questions about why she needed the money or moralize about her spending patterns like her parents would have. After all, she was just following what the advertisements were telling her to do, "Just do it," "Don't deny yourself," and "Indulge." Some of Jane's friends turned down social invitations because it wasn't in their budget, but Jane never missed an opportunity. She went to movies, football games, concerts, stores, and restaurants.

One night, less than one month after getting her first credit card, Jane tried to pay at a restaurant with her credit card and found that the approval wouldn't go through. She had not yet received her first bill, since she had had the card for less than a month, and she couldn't imagine that she had already reached the limit. Several days later the credit card statement arrived in the mail and confirmed that she had indeed reached her initial $500 limit. Jane started to panic but then noticed that all she was required to pay was a $20 minimum payment. This she could handle. In fact, if she could handle one credit card, why not another?

Jane applied for two more credit cards and promptly charged them up to their limits. As she continued to make the minimum payment each month, Jane couldn't believe what a small price she had to pay for so much fun (just like the advertisement promised)! Jane had every intention of continuing her pattern of getting a new credit card every time she had exhausted the credit available on her last card. In fact, the credit card companies were helping her by frequently increasing her available credit limit. Unfortunately, this pattern stopped working after her sixth credit card.

For a reason that she couldn't understand, her applications were now getting turned down. The reason given was that she was "overextended." Jane did not have any idea what that meant. All that Jane understood was that her source of money had suddenly dried up. She had started using cash advances on her sixth credit card as a means to make payments on her other five accounts. She was playing the "credit card shuffle," using one credit card to pay the other. Now how was she supposed to pay her credit card bills?

To make matters worse, her parents' combined income precluded her ability to qualify for a subsidized Stafford loan (Guaranteed Student Loan) and she would have had to get her parents' approval for any other loan program. Telling her parents was not an option. She was sure they would take away her credit cards and put her on a strict budget if they found out, and she couldn't let that happen.

Jane decided to start working part-time at a retail store at the mall in order to have money to pay her credit card bills. Unfortunately, this decision added a seventh credit card to Jane's wallet. She justified the additional card because she could only get store discounts if she made her purchases with the store credit card. She convinced herself that she was saving money by using this credit card.

As her debt accumulated, so did the number of hours Jane was forced to work. Between working and studying, Jane started burning the candle at both ends. In fact, the more she worked part-time, the more she felt she deserved to eat out, enjoy a concert, and hit the clubs with friends. What Jane didn't realize at the time was that she had opened a Pandora's box of rising expectations that could only be satisfied with greater levels of debt and more hours of employment. It became a vicious cycle.

Soon her grades started to suffer because she had less and less time to spend studying. Before she knew it, she was working almost full-time and failing most of her classes. She decided to drop out for the semester and catch up financially. Unfortunately, by only making the minimum payment each month, her debt never seemed to go down. In addition, she had a tremendous amount of guilt because she had been lying to her parents who still thought she was in school.

Jane is living a lie, which will eventually be found out by her parents. The truth will come out and the longer she waits, the longer her college education is being delayed. Right now she is just treading water by making only the minimum payment each month on her $6,000 in total debt. The following example puts into perspective the time it will take Jane to pay off her debt.

If a college freshman with a much lesser balance of $2,000 quits charging on the card and only pays the minimum of $40 due each month at 19 percent interest, he or she could earn a bachelor's degree, complete a master's program, and still have two years left to finish paying off that freshman plastic binge.

Once Jane accepts the fact that her current course of action cannot make a dent in her debt, she will hopefully be more willing to talk to her parents, discuss her situation with a credit counselor, or explore a solution with her school's financial aid office. Until she does so, Jane will continue burning the candle at both ends until it finally burns out. Some danger signs of being overextended are:

- Are you arguing over your bills?
- Are you living from paycheck to paycheck?
- Can you only make the minimum payments on your charge accounts?
- Do you put off medical or dental visits because you don't have the money?
- Would you be in immediate financial difficulty if you lost your job?
- Are you afraid to add up your debt?
- Are you juggling one credit payment to make another?
- Are you receiving past due notices or calls from creditors?
- Are you unable to save?
- Are you running out of money before the next payday?
- Are you using credit cards for normal living expenses?
- Are you borrowing from family and friends?

Jane should have figured out before she started to experience any of these danger signs how much debt she could handle by completing the debt percentage worksheet introduced in Chapter 3. As a refresher, the following guidelines correspond to the percentage of your total monthly debt payments compared to one's net income.

If the debt percentage is:

Under 10 to 15 percent	Relax—Your debt to income percentage is well within acceptable guidelines.

15 to 20 percent	Be cautious—You may want to reduce your current debt loan. Do not take on new debt.
Over 20 percent	Danger—You are heavily in debt and should not under any circumstances take on additional debt!

If Jane had done these calculations prior to getting her first credit card, she would have realized the maximum amount she could have handled per month. Since her net monthly income was only $1,000, Jane could not take on more than 20 percent, or $200 a month, in debt payments. Her car payment was $150 so she could only afford to pay $50 extra in credit card payments. Do you now see why she was forced to play the "credit card shuffle"?

Robbing Peter to pay Paul is never a long-term answer. It may temporarily fix the problem, but in the long run you can't accept a debt level that is in the danger zone! Keep this danger zone in mind when you are confronted with the spending decisions you must now make on your own. Recall one of the lessons from Chapter 2, "Do you really need it or just want it?"

The Freshman Ten

Although the "freshman ten" has usually referred to the extra ten pounds the average college freshman gains during their first year, it also can refer to debt. In the case of Christi, the "freshman ten" referred to the extra $10,000 she charged on credit cards her first year in college.

Credit card companies eagerly seek your business. College students are targeted for many reasons: it is cheaper to conduct mass marketing campaigns on college campuses (about one-half the cost of marketing elsewhere); students forge long-term corporate loyalties (an average of at least fifteen years for credit cards); and their present and future needs include a wide-range of financial services (private student loans, debt consolidation loans, checking accounts, savings accounts, auto loans, and home mortgages). Finally, unlike other nearly saturated credit card "niche" markets, at least one-third of the population of four-year colleges and universities are replenished each year with new students (freshmen and transfers).

The reality is that the United States is a free market society, and when someone is of a legal age, they can be pursued as a customer and held responsible for their debts. This means that as a college student, you will continue to be sought after by credit card companies and other financial institutions. Remember that just because you are offered a credit card doesn't mean that you have to accept it.

Christi's problems all started as a freshman when she found a credit card application that had been placed in her bag at Florida State University's bookstore. She did not have a credit card and thought it would be smart to have one for emergencies. She was far from home, having been born and raised in Illinois, and she felt safer having a credit card in her possession. Unfortunately, Christi's definition of an emergency included meals out, party clothes, and football tickets. She enjoyed going out with her friends, which soon became a daily occurrence.

When she reached the limit on her first credit card she easily obtained another application from a credit card company's booth outside the student union. Christi even got a water bottle and a beach towel for filling out the application. When this card also became charged to the max, Christi went back to the student union and this time got a T-shirt along with her third credit card.

Before it even seemed possible, Christi had accumulated $10,000 on her three credit cards. She never kept track of her spending, so it was easy to get her debt level up this high. So far she had been able to handle the minimum payments by working her part-time waitress job, but now these payments were more than she could handle. She responded by increasing her hours at the restaurant, which left less time to devote to her schoolwork.

By the time summer break arrived, Christi returned home with poor grades and a large debt. She advised her credit card companies of her new address in order to receive her bills over the summer. Her spending habits would have remained a secret if it hadn't been for her brother. He saw a credit card bill arrive one day for Christi and promptly opened it. He wasted no time in telling Christi's parents about the amount of money that she owed.

Her mother and father were livid. They were extremely disappointed and Christi had to endure numerous lectures on her poor money management. But in the end, they paid off her credit cards since they didn't want Christi's credit affected negatively. By the time Christi returned to college in the fall, they had her sincere promise to not apply for any more credit cards. If she did, her parents said she would be on her own to pay them off.

Christi might argue her story had a "happy ending." Her parents paid off her debt and her problem went away. Typically though, when the debtor has someone else pay off their debt, they never learn the lesson. Therefore, the behavior that got them into debt in the first place will probably be repeated. Christi could easily continue her same old spending habits and believe that despite her parents' warning, they would bail her out again if she got into trouble. By relying on her parents to be her financial guardians, Christi could have a difficult time becoming financially independent.

A much happier ending would have been for Christi to have taken a loan from her parents and remain accountable for her debt. She could have paid them back interest free on a payment schedule she could handle. This lingering debt would have served as a reminder of what can happen when credit is not used wisely. Hopefully Christi would then have learned a valuable lesson.

Remember these simple rules regarding credit usage:

1. One or two (at the most) major credit cards is all you need to build a credit history.
2. Set your own credit line/limit. Recommendation—$500 and not more than $1,000.
3. Pay your bills on time.
4. You can build a credit history without carrying an unpaid balance.
5. If you must carry a balance, always pay as much as you can afford each month and try to pay it off within three months.

A Degree in Debt

Credit cards are not the only source of money that needs to be managed wisely in college; student loans and scholarship money can be equally as dangerous. It has become a reality that most students will need to receive financial aid during college since many of their parents have not saved enough to cover all of the costs. In fact, a quarter (26 percent) of parents who say they expect to pay for some or all of their child's college education say they have saved less than $5,000 and a third (32 percent) haven't saved anything specifically for that purpose, according to a poll by Harris Interactive, 2006. This represents only one year of the total cost of attending public universities and only about 6 percent of the cost of private colleges.

Unfortunately, rarely do parents start saving early enough. Many times, they first think about funding their children's college education while the entry applications are being filled out. This reality means that you may have to supplement savings with financial assistance. In the seventies, loans made up 25 percent of government assistance in funding higher education, while grants were the majority. Now loans are about 80 percent or more of the available government assistance.

You will need to apply for loans to make up the difference of what you have available and what you need to pay. This amount should be estimated frugally. You may be eligible for more money than you need. Remember the lesson from Chapter 2: the more money you have, the more you spend. If this pattern holds true for student loans, you may be tempted to borrow too much and spend it on things totally unrelated to school.

Michael had always wanted to attend an Ivy League school, so when he got his acceptance notice from Harvard, he was elated. Even though its tuition was very high, Michael believed that a degree from this prestigious school was well worth the expense. Since his parents couldn't afford to help him pay for the tuition costs, Michael, who had just turned eighteen, had to rely on student loans and a scholarship to foot the bill.

During his freshman semester, the school recorded his student loan and scholarship disbursements electronically in his university account. After the school debited his account to cover tuition, room and board, and other fees, the amount left over was given back to Michael. This amount should have been earmarked for future educational expenses. Instead, Michael considered this money his own private funds to pay for any personal (noneducational) expenses, which might come his way.

These personal funds turned out to be for expenses like drinks for his buddies at the local bar, road trips during the weekends, dinners out with his girlfriend, football tickets, and other daily personal expenditures. Michael felt lucky that he had this extra source of income while his friends seemed to barely have enough money to buy an occasional burger at the local hangout.

When it came time to apply for his student loans for his sophomore year, there was no question that Michael would request the maximum amount available to him, even though his actual school expenses were much lower. He repeated this pattern every year without worry, since he didn't have to start repaying these loans until after he graduated. Eventually that day came to pass and Michael was out on his own working his first post-college full-time job.

His salary of $25,000 was typical for a recent college graduate and it was able to cover his living expenses until he got a bill in the mail six months after he had graduated. This bill was the first monthly payment for his student loans, which he would now be repaying for ten long years. Michael was shocked when he saw the amount he was now required to pay monthly. The reality of the $12,200 in total student loan debt that he owed sent him into a panic.

In fact, when Michael did a monthly budget of his situation based on his student loan obligation plus $2,200 in credit card debt plus monthly living expenses of $2,100, he found out that he would have to earn $38,512 annually in order to break even! His current salary left him $14,000 short. This shortfall quickly put Michael into default since he could not afford his monthly payment.

Michael should have borrowed student loans only up to the amount that he actually needed and not up to the available limit. Since Michael also had received a scholarship, the actual shortage needed to be covered by student loans was not that great. Borrowing more money than was necessary left Michael with a generous slush fund, which allowed him to live a life not like the typical "starving student."

Michael seemed to have forgotten the true purpose of student loans, to pay for school expenses and not personal expenses. Otherwise, they would have been called "personal loans" instead of "student loans."

It is important to realize that student loan debt cannot be discharged, even in bankruptcy. However, a student experiencing repayment difficulty (like Michael) has many options available to them to deal with this debt.

Deferment: You can receive a deferment for certain defined periods. A deferment is a temporary suspension of loan payments for specific situations such as reenrollment in school, unemployment, or economic hardship

Forbearance: Forbearance is a temporary postponement or reduction of payments for a period of time because you are experiencing financial difficulty. You can receive forbearance if you're not eligible for a deferment.

Other forms of payment relief: Graduated and income-sensitive repayment plans are available. Graduated payment plans provide short-term relief through low interest-only payments followed by a gradual increase in payments (usually every two years). An income-sensitive payment plan offers borrowers payments based on yearly income. As that rises and falls, so do the payments.

Consolidation: By consolidating numerous Federal Loans (some private lenders now allow consolidation of private loans), the monthly payment will normally decrease.

Source: U.S. Department of Education

In 2005, the student loan default rate on federal loans was a low 4.5 percent. This is a dramatic reduction from a peak of 22 percent in 1990. The advent of many of the above repayment strategies may have significantly contributed to this reduction.

Leaving the Nest

Moving away from home for the first time is a pivotal moment in your life. It is one of the rites of passage to becoming an adult. Whether your first place is a room in a dorm or in a sorority or fraternity, it is still your own. You can decorate it how you please, invite over whom you want, and stock your refrigerator any way you wish. It is up to you.

Independent spending decisions now become an everyday occurrence, but they also involve an incredible amount of financial freedom that most young adults are not prepared to handle. Living at home usually meant that your parents paid for most living expenses. It is a rude awakening when bills start arriving in the mail once you're on your own. Phone bills, utilities, car payments and credit card bills are just some of the new arrivals you'll find in your mailbox.

It is a good idea to do a budget prior to moving out so that you can anticipate your expenses. If you can't do a budget in advance, it should be done as soon as you start living independently. Estimate your monthly income from all sources (student loans, scholarships, jobs, parent's allowance, and gifts). This should be income left over once you have paid your tuition-related expenses. Then multiply by the percentages given for each expense category to figure out how much you should budget for each expense. If you determine that you can afford a maximum of $200 for food per month, then you need to spend within that limit. That may mean not bringing your dates to expensive restaurants on a regular basis (especially if you are paying for two). Try to live within the limits of each category in order to live within your means.

Income

Monthly net income (after taxes and other deductions)
$______________

Expenses

Category	Percent of Monthly Income	Dollar Amount Budgeted
Housing	31%	$__________
Food	16%	$__________
Clothing	6%	$__________
Health	5%	$__________
Transportation	20%	$__________
Apartment purchases	7%	$__________
Savings	7%	$__________
Miscellaneous	8%	$__________
Total expenses:		**$__________**

The total expenses should be equal to the net income. If you know what your expenses are and the income you have available, you will be more likely to live within your means.

Also keep in mind that there are many first time move-in costs. Some of these costs may not apply if you decide to live in a dorm or a fraternity/sorority. But if you choose an apartment or house, these up-front costs will need to be paid. The following is a worksheet, which lists some of the most common up-front costs:

Up-Front Expenses

Application fee for apartment	$__________
Deposit for apartment	$__________
Deposit for pets	$__________
Deposit for electric service	$__________
Deposit for gas service	$__________
Deposit for telephone service	$__________
Installation fee for cable TV	$__________

First month's rent on apartment $______________

Total Expenses (up-front) $______________

In addition to these up-front costs, if the residence you choose is unfurnished, you will need to come up with the money to equip your place with the furniture, appliances, utensils, and other housewares that you will need—sleeping on the floor gets old and painful after awhile!

Below is a price range for new furniture from a sampling of national furniture retailers. This will help you calculate the amount you'll need to spend. Don't forget that the cost of furnishing your new dwelling can be reduced dramatically by accepting donated furniture from your relatives and shopping garage sales or thrift stores.

New Furniture Costs

Three bedrooms $2,500–$9,400
Three beds, three dressers, six end tables, six lamps

Living room $4,000–$6,800
Sofa (leather), coffee table, two end tables, two lamps

Dining room $3,000–$5,000
Table with eight chairs

Kitchen $500–$3,000
Table with four chairs

Den/office $3,400–$9,000
Computer, desk and shelving, chair

Family room $1,900–$3,600
Sofa, end table, lamp, TV set, pool table

Add it all up and the damage comes to: $15,300 to $36,800

With these estimates as a guideline (or better yet, look at the advertisements in your local paper's inserts), fill in the blanks for the budget below:

Move-In Expenses

Furniture for one bedroom apartment (used)
$_______________

Furniture for one bedroom apartment (new)
$_______________

Dishes, cookware, flatware
$_______________

Decorator items (bedspread, rugs, shower curtain)
$_______________

Cleaning supplies (mop, broom, all-purpose cleaner)
$_______________

Paper towels, toilet paper and incidentals
$_______________

Food (including first time staples- butter, mustard)
$_______________

Total Expenses (move-in) $_______________

Total expenses for first month*
$_______________

*add together the up-front and move-in expenses totals

It doesn't help that today's college students have so much stuff. David Halberstam, the Pulitzer Prize-winning author, recalled that when he went to Harvard in 1951 he unpacked five pairs of pants and two pairs of shoes. Only the most affluent students had hi-fi sets. The reality today is that a young person on their own wants their place to be furnished exactly like the home they just came from, complete with television, stereo, blender, and computer. These items cost money and, more times than not, are paid for with borrowed funds (credit cards or loans). Until this trend is stopped, debt levels will continue to be unacceptably high. Take a look at a partial inventory of one shared dorm room at California Lutheran University:

- 4 computers
- 2 cordless phones
- 2 TVs
- Over 300 CDs
- 2 mini-refrigerators
- 1 microwave oven
- 2 pairs of in-line skates
- 2 secondhand sofas
- 7 pairs of sneakers
- 4 printers
- 3 cell phones
- 3 stereos
- 80 DVDs and 1 DVD rack
- 1 toaster
- 1 vacuum cleaner
- 1 pair of skis and poles
- 15 impressionist posters
- Number of vehicle it took to move in: 7

The comedian George Carlin once said that the only reason we move to bigger houses is because we have more stuff. How much stuff do you have?

Dealing with Peer Pressure

Peer pressure can be a very strong influence in decisions of all kinds. The need to fit in becomes a strong influence on our actions. If we are surrounded by others who are richer than we are, we may feel the need to upgrade our clothes, our cars, and our entertainment choices to match theirs. This upgrading requires money which can become a problem if you're trying to compete with another student whose dad is the CEO of a Fortune 500 company.

Ultimately, self-esteem comes from believing in yourself for the person that you are and not for what you wear. Unfortunately, this is easier said than done. College is a melting pot of students from all backgrounds. For the first time, you may find yourself in contact with others who come from a different economic background than you do. Try to remember that some students have more resources than others and that it is an expensive undertaking to try and keep up with those who are in another financial league.

George was not qualified to enter the big leagues, but he wanted to join the team all the same. George was attending the University of Southern California, a university with tuition of around $20,000 a year. His parents, although not wealthy, had managed to save $40,000 for his education. This amount combined with his student loans should have carried him through his four years. A rational calculation of his necessary budget didn't take into consideration the peer pressure George would encounter.

George grew up in rural Kansas. He was the high school valedictorian and football quarterback. These factors helped him to get accepted to numerous schools. George decided on USC because he had never seen the ocean and the excitement of Los Angeles was in stark contrast to his predictable hometown.

Upon arriving, George immediately felt like he didn't fit in. The majority of the other students came from wealthy families, and George found he didn't have the financial spending means available to him that they took for granted. In order to subsidize his activities as one of the crowd, George turned to credit cards. He felt that people treated him differently when they saw his "Gold Card." At first, it was difficult for him to use his new credit cards since his parents had always preached that debt was bad. But by paying his bills in full, George was able to tell himself that his credit card usage was all right since he wasn't accumulating a balance.

After George got comfortable with using his credit cards, he started to carry a small balance. Over time, this small balance started becoming bigger as his available funds weren't able to cover what was owed each month. To rationalize this running balance, George changed his view of debt as a "bad" thing to something acceptable since it was college debt and that was "good" debt. Wasn't it a fact that everyone had to take on debt to go to college? Wasn't everyone expected to have student loans? Besides, all his peers believed that the great jobs they would be getting after graduation would enable them to pay off their credit card debts.

Now George is a recent college graduate. He is earning an entry-level wage at a large corporation. Although he began with a starting salary of $60,000, George's paycheck is only large enough to pay his rent, car payment, student loans, and credit cards. George continues to rely on his credit cards to pay for gas, groceries, or anything else he wants to buy. Forget savings! He lives in a very small studio apartment in a dangerous part of town since that is all he can afford. The sad thing is that George will be looking forward to making his student loan payments for the next ten years. That's a short time compared to twenty-three years for his credit card payments if he continues to pay at his current rate.

Peer pressure is a hard thing to ignore. It takes a high level of self-esteem to resist conforming to the "crowd." If George wouldn't have felt the pressure to keep up financially with his wealthier classmates, he probably wouldn't have accumulated so much debt. In retrospect, George now realized he had a choice to live a frivolous and lavish lifestyle during college and the life of a pauper afterwards or live the life of a starving student while in school (more acceptable) and a comfortable life after graduation. He now wishes he had made the later choice.

Financing a lifestyle that you can't afford with credit cards will just serve to get you into debt. Take a look at how expensive a simple $50 textbook becomes if you purchase it with your credit card and pay over time.

By Interest Rate and Number of Years

I bet you never realized a textbook could cost so much! A $50 textbook would end up costing $4,579 with accumulated interest at a 22.8 percent interest rate. Wouldn't it have been

Finance Period	10.8%	13.8%	16.8%	19.8%	22.8%
1 year	$55.68	$57.35	$59.08	$60.85	$62.67
4 years	$76.87	$86.56	$97.45	$109.68	$123.41
5 years	$85.59	$99.29	$155.15	$133.48	$154.68
10 years	$146.53	$197.19	$265.17	$356.34	$478.49
15 years	$250.83	$391.59	$610.66	$951.26	$1,480.21
20 years	$429.39	$777.65	$1,406.31	$2,539.46	$4,579.04

*Source: "Credit Cards on Campus," Consumer Federation of America survey

cheaper to have paid cash? A good rule of thumb is "If you don't have the cash, you can't afford it."

Of course there are things that you'll need to finance, like a car or house, but definitely not a sweater, dinner, or a textbook. Paying with credit is easier than paying with cash. Cash seems more real; you have the tendency to be more conservative since it is "real" money as opposed to "plastic." If you do buy on plastic, try and pay off the charges in full when you get the bill. Under all circumstances, resist paying only the minimum payment. The minimum payment trap might cause you to end up paying $4,579 for a $50 textbook.

College Dropout

If you end up making money mistakes while in college, you usually hurt no one else but yourself. However, if you are married or if you share expenses with a roommate, your financial decisions will affect others. For example, if your roommate eats more than you do, is it fair to split the grocery bill in half? If bills can be divided according to the portion of the total bill that each person is responsible for, it is usually equitable. Unfortunately, this amount is sometimes not so easily determined and disagreements result. The worst thing to do is not talk about it. Only when the dispute is discussed can it ever hope to be resolved.

When the sharing of finances involves a spouse or a spouse-to-be, your decisions also will have a lasting impact on the other person, since you will be sharing a life together and not just a semester. Therefore, it becomes even more important to be open and honest about your shared financial responsibilities. Lack of communication can lead to consequences other than financial ones.

Bret and Kim met during their freshman year in college at Berkeley and it was love at first sight. They both were students in the engineering department and had big plans for the future. By their sophomore year, they were engaged. Kim's family was wealthy and she grew up living a privileged lifestyle in a high-income neighborhood in San Francisco. She always attended the best private schools and never lacked for anything she needed or wanted. Bret, on the other hand, was raised in a working class community in Fresno where he attended schools better known for their high dropout rate than a high academic record. Despite his surroundings, Bret studied all the time and was rewarded with a college scholarship.

Bret always felt inferior around Kim's parents and family. He felt he wasn't good enough because of his background and lack of money. These feelings of inadequacy never went away and he became obsessed with proving to them that he was successful. One day, Bret figured out how he could at least get in the race, if not keep up with the Joneses. He applied for his first of many credit cards from an application at the bookstore.

He used this newfound source of money to pay for expensive clothes, designer eyeglasses, and fine dining. These acquisitions came with such ease that he even traded in his used car for a new one financed with a hefty loan. Kim wondered where Bret was getting the money to pay for all these things and he explained that his scholarship money included a very generous living allowance.

This charade worked for a while. He even started to feel comfortable around Kim's parents. One day, Bret received his first of many collector phone calls at his dorm and he knew that the game was over. His debt far exceeded the small living allowance (not the generous one he told Kim) he received from his scholarship. Bret decided to get a part-time job. This helped initially, but unfortunately Bret continued to spend. He had gotten used to living a more privileged lifestyle and he strongly resisted going back.

When he realized he had to work full-time in order to pay his bills, he made the decision to quit school temporarily. When Bret finally confessed his debt to Kim, she was at first confused and then furious. How could Bret drop out of school? What about their high hopes for their future together? Kim couldn't understand the driving force behind Bret's spending. She had never felt the inadequacy that Bret did around people with money. To her it didn't matter whether Bret had money or not. She was completely baffled by his actions and, feeling betrayed, decided to call off the engagement.

If Bret had been honest with Kim about his feelings of inadequacy around her family, maybe Kim could have assured him that it didn't matter to her how much money he had. This knowledge would have hopefully put his fears to rest and prevented his spending spree. If they had had an honest discussion about their upbringings, they could have gained a much deeper understanding of each other. Since attitudes and beliefs about money are very powerful and can determine behavior, Kim's knowledge of Bret's attitudes could have provided the clue to his sudden accumulation of expensive items and lavish spending.

To get insight into your own attitudes toward money, it is helpful to ask the following questions:

- How important is money to me?
- Is being wealthy one of my goals?
- What does money allow me to do?
- How do I handle it when I don't have enough money?

The answers to these questions can provide an initial glimpse into the role that money does and will play in your life.

Where Did the Money Go?

The old saying "Money doesn't grow on trees" could be replaced in modern times by the saying, "Money doesn't just come from the machine." Both of these sayings are trying to convey the fact that money usually has to be worked for. Trying to get money the fast and easy way is usually not a good idea—it may involve something illegal or highly risky. The promise of quick riches is usually just that, a promise.

You never should rely on money as a sure thing, even if it comes from the normal channels like a paycheck, a formal loan, or a scholarship. You could lose your job, default on your loan, or have your scholarship taken away. In the case of other not so formal channels, like a loan shark or gambling, the reliability of receiving the money is even more dubious. Problems can result when you start relying on something (money) that you think is a sure thing when in fact it is quite tenuous.

Samuel never did well academically in school, but he was an excellent athlete. His talent earned him an athletic scholarship to Penn State University. Being on the football team gave him a social status, and Samuel found himself living an active social life in between practices and games. He also joined the Phi Delta Theta fraternity, which added to his social opportunities. His credit cards allowed him to routinely charge $50 bar tabs for his friends and to spend Spring Break in Miami. Without his credit cards, it would have meant "social death."

Samuel's scholarship paid for tuition and a portion of his room and board, but all other expenses were his responsibility. His father had always preached, "If you can't afford it, don't buy it." This advice was for other people though, certainly not for someone on their way to playing professional football and earning millions of dollars.

Between Samuel's social life and the time he devoted to football, he found little time for studying. His grades soon started to plummet. Samuel didn't worry. Since he was a football star, he didn't believe that the university would let him fail. Unfortunately, his confidence was not warranted. Soon, his academic advisor informed him that if his grades didn't improve, he would lose his scholarship. Samuel started studying hard for the first time, but unfortunately it was too late. He was already so far behind that he couldn't catch up. He was put on academic probation and lost his scholarship.

With his scholarship money no longer available to him, Samuel didn't have the money to pay his credit card bills. Summer break was approaching and his roommate, who was on the football team, came up with an idea for a summer business venture. They would coach a summer football camp for kids. This seemed like the answer to their financial woes. They financed the costs for the publicity and the rental of a sports facility with cash advances from their credit cards. Unfortunately, they planned this too late and they ended up not having enough clients to cover their cash advances.

In a financial panic, they followed a tip from a friend that a certain tech stock was going to skyrocket. They took out cash advances on the remaining amount left on their credit cards and invested it all in the stock market, hoping to make up their losses. This risky venture, which amounted to gambling, also failed when the stock plummeted. Samuel ended up having no choice but to drop out of school and take a job at a factory in his hometown. This future was a far cry from the glamorous world of professional sports that had been his dream.

Samuel had looked for the easy way out of his financial dilemma. Fast business schemes without adequate planning and high risk stock market investing are usually a formula for disaster. Both solutions are tantamount to going to Las Vegas and betting all your money on blackjack. Although you might beat the blackjack dealer several times, the odds are stacked against you.

There are usually no fast solutions to money problems. Even solutions like a bankruptcy that may seem fast and painless, usually aren't (see Chapter 14). Samuel should have considered reducing his credit card usage and avoiding further cash advances. He could have dropped off the football team for a season and concentrated on his coursework until his grades improved. Raising his grades would have probably made him eligible for his scholarship again. The old adage "You can't get something for nothing" usually applies in most instances and Samuel's case was no exception.

What Do You Mean You Don't Gamble?

College campuses have become a hotbed of financial recklessness. With the advent of easy-to-open online accounts, daredevil sports gambling and on-line day trading is practically a badge of honor among college students. In some cases, students are gambling with their student loans in an attempt to double the value of the loans. In the case of day trading, the risk seems minimal since the stock market has more or less had a continuous climb over the years. But this becomes very risky business when the market dives, or when the latest hot Internet start-up cools down or a hedge fund becomes worthless.

The dangers of gambling are overlooked by reports of students boasting after their tech stock doubled in one day. The more common incidents of stocks tumbling are usually not reported, so it appears that everyone is making money. The sentiment becomes "I would be a fool to not join in."

The first thing Francis checked when he turned on his computer was his stock portfolio. It always cheered him up, no matter how bad his day had been. Francis was in business school working on his MBA at Wharton. He was under a lot of stress since this program was a very demanding and prestigious one and his grades were poor. He found that a good way to reduce his stress and raise his self-esteem was to follow his stock portfolio.

After starting with $5,000 he had diligently saved from summer jobs, he had pushed this amount up to $12,000 by trading stocks online. Francis had been able to finance a summer trip to Europe and purchase a new computer through his gains. He thought nothing of picking up the bar tab for his friends when they went out, and they had come to count on it.

Francis's arrogance caused him to start investing in volatile stocks that he knew little about. On a tip from a friend about a medical breakthrough drug, he invested his whole portfolio in one company in order to realize huge profits. He even dreamed about dropping out of school with his earnings, figuring that with all his newfound wealth, college would become unnecessary.

As he was daydreaming about sailing in Greece, he noticed the stock price start to plummet on his computer monitor. He frantically tried to place a sell order, but since everyone else was trying to sell at the same time, his order didn't get filled until the stock had become basically worthless. Francis knew that he needed money in order to make money, so in desperation he bought a very high-risk stock in hopes of recouping his losses. However, this stock also performed badly. Before he knew it, he had lost almost all of his money. He had to borrow money from his dad in order to make it through the semester. By not following a long-range strategy (see Chapter 13), Francis had approached investing much like gambling.

One rule of thumb for deciding what investments to make is to add a percent sign to your age. You should have no more than that percentage of your money in fixed-income investments like bonds or CDs. The rest should be in stocks. For instance, if you are twenty years old, you should have no more than 20 percent of your long-term savings in fixed-income investments and 80 percent in a variety of stocks.

The willingness among college students to take risks is fueled by a perception that upon graduation they will have numerous high-paying job offers to choose from. It is no big deal if they lose money now since they will easily make it up once they start working. This strategy only works if that high-paying job materializes and their risky behavior stops. Unfortunately, this behavior, more times than not, becomes habit forming.

With today's college students having access to a credit card and an Internet connection, day trading or online gambling becomes as easy as a click of a mouse. Online sports gambling sites have diverted students' attention away from studying. Instead, they become fixated to the game on television and ignore their homework and social life in favor of the latest sports event. Grades suffer as do most of their pocketbooks. There have been stories of students copying down their roommates' or parents' credit card numbers in order to try and recoup their losses once their credit cards have reached the limit.

Although gambling/day trading has become a "cool thing to do," the risks need to be realized. It is not cool to have to drop out of school to work and pay off your losses, to beg for money from your parents, or, in the worst cases, steal credit card numbers to continue the habit. Investing wisely is the smartest way to go.

Financial Aid

It is necessary to realize that financing your education with your credit cards, day trading, or gambling are potentially the most expensive and risky things you can do. You need to research other forms of financial aid. The biggest problem in students securing financial assistance is that they are not always aware of what's available. Most colleges provide a variety of financial aid programs. Too many students wrongly assume they won't qualify. The truth is there are plenty of sources for grants, work-study programs, scholarships, and low-interest loans. The following is a chart summarizing Federal Aid options, according to the U.S. Department of Education:

Federal Student Aid Summary Chart			
Federal Student Aid Program	**Type of Aid**	**Program Details**	**Annual Award Limits**
Federal Pell Grant	Grant: does not have to be repaid	Available almost exclusively to undergraduates; all eligible students will receive the Federal Pell Grant amount they quality for	$400 to $4500 for 2006-
Federal Supplemental Educational Opportunity Grant (FSEOG)	Grant: does not have to be repaid	For undergraduates with exceptional financial need; priority is given to Federal Pell Grant recipients; funds depend on availability at school	$100 to $400
Academic Competitiveness Grant (ACG)	Grant: does not have to be repaid	For undergraduates receiving Pell grants who are U.S. citizens enrolled full-time in their first or second academic year* of study. For first academic year* students who have completed a rigorous secondary school program of study, graduated for high school after Jan. 1, 2006, and have not been previously enrolled in an undergraduate program. For second academic year* students who have completed a rigorous secondary school program of study, graduation from high school after Jan. 1, 2005, and have at least a 3.0 cumulative GPA at the completion of their first year of postsecondary study.	First academic year* students: up to $750 Second academic year* students: up to $1,300
National Science and Mathematics Access to Retain Talent Grant (National SMART Grant)	Grant: does not have to be repaid	For undergraduates receiving Pell Grants, who are U.S. citizens enrolled full-time in their third or fourth academic year* of an eligible degree program majoring in physical life, or computer sciences, engineering, technology, mathematics or a critical-need foreign language and have at least a 3.0 cumulative GPA.	Up to 4,000 for each of the third and fourth academic years*
Federal Work-Study (FWS)	Money is earned while attending school; does not have to be repaid	For undergraduate and graduate students; jobs can be on campus or off campus; students are paid at least federal minimum wage.	No annual minimum or maximum award amounts
Federal Perkins Loan	Loan: must be repaid	Interest charged on this loan is 5 percent for both undergraduate and graduate students; payment is owed to the school that made the loan.	$4,000 maximum for undergraduate students; $6,000 maximum for graduate and professional degree students; no minimum award amount

(Continued)

Subsidized Direct or FFEL Stafford Loan	Loan: must be repaid	Subsidized: U.S. Department of Education pays interest while borrower is in school and during grace and deferment periods; you must be at least a half-time* student and have financial need.	$3,500 to $8,500, depending on grade level
Unsubsidized Direct or FFEL Stafford Loan	Loan: must be repaid	Unsubsidized: Borrower is responsible for interest during the life of the loan; you must be at least a half-time* student; financial need is not a requirement.	$3,500 to $20,500 (less any subsidized amounts received for the same period), depending on grade level and dependency status
Direct of FFEL PLUS Loan	Loan: must be repaid	Available to parents of dependent undergraduate students who are enrolled at least half-time.* The PLUS Loan Program is now also available to graduate and professional degree students. Financial need is not a requirement. PLUS Loans are unsubsidized: Borrower is responsible for interest during the life of the loan.	Maximum amount is cost of attendance* minus any other financial aid the student receives; no minimum award amount

There's a single form that all colleges use called the Free Application for Federal Student Assistance (FAFSA). Most financial aid information is easily available online from the school you are planning on attending. Generally there will be a connection or a link to web resources for scholarships and other types of aid. After you've submitted your FAFSA, you will start getting requests for information. You need to respond quickly and provide all the information that's requested. That way, you'll stay on time and get the best aid available.

Grants or scholarships generally don't have to be repaid, but loans do. The repayment doesn't start until six months after graduation. If you continue onto graduate school, these payments can be deferred (delayed) until your schooling is complete. The interest on student loans is usually much lower than that of a conventional loan and definitely much lower than the interest on credit card debt. Keep in mind that most student loans can also be deferred if you suffer a hardship situation like the loss of a job.

In recent times, private loans have entered the marketplace. These are loans that exist outside of the federal student loan system and are not guaranteed by the federal government. These loans may be provided by banks, nonprofit agencies, or other financial institutions. The increasing significance of private loans can be seen in their vast growth: currently the yearly growth rate of private loans is outpacing that of federal loans.

Words of Wisdom

By understanding the special financial situations you may encounter in college, you will be able to handle them more intelligently. You should take the following "words of wisdom" with you from this chapter:

- Recognize the danger signs of being overextended.
- Calculate the debt level your income can handle.
- Try to pay your credit card bills in full.
- Resist peer pressure.
- Research financial aid options.
- Communicate with your parents, partner, and creditors if you experience financial problems.
- Avoid gambling.
- Follow a long-term investment strategy.
- Create a moving-out budget.
- Don't drop out of school.

6

What Do You Want to Be When You Grow Up?

If you don't know where you're going,
any road will take you there.

—*Alice in Wonderland*

In Chapter 2, we learned that there are only two ways to make your financial situation better, make more money or spend less. If you can't possibly cut down your expenses any further, you may want to concentrate on ways to increase your income. To clarify what defines income, it is money you have received free and clear or earned but not borrowed. Don't make the mistake of believing that credit (see Chapter 3) is an extension of your available income.

In 2005, teens (twelve through nineteen years old) had a combined income of $159 billion, according to Teenage Research Unlimited. Teens obtained their money from a variety of sources:

- From parents when needed
- Odd jobs
- Gifts
- Regular allowance
- Full-time jobs
- Part-time jobs

Even though teens' spending power is significant, compared to the previous year they are spending less. There are several factors that contribute to this. Parents are worried about unemployment, so they're not spreading the wealth around like they used to. And historically high gas prices mean that teens who drive are watching an unprecedented amount of their budget flowing directly into their gas tanks. Even though sixteen is legally the age in which a person is allowed to start working, teens younger than that are participating in some kind of work. Half of all fourteen year olds work in freelance jobs such as babysitting or doing yard work. By the time they reach fifteen, nearly two-thirds will be working.

Because of the high cost of a college education, many teens continue to work part-time jobs during high school or full-time jobs during the summer to help pay for their tuitions. Once they get to college, they keep on earning money, whether it's through a work-study job or a part-time job at a local business.

The transition to full-time employment is often made upon graduation. As you acquire more education and experience, you will find your income will increase accordingly. Workers with a bachelor's, master's, and doctoral or professional degree usually have higher incomes than do workers with less education. According to the U.S. Bureau of Labor Statistics, a college graduate makes 43 percent more per year than a person who doesn't have a high school diploma.

This chapter will examine the different choices you will confront when having to make employment related decisions. Your future earning potential can be seriously affected by unwise actions, such as:

- Deciding not to continue your education

- Not making enough money to pay your debts
- Choosing a career that is not in demand
- Budgeting based on your gross income instead of your net income
- Not understanding taxation

Off to Work We Go

The decision to go to college after high school can be influenced by many factors. The percentage of graduates going on to college from your high school can play a big role. If a large number of your classmates are college bound, it increases the likelihood that you will consider attending college. Additionally, if your parents are college graduates, your likelihood of going to college increases.

The reality is that increased education and increased pay go hand-in-hand. The statistics show that the higher educational level you attain, the higher salary you will command. Take a look at the U.S. Bureau of Labor Statistics' 2006 findings relating to earnings by educational attainment:

Highest Level	Weekly Earnings	Annual Earnings	Unemployment Rate
Some high school	$419	$21,788	6.8%
High School Graduate	$595	$30,940	4.3%
Bachelor's degree	$962	$50,024	2.3%
Master's degree	$1,140	$59,280	1.7%
Ph.D.	$1,441	$74,932	1.4%
Professional degree	$1,474	$76,648	1.1%

A "diploma premium" is attached to each advanced educational level. The average salary of someone with a master's degree is almost double that of someone with only a high school diploma;

someone with a professional degree averages four times more than someone with a high school diploma.

Brent's dad Walter had an undergraduate degree and always preached to Brent the value of going to college. Over the years, Walter had been passed over for promotions three times by people who were less qualified but had higher degrees. These disappointments frustrated him and he wished he had stayed in school longer. Walter didn't want his son to miss out on advancement opportunities, so he encouraged Brent to go to college.

However, his son did not share Walter's dream. Brent, at eighteen, thought college was a waste of time when the alternative was to earn "big bucks" immediately. His older brother was a starving student, and Brent did not find that lifestyle attractive. He didn't believe that a college degree had anything to do with making money, Brent's No. 1 priority was "a well-paying job." In fact, 81 percent of teen males chose "a well-paying job" as their number one future goal, according to *Men's Health.*

Brent began by selling health club memberships at a new fitness club. He made good money because he was paid a commission on each person he enrolled. The new members joined since this neighborhood had been underserved before; the closest gym had been a twenty-minute drive away. As the new members flocked to the club, Brent saw his paycheck get bigger and bigger, reinforcing his belief that he had made the right decision in choosing not to go to college. He would be studying and writing term papers right now instead of earning and spending money.

The good times did not last forever. As the club became saturated with new members, the new enrollees dwindled along with Brent's paycheck. His income leveled out to an amount that was far below what he felt he deserved to make. So Brent quit and started looking for another job. He thought that a different industry would prove to be the solution.

As he applied for jobs, he noticed that many required a college degree. He could apply only for those jobs that required a high school diploma. After failing to earn the money he wanted, Brent started to wonder if maybe his dad had been right. When he came to his dad for advice, Walter had the urge to say, "I told you so" but didn't because he knew his son had to make this discovery on his own.

After a long discussion, Brent decided to go to college after all. In fact, in convincing his son to go to school, Walter also convinced himself. He found an evening program that allowed him to continue working full-time and get his master's degree at the same time. As Walter lectured Brent about the need to delay gratification while making sacrifices in the present, he was also lecturing himself. He knew that his decision to go back to school would not be an easy one.

The short-term difficulties of juggling a job and an education can pay off well in the long-term. There are many training programs to increase your skills in a specific area, which could also make you more marketable and increase your salary. There are also many colleges and universities that cater to the working adult. You can continue to work and also receive your education at the same time. Achieving this is not always easy, but people who have disciplined themselves to complete this undertaking are almost never sorry.

The Education Reporter Gets an Education

If you are spending a minimum of forty hours a week at a job, you should try and pick a profession you enjoy. Choosing an occupation that you are ill suited for may make you frustrated and unsuccessful in your career ambitions. Since we all have different skills and strengths, it is worthwhile to decide upon a career path that allows you to use your talents to the best of your ability.

Although we can argue that no job skill should be worth more than another, the fact remains that a doctor's skills are more highly compensated than a teacher's. If you find that the job of your dreams does not pay well, that fact should not detract you from pursuing it. When people decide upon professions solely for the financial reward, they often find themselves miserable in a job for which they feel no passion.

Once you have answered the difficult question "What do you want to be when you grow up?" you then need to do some research. Find the answers to the following questions:

- How much education is necessary for this profession?
- Do you need an advanced degree?
- How much will this education cost you?
- How much can you expect to earn?

Joan had decided upon her profession when she was a little girl. She always interviewed everyone around her. Joan loved to ask questions and had an inquisitive mind. She became the editor of her high school newspaper and was responsible for the paper winning several awards. It was therefore no great surprise to her parents when she decided to become a journalist.

She enrolled in Northwestern University's school of journalism and graduated near the top of her class. Upon graduation, at twenty-four, she started working as a reporter for a local newspaper in a Los Angeles suburb. Unfortunately, this dream job did not offer a dream salary. She made only $28,000 a year. Joan found it very difficult to survive on this salary in a very expensive city along with the $30,000 in student loans she had started repaying.

Since her beat was "education," she decided to write a story which compared average salaries for different jobs. The median salary for her profession "journalism" was $41,900, about equal to what a social worker earns. Joan was surprised by many of her findings when she did a random sampling from the Department of Labor's statistics:

Occupation	Average Annual Salary
Postsecondary Teachers	$64,610
Operations Managers	$99,280
Elementary School Teachers	$48,700
Accountants/ Auditors	$60,670
Computer Software Engineers	$82,000
Physicians/ Surgeons	$142,220
Network Systems Analysts	$67,460
Police Officer	$48,410
Lawyers	$113,660
Cooks, restaurant	$21,020
Fishing Workers	$28,510
Child Social Workers	$40,640
Personal Finance Advisors	$86,730
Radio Announcer	$36,120
Funeral Director	$57,250

For her story, Joan interviewed a young woman, Claire, who had graduated from law school two years earlier. After receiving her law degree, Claire promptly took the bar exam and flunked it. While she studied to prepare for her second attempt, she worked as a paralegal. While "lawyer" was the second-highest paying profession Joan's earning list at an average salary of $113,660, Claire's legal assistant job only paid her $45,460.

$113,660, Claire's legal assistant job only paid her $45,460. She had been relying on the higher salary to pay her student loans, which totaled $70,000. Now Claire found herself unable to make the monthly payments on her loans and was in default. She was scheduled to retake the bar exam the following week. If she didn't pass the second time, she knew she would be in a lot of trouble.

After hearing Claire explain that a higher paying job would be the solution to her problems, Joan went back to researching jobs and their respective salaries. She discovered that she could work as a technical writer and make more money, averaging $60,850 annually. Although her heart was in reporting, Joan decided that her more immediate concern was being able to repay her student loans. So she put her dream on hold and found a job as a technical writer.

When you are considering various professions, you should always take salaries into account in addition to considering other factors. The following is a career action plan to assist you in choosing a profession which will be a good fit for you. For each of the following elements of career planning:

a) Describe your current situation in this area.

b) State a specific goal you have in this area.

c) Describe the time frame for accomplishing this goal.

d) Indicate actions to achieve this goal.

1) Personal interests:

a)____

b)____

c)____

d)____

2) Career skills:

a)____________________________________

b)____________________________________

c)____________________________________

d)____________________________________

3) Education:

a)____________________________________

b)____________________________________

c)____________________________________

d)____________________________________

4) Employment position:

a)____________________________________

b)____________________________________

c)____________________________________

d)____________________________________

After you have answered question 4 and have identified career fields of interest to you, make a list of actual jobs within this field and their corresponding salaries. To aid you in your job search, you can consult the following sources:

- Library (career publications, government materials)
- Professional Associations (publications and meetings)
- Job training and employment offices
- Business contacts (teachers, former and potential employers)
- Personal contacts (relatives, friends)
- College campus career placement office
- Media (online employment services, newspaper articles, company websites)

The Bureau of Labor Statistics has a detailed listing of hundreds of jobs along with their average earnings (see Appendix).

Job	Average Salary
______________________	______________________
______________________	______________________
______________________	______________________
______________________	______________________
______________________	______________________
______________________	______________________

Once you have created your career action plan and identified jobs that are a good match for your skills, interests, and financial needs, you will be in a better position to make the right choice. If you decide to skip those steps and figure it out as you go along, you might eventually stumble upon your dream job, but you will waste a lot of time along the way.

Do You Know of Any Philosophy Jobs?

Once you have done some soul searching and investigation and have an idea of what your dream job might be, you must do one last piece of research. You need to find out if this job is in demand. If you have decided upon the perfect job but can't find employment, you might have to alter your career path.

As a young girl, Beatrice was always asking her parents questions that started with "Why." As she got older, she loved to analyze every situation to try to understand its complexities. This curiosity about the meaning of life extended to her studies after she started college. Beatrice enrolled in every philosophy class that was offered. She loved the process of learning and couldn't imagine stopping. By the time she was twenty-seven years old, she had received both her master's and doctorate degree in philosophy.

Having attained the highest education level possible, she had exhausted her days as a student and now had to make the transition to an employee. This turned out to be difficult. Beatrice searched for six months without any success finding employment in her chosen field. Any time she looked in the job classified section for a category called "philosophy" or typed in that word for a computer search of jobs, she came up with no matches.

Beatrice was getting nervous about her job prospects, especially since her student loan repayment had reached the end of its six-month grace period. Not knowing what to do, Beatrice scheduled an appointment with her former academic advisor in the philosophy department. This meeting provided her with more than just advice. She found out about the scheduled retirement of one of the members of the faculty. Beatrice applied for the vacancy and got the job.

Even though the starting pay was relatively low, what really made Beatrice feel trapped was the lack of other alternatives. She was able to afford her student loan payments only by living an extremely frugal lifestyle. She took her bicycle to class, even in the snow, and lived a lifestyle not unlike that of the "starving student."

Beatrice had failed to consider the question "How much in demand is a degree in philosophy?" If she had done some research, she would have probably discovered that this degree, like similar degrees in ancient history, Latin studies, or Shakespeare, had a limited demand. While these are all important and respectable areas of study, if obtaining a high salary is important to you, you will need to become trained in a more sought-after field.

According to the U.S. Bureau of Labor Statistics' "Employment Projections," here is a partial list of some of the jobs with the highest projected growth rates from 2004 to 2014:

Jobs	Employment Change by %
Home health aides	56%
Network systems and data communications analysts	54%
Medical assistants	52%
Physician assistants	49%
Computer software engineers, applications	48%
Physician therapist assistants	44%
Dental hygienists	43%
Computer software engineers, systems software	43%
Dental assistants	42%
Database administrators	38%
Physical therapists	36%
Forensic science technicians	36%
Veterinary technicians	35%
Preschool teachers, except special education	33%
Postsecondary teachers	32%
Hazardous materials removal workers	31%
Employment recruitment and placement specialists	30%
Environmental engineers	30%
Paralegals and legal assistants	29%

Although not all the highest growth rate jobs in this chart have correspondingly high salaries, at least you can be assured job openings will exist. Doing research into your career's desirability is well worth the effort. It could make the difference between having multiple job offers upon graduation and a visit to the unemployment office.

Who Is FICA and Why Are They Taking My Money?

The old adage "There are two things in life that are inevitable, death and taxes," still holds true today. The impact of taxes on your income can be quite significant. Neglecting to consider this influence can result in unrealistic salary expectations. Don't make the same mistake as Aileen, who forgot to add taxes into the equation.

When Aileen got her first full-time "real" job after college, she was told that her annual salary was going to be slightly over $27,000 a year. She promptly went home after accepting the job offer and calculated how much she was going to make from each paycheck. She received quite a shock when the actual amount listed on her check did not correspond to what she had anticipated. No one had ever explained to her the difference between "gross" and "net." Aileen did not realize that "gross" income is reduced by taxes and benefits to arrive at the "net" income, the amount she actually took home. Based on the U.S tax brackets for 2006, Aileen's income put her in the 15 percent tax bracket.

U.S. Tax Brackets-2006	
Single Taxpayer	**Rate**
$0-$7,550	10%
$7,551-$30,650	15%
$30,651-$74,200	25%
$74,201-$154,800	28%
$154,801-$336,550	33%
$336,551-and above	35%

Below is a breakdown of the actual deductions taken from her gross income:

Aileen's Bi-weekly Paycheck After Deductions

Earnings	Hourly Rate	Total Hours	This period	Year to date
Regular	13.02	80	$1,041.60	$12,323.81
Gross Pay			**$1,041.60**	**$12,323.81**
Deduction				
Federal Income Tax			$82.19	$959.85
Social Security Tax			$64.59	$764.08
Medicare Tax			$15.11	$178.70
State Income Tax			$34.27	$402.34
City Income Tax			$3.14	$34.50
Company 401(k) Retirement Plan			$31.25	$375.00
Medical Insurance			$25.00	$300.00
Net Pay			**$786.05**	**$9,309.34**

Since Aileen was not expecting money to be taken out of her check and diverted elsewhere, she had planned her budget considering the higher "gross" amount. As the result of this mistaken assumption, she had budgeted $255.55 more for each paycheck than she actually received. Unfortunately, Aileen had already signed an apartment lease based on the gross salary.

She desperately needed to make more money and thought she had found the perfect solution. Since taxes were the cause of her income reduction, she rationalized that she could adjust her withholdings on her W-2 form and get the money back. Aileen promptly went to the personnel department and changed her withholdings to "exempt." This allowed her to have the least amount of tax deductions taken out of her check. Although this change provided immediate relief by increasing the net income she received, it created a much larger problem in the long run.

When it came time to do her taxes, Aileen's accountant gave her the bad news. She owed the IRS $2,000. Since Aileen did not have the money to pay this amount, she just ignored it. The next year came and again she owed $2,000. Now her total debt to the IRS was $4,000. This did not include all the extra penalties that were assessed for being overdue. The IRS was starting to pursue Aileen for this money.

The collection methods available to the IRS are more aggressive than normal creditors. While normal creditors can legally garnish (take) only up to 25 percent of your disposable income, if you run afoul of Uncle Sam (taxes), he can take out as much as he wants from your daily wages. In addition, debts owed to the IRS are not dischargeable in a bankruptcy. Therefore, Aileen had no way to make this debt go away. The longer she ignored it, the worse her situation would become.

Aileen ended up making long-term payment arrangements with the IRS to catch up on the taxes she owed. She also went back to personnel and changed her W-2 form to the correct amount of withholdings that she should have been claiming. Finally, she moved out of her apartment into another one with a much lower rent. These changes were enough to make her financial situation manageable.

Aileen learned some important facts about taxation in the process:

- Money is withheld for federal, state, and sometimes city income taxes for reasons such as police, roads, and disaster relief.
- The FICA (Federal Insurance Contributions Act) tax pays for Social Security and Medicare.
- Additional deductions may be made for unemployment insurance, parking fees, dues, medical insurance, and an employer retirement plan.

Aileen also learned that a "progressive" income tax system means that as your income increases, so does the percentage of your income that is taxed. As Aileen earns more money throughout her career, the percentage of tax paid on her income will be greater.

While examining her employee manual, Aileen also discovered that she was receiving benefits that were included in her salary and not deducted from her paycheck. These benefits included sick days, holiday pay, and paid vacation. The value of these "fringe" benefits can be worth an additional 25 to 50 percent of an employee's salary. Common employer-provided fringe benefits include:

- Paid vacation
- Paid sick and maternity leave
- Holiday days
- Retirement plans (a company may match your contributions)
- Life insurance
- Reimbursement of educational expenses
- Employee discounts

Aileen never thought to include the value of these fringe benefits in her salary. Her best friend Susanna, who is self-employed, emphasized to Aileen that none of the benefits Aileen took for granted were available to her. Whenever she wanted to take a vacation, for example, she had to stop working and therefore reduce her income. Since employers vary in the benefits they offer their employees, you should consider these benefits carefully when making job decisions. The actual salary might not tell the whole story if the employer has a generous benefits package to go along with it.

Both income deductions and additions to the gross salary should be analyzed carefully to understand where your money is being directed. As you have seen, the bottom line of what you actually receive is not always as clear-cut as what you might have initially thought.

Words of Wisdom

Regardless of your chosen field, your earning power is probably your most valuable asset. Many people will earn more than $1 million during their working years. Follow the advice in this chapter to maximize your earning potential by:

- Continuing your education.
- Choosing a job that matches your skills and interests.
- Conducting detailed research on various job possibilities.
- Following a career action plan.
- Choosing a career path that is in demand.
- Factoring taxation into your financial plan.
- Comparing fringe benefits from different jobs.

7

Returning to the Nest

The trouble with having money to burn is that it usually comes after the fire has gone out.

—*A man at his retirement party*

Not surprisingly, most young adults look forward to financial independence. This desire to cut the umbilical cord of dependence upon their parents is also reinforced by their certainty that their parents are not going to support them forever. In fact, Charles Schwab's annual survey of "Teens and Money" found that 86 percent of teens expected their parents to stop supporting them before age twenty-five. However, the desire to cut the cord and the actual "ability" to cut the cord have created a very different reality for many young adults.

In a recent *Newsweek* poll, almost half of all college students graduating in 2006 said they were moving back into their parents' home after graduation. This boomerang effect is becoming increasingly common. In a number of instances, many "return to the nest" for financial reasons. Young adults may decide to come home because they cannot afford to be on their own or because they do not have marketable skills to find sustainable employment.

Even those who have been fortunate enough to find gainful employment sometimes end up having financial challenges because of their lack of financial knowledge and experience. This tends to result in young adults having a difficult time dealing with personal finance and consequently making unwise money decisions. In fact, 75 percent of students admitted to having made mistakes with their money when they arrived on campus, according to the 2006 KeyBank poll.

Ignorance is only part of the problem. College graduates in particular face special challenges because a time lag often occurs in finding employment. Six months after you have received your diploma, you are obligated to start repaying your student loans. This monthly amount is often significant since college graduates today borrow heavily to finance their college educations. Adding to student loan debt is the additional money a student may owe from credit card usage. A recent survey by Sallie Mae found that half of college students accumulated more than $5,000 in credit card debt while in school. And one-third of the thirteen thousand respondents had piled on more than $10,000 in credit card debt while in college.

Despite these debt realities, most young adults seem unconcerned about their ability to repay their debt obligations. This may be due to a sense of optimism. The Schwab survey revealed that nearly three-quarters of teens polled believed they would be earning "plenty of money" when they're out on their own. In fact, they expected to be earning an average annual salary of $145,500. In reality, only 5 percent of the U.S. population currently earns a six-figure income. And the average national wage is only $40,000.

Without the skills to handle their finances on their own or sufficient income to deal with their debt obligations, many young adults eventually fail to make their payments on time or at all. The free lodging, food, and services they receive at home suddenly become very appealing. In other cases, many find no other choice than to move back home with their parents. In fact, "returning to the nest" is starting to become as commonplace as "leaving the nest." Unfortunately, the excitement that accompanies the first time a young adult moves away from home is seldom repeated when they find they must now move back.

This chapter will profile the various situations that led young adults to move back home. Reasons such as:

- Not following a budget
- Not prioritizing "needs" before "wants"
- Not doing cost of living research
- Not being able to afford the big city
- Not expecting and preparing for "life events"

Three Strikes and You're Out

Before you move out on your own, it is essential to draw up a budget. After doing so, you must calculate moving expenses. The resulting bottom line figures will affect all your decisions. It will determine where you move, whom you live with, the furnishings you obtain, and even the type of cable service you choose. Knowing how much money is available in comparison to your expenses is crucial information if you want to make wise financial decisions. Not choosing to know this information will only guarantee decisions made in the dark. These choices will not be based in reality and will often not be sustainable. When Christopher decided to move out, he discovered the price he had to pay for not doing his homework.

Christopher was eighteen years old when he moved away from home for the first time. The going away party for Christopher was quite an event. All of his relatives came to celebrate his transition to manhood. His departure was accompanied by a lot of fanfare as he finally drove away in his pickup, which was overflowing with all of his belongings.

After he had driven out of sight, his mom Sara looked for her husband James and couldn't find him. She searched everywhere and finally found him in Christopher's room crying. This took her by surprise since James rarely showed emotion. He sobbed, "Our baby boy has left us." His sorrow was short lived. Three months later, Christopher moved back in.

Christopher ended up staying with his parents for one year. The second time he moved out, this event wasn't accompanied by as much fanfare. As Christopher left the house and the door closed behind him, James turned to Sara and said, "Honey, open a bottle of wine. I need a drink."

Three months later, Christopher was back. This time, he again stayed for one year. By now, James had gotten over the sorrow of losing his son and was beginning to think that his son would end up living with them forever. When it came time for Christopher to move out the third time, there was no fanfare at all. As soon as the door closed behind his son, James said, "Sara, call a locksmith fast and change the locks!"

Nowadays, parents shouldn't expect to become empty nesters when their youngest child turns eighteen. According to the Bureau of the Census, most children do not leave home until the age of twenty-four. I've recently talked to numerous parents who say their children last approximately ninety days on their own the first time they move out. Why ninety days? It might have something to do with the fact that after ninety days of nonpayment, the credit card companies start calling you to find out when you intend to pay. It also takes around ninety days to have your phone and utility services disconnected for nonpayment. At the end of ninety days, the stack of dirty laundry is probably very high and the refrigerator very empty. Suddenly, living under your parents' rule doesn't seem quite so bad.

Sara and James' increasing frustration with their son's annual return home was most certainly also felt by

Christopher. It must have been embarrassing to find himself moving out on three different occasions, not to mention the hassle of the move itself.

Christopher ended up back with his parents because he didn't know how to manage his money. He had been used to buying almost anything he wanted with the money he earned while living at home. It was a very difficult adjustment for him to have to share that "fun" money with bills like rent, utilities, and car insurance. Instead of paying these bills first, Christopher kept spending his money on entertainment, music, and clothes like he always had. When the bills arrived, he had no money left over from his paycheck to afford the necessities.

Christopher was spending his money backwards. He was paying for his "wants" before his "needs." Learning to make this distinction is fundamental to effective money management. As a practice exercise, put a check in the column which most accurately defines the following expenses. Are they primarily a want, a need, or both?

Expense	Want	Need
Car insurance		
Groceries		
Going out to eat		
Cable/Satellite TV		
Mobile phone		
Concert tickets		
New clothes		
Spring break in Florida		
Income taxes owed		
Student loans		
Premium gas for your car		
Football season tickets		
Rent		

Some expenses like rent are indisputably a "need." Other expenses like "Spring break in Florida" are more a "want" than a "need." But there are other expenses that you might want to debate. You may feel that season football tickets are a "need" while your mother might believe otherwise. However, your dad may take your side.

Someone you trust should review your perception of which category an expense should be placed in. As an impartial observer, this trusted person might point out that season football tickets equal the cost of your car insurance for an entire year. Your love of football may cause you to see this expense as more of a "need" as opposed to a "want." But if you have limited money and have to make a choice, car insurance should definitely be paid before season football tickets. And if your dad still classifies football tickets as a "need," then he can buy them for you.

If Christopher had made out a budget, he would have known how much money he had left over after he paid his bills and living expenses. This money was all that he could spend before he got his next paycheck. If he wanted to spend more money than he had available (according to his budget), he would know he wouldn't have rent money for next month. The inconvenience of denying himself something he wanted would be minor compared to the inconvenience of having to live once again under his parents' rules.

No More Free Ride

Parents usually look forward to the time when their children become independent and move out on their own. The majority of parents long for the time when their house is finally clean and quiet and they have the freedom to do what they want as a couple.

Most young adults also eagerly look forward to the time

when they can become independent. With no more rules to live by, curfews, or monitoring of their activities, young adults find that the financial costs of living on their own are outweighed by the benefits of this independence. For some young adults, though, these costs and benefits are reversed. They are not ready for the financial responsibility of living on their own, and prefer to be sheltered and taken care of by their parents. This nesting preference was the reason behind the Millers' financial problems.

When the Millers came in for their credit counseling appointment, they appeared to be extremely stressed. After the counselor had an opportunity to examine their budget, she discovered that they were $500 short each month. The Millers were two months behind on their mortgage payment and the bank was threatening foreclosure.

The counselor noticed that some of their expenses seemed rather high. For example their food, electric, and water bills were higher than the average for two people. When the counselor pointed this out, the Millers informed the counselor that their adult daughter Rebecca, twenty-two years old, and her boyfriend lived with them. The daughter worked while her boyfriend spent the day at home. Even though the parents didn't require them to pay any rent, they had access to as much food as they desired and free use of electricity and water services.

The counselor suggested that the Millers charge their daughter and her boyfriend $700 for rent. This way they would be able to pay their mortgage and still have some money left over to start a savings account. At first, the Millers resisted this idea, since their daughter and her boyfriend were family and not tenants. In the end, they changed their mind after they realized it was their best and possibly only solution to their money troubles.

Several months went by and one day a young couple came into the credit counselor's office. They were hostile from the minute they walked in. The counselor soon discovered that this couple was Rebecca and her boyfriend. The young couple was extremely angry with the counselor for suggesting that they be charged rent. Rebecca explained that now they too were having financial problems since they had to pay an extra $700 each month, and she blamed the counselor.

The counselor, after calming them down, put together a list of typical expenses along with their average monthly costs. For the average person who is not familiar with the costs of living, the best way to figure this out is by doing research. For example, to determine rent costs in various neighborhoods, you can pick up a local newspaper. Go to the classified rental section and write down the price ranges you find.

Location A

$ ________________ Studios

$ ________________ One bedrooms

$ ________________ Two bedrooms

$ ________________ Group homes

$ ________________ Sharing with a roommate

Location B

$ ________________ Studios

$ ________________ One bedrooms

$ ________________ Two bedrooms

$ ________________ Group homes

$ ________________ Sharing with a roommate

You will discover that these price ranges vary significantly depending on the locations you are comparing. You may prefer one location because it is convenient and trendy, but ultimately settle upon another location (even though it is in a less desirable neighborhood) because it is within the price range you can afford. The price you are able to pay also will affect the size of the rental. You may prefer a single-bedroom apartment, but might only be able to afford a studio. You may also decide you want your own place, but realistically need a roommate to split expenses.

You then can research the expenses that go along with the residence you chose. You can get insurance quotes for your contents, estimates from the phone company for service, and different package deals from the cable or satellite television provider. Attempt to get monthly estimates for the following expenses related to your shelter:

$ ________________ Rent or mortgage

$ ________________ Property tax (only if you have a mortgage)

$ ________________ Insurance (home owners or renters)

$ ________________ Gas and Electric (may be included in your rent)

$ ________________ Water, sewer, and garbage (may be included in your rent)

$ ________________ Association/Complex dues

$ ________________ Storage rental space

$ ________________ Gardening

$ ________________ Telephone/DSL

$ ________________ Cable/Satellite TV

$ ________________ Cleaning supplies/maid service

$ ________________ Other

$ ________________ **TOTAL**

When Rebecca and her boyfriend were shown the estimate for their shelter costs in addition to other living expenses, the total came to $1,200. This was a conservative estimate and would have required that they move into a one bedroom unfurnished apartment that would probably stay unfurnished for a while since they could not afford furniture. No furniture also meant no appliances such as a television, washing machine and dryer, stereo, or dishwasher!

They realized that their current rent was quite a bargain! They lived in a comfortable house with a yard and even had their meals prepared for them. All of a sudden, $700 seemed like a small amount to pay for these conveniences. The counselor hoped that she had inspired them, from the revelation of their good deal, to become better tenants.

The Millers always had approached money as a taboo subject. It was very uncomfortable for them to talk about the family finances. They assumed that Rebecca had learned about money in school. Unfortunately, no personal finance course existed in her school's curriculum. Since Rebecca had never heard her parents discuss the household expenses, she had no concept of mortgage payments or utility bills.

Many times, parents that are better off financially demand the least from their adult nesters. They might never dream to charge them room and board. But by living in an unreal situation with no bills or financial responsibilities, their children are the least equipped to handle themselves once they enter the real world. A mother once told me that she kept raising the rent she charged her daughter who had moved back in after college. When the rent got high enough, her daughter found her own place. With increased education and responsibility, the incidents of returning to the nest or staying in the nest will be reduced dramatically.

Big City Living

Moving out for the first time is difficult. It becomes even more challenging when you need to live in a large city. Most large cities are expensive places to live. A starting salary of $25,000 might allow you to enjoy a life of relative comfort while living with your parents. However, on your own, this salary may barely cover rent and food.

Reginald knew the financial realities of moving to Washington, D.C. He had done his research and a complete budget. The bottom line told him that it would be very difficult to afford the move on his starting salary of $27,500 as a low-level staffer on the Hill. Reginald, at twenty-two, had just graduated from Penn State University and had moved back to his parents' house in Maryland.

Many students move home after graduation, unable to afford to live on their own because of excessive debt obligations. Credit card debt and student loan debt can be daunting for a young college graduate to pay with a low starting salary. The addition of normal living expenses like rent, food, and utilities can make unrealistic the desire to live on one's own.

Reginald had become used to living alone while in college and having now to live under his parents' rules once again had been a very difficult transition. He was desperate to move to the Nation's Capitol. Although his budget told him it wasn't possible, Reginald was determined to figure out a way. He started by examining his budget in detail, trying to reduce any expenses that he could. If he could change his bottom line from being negative to positive, he would move.

Let's examine the expense categories that Reginald was able to reduce:

- Rent—by moving into a group house with three other roommates and by settling for a neighborhood that was not as convenient or trendy.
- Car payment—by selling his car he eliminated his car payment. Besides, there was nowhere to park it in the city and the subway (metro) system was very accesible.
- Insurance—by selling his car he also eliminated his car insurance payment.
- Credit card debts—by consolidating his four credit cards into one credit card with a lower interest rate, he lowered his monthly payment (he wisely remembered to cut up the newly paid-off cards and close their accounts).
- Student loans—by consolidating his Federal student loans through Sallie Mae (Student Loan Marketing Association), he was able to reduce his monthly payments. For his private student loans, he changed his

level payment plan to a graduated one, which allowed him to pay less at first and have his payments gradually increase over time. He was counting on the belief that his salary would also increase with time.

- Utilities—by splitting the electric, phone, and cable TV bills between four roommates, each paid a smaller percentage of the set fees.
- Groceries—by deciding to cook more often and go out to eat only two times a week, he cut down on his food costs.
- Dry cleaning—by ironing his clothes after wearing them, he didn't have to dry clean as often.
- Transportation—by taking the metro instead of taxis.

These reductions were enough to enable Reginald to move out. He knew that he would have to be disciplined, but he was willing to make these sacrifices. An added bonus to his move was that his relationship with his parents improved. As he started viewing himself more as an adult, Reginald found his parents began to treat him accordingly.

Murphy's Law

Major life events are not calculated into our normal day-to-day cost of living. Since we don't have a crystal ball, most life events are surprises. Funding an emergency savings account to handle extra expenses may not have been a priority and you may find yourself unable to handle the expense. As a consequence, life events can lead to moving back in with your parents.

If you think that life events don't or won't happen, look at the following list and identify those that have already occurred to you or your parents:

- Divorce
- Loss of job

- Pay cut
- Unexpected pregnancy
- Car accident
- Injury
- Natural disaster
- Home/car repairs
- Funeral
- Elder care
- Small business failure
- Legal problems
- Traffic/parking tickets
- Relocation

Have you experienced any of these life events? Most are unexpected. When walking down the aisle, nobody believes that their marriage will eventually end in divorce. But reality has shown that in certain parts of the country, one out of every two marriages end in divorce. Another example is returning to your car and finding a parking ticket waiting on your windshield. Obviously, some life events are more expensive than others. While a parking ticket may cause a temporary financial inconvenience, a divorce can have lasting consequences.

We can do our best to avoid "life events" by taking precautions. Driving under the speed limit is a good way to avoid getting a speeding ticket. Not living in Los Angeles is a tactic to reduce the probability of experiencing an earthquake. One of the best approaches to dealing with "life events" is to remember Murphy's Law, "What can go wrong probably will." While we always hope for the best, it is important to be prepared if things go wrong. In Patty's case, this advice would have served her well.

Patty and Andrew, who were in their early twenties, had been married for only three years and already had two children.

They hadn't planned on expanding their family so quickly, and the extra mouths to feed and clothe had strained the family's finances. It hadn't helped that Patty's income was lost after she decided to stay home full-time with the children.

By paying only for the essentials, they tried to make ends meet. This meant giving up the "fun" from their budget. Even after they eliminated the "fun," they still needed to cut out more. They decided that they would discontinue paying for life insurance for themselves. They just couldn't afford it anymore and besides, it really wasn't absolutely necessary. Since they were both young, what were the odds that they would die soon?

It turned out that their bet didn't pay off. Andrew was the victim of a hit and run accident and died on the scene. Patty was still in shock over Andrew's death when she received the additional shock of the cost of the funeral. There was no way she could pay for it. Since they had stopped paying for their life insurance, there was no policy to collect. Andrew was self-employed, so she didn't even have the possibility of collecting a company death benefit.

Patty's parents ended up paying for the funeral, and this payment became the first of their many payments to Patty's creditors. Unable to leave her children after the tragedy, Patty couldn't work and ended up on welfare. The welfare payments were much lower than Andrew's wages and she found herself unable to pay her living expenses. Faced with no other option, she moved back in with her parents.

This proved to be a hardship to everyone involved, since her parents had downsized their home after Patty and her brothers had married and left home. Her parents now lived in a small two-bedroom house. Patty was forced to share the second bedroom with her two children. One benefit of living with her parents was that her mother could watch her children during the day, which allowed Patty to start working at least part-time. She eventually increased her hours to full-time after she felt enough time had passed for her children to adjust to the loss of their father.

It took six years of living with her parents before Patty could move out on her own again. These six years sometimes seemed like sixty years for both Patty and her parents. Although they loved each other, the lack of privacy and Patty's dependence on her parents had increasingly strained their relationship. When she finally moved out and gained her financial independence, Patty swore that she would never put her children into that situation again. One item that she religiously paid each month was her life insurance policy.

The tragedy of Andrew's death did not have to be followed by a financial catastrophe as well. Insurance is not something that is an option. Anyone dealing with a tragedy like Patty's is much better served by not having to also face financial burdens at the same time. An insurance payment would have solved her immediate financial needs and given her some time to plan for the future.

Words of Wisdom

Personal finance is a life skill that is rarely taught. Few young adults are exposed to personal finance instruction in school and those who are lucky enough to have instruction from their parents might not be learning the right lessons. If their parents have never learned about money, how can they be expected to be good teachers? The alternative is to continue young adult's education about money in the school of hard knocks—trial and error. This school has a very expensive tuition!

Without this proper education in personal finance, young adults find they are not equipped to handle themselves independently. Personal finance is confusing and complex. The financial world has become complicated and you must learn to navigate it, for the most part, on your own. You are exposed to lines of credit, must make complex decisions regarding your 401(k)/retirement plans, must choose between different types of insurance, must be able to handle your checking account without having NSF (not sufficient funds) fees, and must be able to pay your bills on time to avoid negative marks on your credit reports.

Despite the fact that you may feel ill prepared, you can successfully make the move out of the nest. Once you are out, you should follow the lessons in this chapter to make sure you do not boomerang back:

- Create a moving out budget.
- Conduct research to find out anticipated expenses.
- Always pay needs before wants.
- Do not live a lifestyle you cannot afford.
- Be willing to decrease your standard of living.
- Take precautions to be ready for life events.

8

Loaning Money? Call It a Gift

If you want to know what a dollar is worth, try to borrow one.

Chances are that throughout your life people have asked to borrow money from you. Think back to grammar school, did any of your friends ever forget their lunch money? What about when you went out to eat with friends, were they ever short on cash? Did anyone ever have their credit card declined because they were up to the limit and you had to step in? As you got older and had more money to lend, did anyone ever ask for help making his or her rent payment or ask you to cosign on a loan?

If you did decide to loan your money for any of these reasons, did you get it back? Did you lend the money because you wished to help or because you were made to feel guilty? Did it cause friction in the relationship? Did lending money put you into financial difficulty if it was not repaid?

Giving to others has long been one of the enduring religious and moral teachings. U.S. giving has represented abut 2 percent of gross domestic product for four decades, according to the Center on Philanthrophy at Indiana University. And young adults are among these charitable givers. Barna

Research found that 38 percent of teens donated some of their money to a church on a weekly basis. To be charitable is honorable and virtuous, but under what circumstances can "giving" create a situation where the giver then becomes the one in need of assistance?

This chapter will explain all of the ramifications of lending money including:

- When you need a cosigner
- Considerations before cosigning
- Your legal obligations as a cosigner
- When the borrower has no intention to repay
- How to collect money lent to others

Money is not just a transaction when lent to a friend, there are also emotional bonds attached. This distinction makes both the giving and the receiving more complicated than a formal bank transaction. The story of Devin and Rhonda illustrates this problem.

Will You Cosign On My Car?

When friends become bankers, it is a risky relationship. The bonds of friendship are strong, but our feelings about money are also powerful. Since money affects so many areas of our lives, it sets up a dangerous link to have your friend in control of your finances. Your friend may end up being responsible for your losing your car, not being able to pay your bills, or ruining your credit. When these consequences result after money promised is not received, trust is broken. Once trust is lost, it is very hard, if not impossible, to regain.

Devin and Rhonda were in their mid-twenties and had been friends since childhood. They grew up next door to one another and went to the same college. People thought they were brother and sister because they were so close. In fact, Devin considered himself to be a brother to Rhonda. He looked out for her and became very protective; especially when it came to the men she dated! Rhonda also looked out for Devin, but it was in the area of his finances that she gave Devin the most assistance. In fact, it seemed to her that she was always coming to Devin's financial rescue.

Usually, it was just a couple of bucks to cover a restaurant tab or to get Devin into the movies. Rhonda was sure that these small sums probably added up to quite a sizable amount over the years, but she was happy to help. After all, isn't that the meaning of friendship?

In their senior year in college, Devin got an internship that required him to work two days a week. Devin had never needed a car before since all his classes had been within walking distance. This time, his internship was not nearby and it wasn't possible to get there by public transportation. When Devin went to buy a used car from a dealer, he had no idea that he wouldn't qualify.

Devin had acquired the habit of spending money faster than he made it. It was never really a problem, and Rhonda always was there when he was short of funds. But Rhonda wasn't there when Devin's bills came in the mail. When he didn't have the money, he just ignored the bills. He got letters from time to time telling him he was delinquent, but he usually caught up. There were instances, though, when he didn't pay his debts quickly enough and arrived home to find his phone or utility service disconnected. That also wasn't a problem since Devin always had roommates who could get the service reinstated in their names.

Devin never realized there were consequences from his poor bill-paying record. He learned a hard lesson when the car dealer told him that his credit record was so bad that in order for him to purchase a car, someone with a good credit rating would have to cosign for him. After hearing this news, Devin relaxed. "I'll just get Rhonda to cosign for me," he thought.

Rhonda was hesitant when Devin sought her help. She knew that cosigning for someone meant being responsible for the loan if Devin stopped paying. But Devin assured her that he would make all his payments on time. Rhonda finally agreed, telling herself that she was being selfish by not helping out her best friend. She signed the loan papers and received a "cosigner's notice" (required under federal law) that explained her obligations:

- You are being asked to guarantee this debt. Think carefully before you do. If the borrower does not pay the debt, you will have to do so. Be sure you can afford to pay if you have to, and that you want to accept this responsibility.
- You may have to pay up to the full amount of the debt if the borrower does not pay. You may also have to pay late fees or collection costs, which increase this amount.
- The creditor may be able to collect this debt from you without first trying to collect from the borrower (depending on which state you live in, this rule may not apply). The creditor can use the same collection methods against you that can be used against the borrower, such as suing you, garnishing your wages, etc. If this debt is ever in default, that fact may become a part of your credit record.
- This notice is not the contract that makes you liable for the debt.

Rhonda skimmed this notice quickly, but didn't give it much thought since she was convinced that cosigning would

prove to be no more than a formality and that the loan was really Devin's. After three months, Rhonda had almost forgotten about the loan when she received a notice in the mail saying the loan was three months delinquent. Rhonda was furious and called Devin, who assured her he would pay the money owed. He explained he had to buy some business suits due to the dress code at his new internship. He promised he would get the loan current.

The next month, Rhonda was at home studying when the phone rang. It was the car dealership's collection's department who explained that they were now left with no other option than to repossess Devin's car. His car payment was now four months delinquent. This repossession could be avoided in addition to its appearance on Rhonda's credit report if the amount owed could be paid immediately.

Rhonda again confronted Devin who had more excuses as to why he hadn't paid. He promised to pay the amount right away. A few days later, Rhonda got a call from Devin who needed a ride home from his internship. He explained that someone must have stolen his car while he was at work. When he went to the parking lot to leave for the day, his car was gone!

It turned out to be a repossessor and not a thief who took Devin's vehicle. Because of the repossession, both Devin's and Rhonda's credit have suffered. Since a repossession stays on a credit report for seven years, both of their credit reports will have this negative mark for a long time. Devin was able to get another car by agreeing to an interest rate of 31 percent. This high interest rate was not a concern to Devin since he did not grasp the concepts of interest and the true cost of credit.

Rhonda, who otherwise had spotless credit, now had a significant blemish. She found it difficult to get additional credit, rent an apartment, or trade in her car for a newer model.

Explaining that she wasn't the one responsible didn't work because she was in fact equally responsible.

Rhonda hasn't spoken to Devin for three years. Their long and close friendship has been ruined by this experience. Of course, not every story ends as sadly as theirs, but the important thing to remember is that when friends enter into financial agreements, there is more than money at stake.

Follow these do's and don'ts and be aware of the risks before you decide to loan or borrow money from friends.

When you loan a friend money:

- Do have them sign an agreement. When it's in writing, the obligation to repay is stronger.
- Do discuss what will happen if they can't repay you.
- Don't make them feel bad because they can't handle their money affairs on their own.
- Don't lose your temper if they aren't repaying you.
- Do try to act rationally and see if you can work out a postponement or another repayment schedule.
- Do remember that it is only money, which comes and goes. Good friendships are hard to find.

When you decide to borrow money from a friend:

- Do look at other options. Can you cut some of your expenses, earn extra money, or sell something you own before you ask a friend for a loan?
- Do ask yourself if you really need the item you are borrowing money for. Is it a want or a need?
- Do figure out a realistic plan for repayment. Remember that breaking a promise usually will not earn points with your friend.
- Don't avoid your friend when you find out you can't pay them back.

- Do try and pay back whatever amount you can. Usually receiving something is better than nothing.
- Don't lie to you friend. Be honest about why you can't repay them right now.
- Do thank them for loaning you the money and promise to do your best to repay them as soon as possible.
- Don't let a friendship be lost over money.

It is normal to feel hurt and disappointed when the borrower doesn't repay the loan. Broken promises and avoidance often compound these feelings. When your friend or relative avoids your phone calls, won't answer your requests for payment, or stops all contact with you, it is hard not to feel betrayed.

When this happens, you must decide if the relationship is more important than the money. If that is the case, you may want to, in effect, write-off the loan. The danger in doing so is to establish a pattern of loaning money and not expecting it to be repaid. This can result in a financial parent/child relationship. A dependency upon the financial parent can cause the financial child to lose their willingness to become self-sufficient.

Rhonda failed to understand that sometimes the best way to help a friend is not to help them at all. Rhonda knew Devin very well and should have realized that old habits die hard. When he didn't make his car payment, he was continuing his previous behavior. By enabling Devin to continue on with his irresponsible financial behavior, Rhonda was not helping Devin as she thought she was. Ironically, she was actually hurting him. Since he was never responsible for the consequences of his actions, he was never forced to change.

Best friends can be more honest with one another than can casual acquaintances. The truth can be blunt, but it hurts less than a broken friendship. If Rhonda had been honest with

Devin about his financial irresponsibility, maybe he would have been forced to confront the reasons why he was so careless. If she had denied him assistance, Devin would have been forced to solve his own dilemma. Like a child learning to ride a bike, Devin would have most certainly fallen several times at first, but eventually he would have learned to ride steadily on his own.

America: Home of the Free—But Not For Free

Collecting money you have lent to a friend is hard enough. When you add the extra complication of having to retrieve it from someone who has left the country, it is almost impossible. Legally, there is little that the courts can do when the borrower has left their jurisdiction. If the borrower returns, they will find bad credit or lawsuits await them. If they have no intention of returning, this is not a deterrent.

You may feel that lending money to a friend or relative from another country is a safe proposition. They are family, you convince yourself; they will never abandon me with their debts. Maria felt she would have no problem when she decided to loan her relatives money.

Maria had immigrated to the United States from the Philippines seven years ago when she was just sixteen years old. She was sent to live with a distant relative so that she could go to school in America and receive a good education. At first, she missed her family desperately, but over time she made friends and started to feel comfortable in her adopted country.

After graduation from high school, Maria had to choose between working full-time and going on to college. Since her family was struggling financially in the Philippines, she decided to work and send her family as much of her salary as she could afford. In time, Maria became her family's main breadwinner as a catering manager for a large hotel. Because of Maria, her family had a comfortable life and she was proud to help provide it for them.

After seven years, Maria started feeling more at home in Los Angeles than in the Philippines. During her infrequent trips home, she would brag about how the United States was a land of opportunity, with jobs available for anyone who was willing to work. This picture she painted was appealing to some of her relatives who were struggling to find employment in the Philippines. Several decided to move to Los Angeles to share in the wealth.

Maria was more than willing to be their mentor when they arrived. She helped them find employment and let them stay with her until they got settled on their own. She even gladly cosigned on their loans and credit cards so they could establish credit. Because of Maria, her relatives were able to get credit cards, car loans, and even small business loans.

Three years later, when Maria entered the office for her credit counseling appointment, she was eight months pregnant and a nervous wreck. Not only had her boyfriend and father of her child decided to abandon her, but so had her relatives. Maria explained to the counselor that her relatives did not grow to love the United States like she had and decided to go back to the Philippines. They left behind large balances on their credit cards and unpaid loans. Maria was now being contacted by the lenders to pay these outstanding balances. Since she had cosigned on these loans, she was responsible for their payment even though her relatives were gone.

Maria's situation was even more desperate because her stress was affecting her health and possibly that of her unborn baby. Her doctors encouraged her to relax but it was hard because she received letters and daily phone calls from collectors. She did not know how she could pay for her relatives' debt and the extra expenses of a newborn all by herself.

Maria was so pressed that she even contemplated going back to the Philippines as a way to escape her debt obligations—something she did not want to do. Maria was glad that she was so pregnant they wouldn't allow her to fly in a plane. With no obvious solution, Maria sought out a credit counselor whom she hoped would give her other options.

Maria knew that moving to a foreign country was a huge adjustment. Her first year in America was very hard and she contemplated moving back home almost every day. Knowing this, Maria should have acted like a bail bondsman when deciding to cosign on her relatives' loans. How great of a flight risk were they? Surveys of cosigned loans that go into default show that as many as three out of four cosigners are asked to repay the loan. When you cosign, you are being asked to take a risk that a professional lender wouldn't take. If the borrower had met the criteria and had been a good credit risk, the lender wouldn't have required a cosigner.

Before you decide to cosign, consider the following carefully:

- Be sure you can afford to pay the loan. If you're asked to pay and can't, you could be sued or your credit rating could be damaged.
- Even if you're not asked to repay the debt, your liability for the loan may keep you from getting other credit because creditors will consider the cosigned loan as one of your obligations.
- Before you pledge property to secure the loan, such as your car or furniture, make sure you understand the consequences. If the borrower defaults, you could lose these items.
- Ask the lender to calculate the amount of money you

might owe (the lender isn't required to do this but may if asked).

- You may also be able to negotiate the specific terms of your obligation. For example, you may want to limit your liability only to the principal on the loan, and not include late charges, court costs, or attorney fees. In this case, ask the lender to include a statement in the contract similar to "The cosigner will be responsible only for the principle balance on this loan at the time of default."
- Ask the lender to agree, in writing, to notify you if the borrower misses a payment. That will give you time to deal with the problem or make back payments without having to repay the entire amount immediately.
- Make sure you get copies of all your important papers, such as the loan contract, the Truth-in-Lending Disclosure Statement, and any warranties. You may need these documents if there's a dispute between the borrower and the seller (the lender is not required to give you these papers; you may have to get copies from the borrower). Check your state law for additional cosigner rights.

*Source: Federal Trade Commission

Maria hadn't considered the responsibility of being a cosigner before she agreed to help her relatives. After they fled the country, Maria should have been honest with her family in the Philippines about the liabilities they had left her with. Maria didn't share this information with them, and therefore they assumed she was doing fine. If they would have known, maybe they could have persuaded her relatives who owed the money to assist Maria in paying off their responsibilities.

By contacting her creditors and explaining her situation, Maria was able to get some of her interest waived or reduced. Her monthly payments were then renegotiated to an amount that she could handle. While she is now more in control of the situation, paying back her relatives' loans made Maria feel like she had been sent to jail for someone else's crime. Cosigning can make you feel like you are a conspirator to a crime. Both parties share responsibility on a cosigned loan, so be sure your interests are protected.

Parenthood: A Lifetime Responsibility

To be a parent is a commitment for your entire life—not just until your child turns eighteen years old. Does that lifetime responsibility include financial commitments also? When does the parent step in to offer financial assistance? If this assistance is given, does it end up fostering dependency?

Dave was contemplating those questions as he cosigned for his twenty-nine-year-old son's car. His son Tim had survived a messy divorce and now had full-time custody of his two children. Tim had had no success in collecting child support from his ex-wife who had disappeared with a Brazilian man (to Brazil, Tim assumed). Tim had childcare expenses, groceries for three, hockey dues, and tripled electricity and water bills.

Tim called his father almost every month with pleas for help. First, it was money for food, then the phone bill, and then he needed a cosigner for his car. One month, he needed a down payment to start a small business, which would allow him more flexible hours to care for his children. This down payment would be paid back, Tim promised, after the business became profitable.

Dave wondered when it was going to end. He started to tell Tim that he could no longer give him money, but then he didn't have the heart to go through with it when the next request for help came. While he was not happy about giving away so much money, he also couldn't deny help to his son and grandchildren.

The money Dave provided started becoming an expected part of Tim's budget. No longer was this money just a source of emergency funds, but it had become an anticipated income source to pay for normal monthly expenses. Dave had retired six months ago, but found himself returning to work since his lowered retirement income wasn't enough to support his son's needs. He told himself that he was bored by retirement, and going back to work was something he would have done anyway. But however hard he tried, he couldn't convince himself that this was true.

From Dave's point of view, his son was always in a crisis situation. He invariably needed money. Dave assumed that the cost of raising the children was too much for Tim to handle. In reality, Tim's financial problems had more to do with his spending habits than his childcare expenses.

Tim was desperate to find another wife and he wanted to make sure that he was a "good catch." He spent lots of money on expensive clothes as well as taking women out to dinner. If Dave had sat down with Tim and discussed his finances, instead of just giving him money whenever he asked, they could have worked out a plan that was beneficial to everyone. Dave could have helped Tim to see where he could manage his money better and rely on Dave less.

Out of Sight but Not Out of Mind

When you first have an indication that the borrower might not repay you, action should be taken. Your fears may have been triggered by their procrastination in starting the repayment or because the repayment is sporadic. You should not ignore these danger signs. Have an immediate discussion about the repayment schedule.

You should try to convince the borrower to commit to regular disbursements. If the borrower does not agree to these arrangements or does agree and then does not follow through, you should again ask why the agreement has been broken. After repeated attempts to collect the money through requests, pleading, or anger, you may choose to turn over the collection process to someone else. You should not seek legal recourse unless you have exhausted all of your other options. Getting the court involved will most certainly put a strain on your relationship and an additional strain on your pocketbook. When the situation has reached that point, your relationship has probably already been damaged.

When Lisa loaned Billy money, she thought she was in love with him. She would have done anything for Billy. Lisa had met him in college and she assumed they would eventually get married. Even though they weren't engaged, she still felt that their relationship was a fully committed one. So when Billy's car broke down and he needed $500 to fix it, she was happy to be able to help him out. Even though $500 was a lot of money at that time for her, she didn't hesitate.

Billy assured her that as soon as he caught up he would pay her back. The problem was that Billy never seemed to catch up. He changed jobs frequently so he rarely received a consistent paycheck for long. One day he broke the news to Lisa that a great job opportunity had come up and he was going to move from San Francisco to Los Angeles. He didn't want Lisa to relocate with him just yet. Billy said he wanted to make sure that the job worked out before she quit her job to follow him.

Lisa was very sad, but Billy assured her that with his new higher salary, he could afford to visit her regularly. At first, they saw each other at least once a month, but eventually they would go months without seeing one another, and Lisa could feel they were growing apart. Finally, Billy confessed that he had met someone else and he wanted to end their relationship. Lisa felt angry and betrayed. Billy thought it best to break all ties and suggested that they return all items each had borrowed from the other. Lisa responded that she wanted her $500.

"What?!" Billy exclaimed. He had forgotten about the loan since it had been over a year since it had been mentioned. But Lisa hadn't forgotten about it. Billy said that he didn't have the money, but would send it as soon as he could. After five months of patiently waiting, Lisa decided she had no other option but to take Billy to small claims court.

Small claims court basics in Los Angeles County (rules may vary from state to state):

- A person who sues in small claims court must first make a demand if possible. This means that you have asked the defendant to pay, and the defendant has refused.
- The claim limit is $7,500 each calendar year.
- If you are suing a guarantor, the maximum is $4,000. A guarantor is one who promises to be responsible for the debt of another.
- You can file as many claims as you want for up to $2,500 each. However, you can only file two claims in a calendar year for more than $2,500.
- You must sue in the right court and judicial district. This rule is called venue. The right district may be where the defendant lives or where the business involved is located.
- The correct way of telling the defendant about the lawsuit is called service of process. This means giving the defendant a copy of the claim. You cannot do this yourself.
- You must appear at the small claims hearing yourself.

Lisa went to the courthouse and filled out the necessary paperwork. She then waited for the marshals to notify her that

Billy had been served the small claims papers. Unfortunately, the marshals had a hard time finding Billy. His company had a policy of not accepting personal deliveries on the job and the sheriff's marshal only visited his apartment during business hours, when he was not home. After three tries, they gave up.

Lisa's eventually had her friend to go to the hotel where Billy worked as a front desk manager and serve him the papers directly. Her friend asked for Billy at the front desk and when he eagerly came over to help her, she said that they had a mutual friend in common and that she had a gift for him. He excitedly asked, "What is it?" She handed him the papers and said, "You are served!"

Billy eventually paid and wanted to forget the past, but Lisa couldn't. She always felt that he paid her only because he was forced to do so. Why couldn't he have just paid her back slowly? Even small payments would have shown that he was living up to his promise. She hated having been forced to seek legal recourse. She found she had too many hurt feelings to continue their friendship. So Billy got his wish and she did sever all ties.

Lisa thought she was in love with Billy when she loaned him money. Love can definitely be blind and cloud judgment. Lisa would have held her friends accountable to a much higher standard than to the one she held Billy. She didn't even hesitate when he asked her if he could borrow money.

Since emotions run high in love relationships, it's a good idea to give a lot of consideration to any decisions which could be regretted later. Lisa should have said no to Billy, or she should have insisted on a written signed agreement that included a regular repayment schedule. That ending would have gotten Lisa her money back and hopefully salvaged their friendship after the romantic relationship ended.

Words of Wisdom

Problems occur when you perceive a loan to a friend or relative as a normal business transaction, which requires repayment. When the repayment doesn't happen, hurt feelings enter the equation since the borrower isn't a faceless person. You feel betrayed because you know the person and expect your friendship to be a prime motivation for them to repay their obligations. A bank is an impersonal entity, but you aren't.

The only way to truly avoid hurt feelings over anticipated returns is to adopt the philosophy, "When loaning money, consider it a gift." If you never expect repayment, you can avoid any hurt, betrayal, and sense of being taken advantage of. Giving gifts needs to be prefaced with the caveat, "Be cautious of being overly generous." There is a difference between being nice and being a target.

Despite the risks, you may decide to be a cosigner anyway. If you make this decision, remember the following lessons from this chapter:

- Be sure you can afford to repay the loan.
- Read your obligations carefully.
- Be aware of the possible adverse consequences to your credit report, loss of property, lawsuits, etc.
- Be careful not to create a financial dependency pattern.

9

Mind over Money

People who say money can't buy happiness
just don't know where to shop.
—*Tom Shivers*

Managing money involves a rational mind, but how we react to money is seldom rational. Let's take the simple concept of "Don't spend more than you make." The logic behind this statement is easy to understand. Then why do so many people spend money they do not have?

The answer is that our emotions get in the way. We can spend more than we make because spending can be triggered by feelings of depression, love, guilt, joy, reward, loneliness, and almost any other emotion you can imagine. When emotion is stronger than your rational mind, the emotion wins out.

People usually relate to money in one or more of the following four categories: Love, Freedom, Power, and Security. This chapter will tell stories that illustrate the extremes of each of the four psychological relationships to money. Each of the categories has admirable characteristics when approached in moderation; it is the extremes that should be avoided:

- LOVE—it is admirable to give to others who are in need.
- FREEDOM—it is admirable to take a chance and to dream big.

- POWER—it is admirable to use money as a means to increase your sense of control over your life.
- SECURITY—it is admirable to live within a budget and save your money.

The category you identify with the strongest has a lot to do with your personality, fears, and tendencies. The danger lies in taking any of these categories to the extreme. When that happens, addictive behavior can result. Once your actions toward money turn into an addiction, the logical and rational mind that is necessary to make wise money decisions will take a back seat to your emotions. Many decisions based solely on emotions are not the most prudent course of action.

By identifying your particular classification, you will have a better understanding of what motivates your actions in regard to money. What does money mean to you? What sparks that urge to make or spend it? To fight about it? Many people already can guess which category applies to them even before they answer the first question.

Take a few minutes to complete this test by answering the following questions. (While it may seem obvious which answers correspond to which categories, it is important to answer each question honestly in order to get accurate results.)

Discover Your Primary Money Drives

1) Money lets me...
    a) do what I want.
    b) feel safe and sound.
    c) become successful.
    d) buy things for others.
2) My approach to saving money is, I...
    a) don't have a plan and rarely save.
    b) develop a plan and follow it closely.

c) manage to save despite not having a plan.
d) routinely answer my friends' pleas for money so I have none left over to save.

3) Money allows me to...
a) have free time.
b) solve my problems.
c) reach my goals.
d) have better relationships.

4) When making a major purchase, I...
a) follow my intuition.
b) research and compare before buying.
c) am the boss—it's my money after all.
d) rely on my friends' and family's advice first.

5) If I found out a friend paid less for something than I did, I...
a) couldn't care less.
b) would think it's only fair since I also find good deals at times.
c) would imagine he spent more time shopping and time is (wasted) money.
d) would be upset he didn't tell about the bargain.

6) When it comes to paying bills, I...
a) procrastinate and occasionally forget to pay.
b) pay them before they are due, never late.
c) pay when I have the time, but don't want to be reminded.
d) am concerned about ruining my credit if I miss a payment or pay late.

7) If I have extra money, I...
a) have fun and celebrate.
b) put it in the bank.
c) add to my investment portfolio.
d) buy a gift for someone special.

8) On the subject of borrowing money, I...
   a) won't ever consider it since I don't like to feel indebted.
   b) will only borrow if all of my other options fall through.
   c) prefer to borrow from a bank instead of a friend.
   d) don't hesitate to borrow from friends/family because I know I'll pay them back.

9) When it comes to tipping, I...
   a) tip depending on the service.
   b) never do.
   c) always tip the right amount, but resent having to pay extra.
   d) always tip generously.

10) If I suddenly received a huge inheritance, I...
   a) would quit my job.
   b) wouldn't have to worry about the future.
   c) could invest more into my business.
   d) would give a lot away to my family and friends.

11) After receiving the restaurant bill with friends, I prefer to...
   a) have each person pay for their share.
   b) ask for separate checks.
   c) charge the entire bill to my credit card and have the others pay me cash.
   d) pick up the whole tab since I like to treat my friends.

12) When unable to make up my mind about a purchase, I tell myself...
   a) it's only money.
   b) it's a good deal.
   c) it's a good investment.
   d) it will be a great gift.

13) If I share money...
   a) I handle all the money and pay all the bills.
   b) my partner takes care of everything.
   c) we are each responsible for our own bills.
   d) we sit down together and pay bills.

Answer Key

<u>If you answered mostly "A" you:</u>

- See money as a source of **Freedom**.
- Relate to money as a way to expand your options.
- Would trade love and security for the ability to go anywhere and do anything.

<u>If you answered mostly "B" you:</u>

- See money primarily as a source of **Security**.
- Yearn for safety.
- Equate money with stability.
- Spend money responsibly.
- Have a hard time passing up a bargain.

<u>If you answered mostly "C" you:</u>

- See money primarily as a source of **Power**.
- Want success and the status symbols to prove it.
- Are thorough and to the point, very businesslike.
- See money as a means of control over people.

<u>If you answered mostly "D" you:</u>

- See money as a means of showing your **Love**.
- Value friends and family above all else and use money to enhance those relationships.
- Are generous and dependable.
- Use money to make life better for your family/friends.

*Source: This quiz was amended by Consumer Credit Counseling Service from a quiz that originally appeared in *Couples and Money: A Couples' Guide for the New Millennium*.

Did you end up in the category you thought you would? You can have traits from several types, but unless there was a tie, a category should predominate. We will now see the meaning behind each category. The first money drive we are going to explore is love.

Love: Giving 'Til It Hurts

Do you believe the expression, "You can't buy love"? Some people use their wealth to attract friends or even the person they will marry. The allure of money is very difficult for some to resist. People can even talk themselves into marrying someone whom they are not attracted to, all for the love of money.

Eventually, the reality of a loveless marriage or fake friendship surfaces and no amount of money will make the charade worth it any longer. Using money as a way to attract others or make them love you often indicates a person with low self-esteem. They do not believe that someone could actually love them for who they are; they can only be loved for what they have.

Another way that money and love go together is in the genuine desire to give to others who you care for to make their lives easier. It feels good to share your good fortune with your friends and family who are struggling financially. The joy you get out of this charitable act is rewarding.

It is fine to give for love as long as you do not forget the lesson learned in the previous chapter, giving too much. It becomes too much when you are continually bailing out someone or if your standard of living becomes drastically reduced, not having enough money left over for your own needs.

The important distinction to remember in using money for love is that money can never take the place of love. It can be used to enhance your love, but not as a substitute. If Ben's dad Charles had understood this difference, he hopefully would have avoided the financial crisis this belief caused him.

Ben's parents had been divorced for three years. He was a freshman in high school when his dad Charles first moved out. Ben missed his dad since under the custody arrangement he saw his father only every other weekend. His mother Susan seemed to relish the fact that she was developing a much stronger bond with Ben and his sister Virginia than their father was. Susan continually pointed out the fact that it was she who attended the PTA meetings, their sports practices, their doctor's appointments, and all the other daily routines that took place when Charles was not around.

His mom was trying to make herself more important than Charles in their children's lives and it was working. Charles felt so inadequate that whenever he saw his children he tried to make up for his time away from them by showering them with gifts. He would take them out to expensive restaurants, take them away on weekend vacations, and buy them anything they wanted at the shopping mall.

Deducing Charles's psychological connection to money is obvious by looking at his spending pattern. He spent money to cover up the guilt he felt over not spending enough time with Ben and Virginia. Like Charles, most people tend to have a certain mood, which may trigger spending money. In order to figure out your mood, the next time you are shopping for the wants (not needs) in life, what mood tends to predominate? Do you shop when you are bored, depressed, or celebrating? Keeping a journal of your money moods while you are spending money will help you figure out your tendencies:

Date	Activity	Mood	Comments
Example: July 22, 2007	Shopping at the mall	Depressed	Boyfriend dumped me
August 22, 2007	Purchasing art	Lonely	Haven't had a date in a month

By consciously observing your moods when you spend money, you may discover a pattern. If, for example, you find that you tend to spend money when you are depressed, you may want to avoid a shopping mall at all costs when feeling this way. By substituting the activity of shopping with another less destructive activity like exercise, you may succeed in reducing your spending compulsions during times of depression.

Ben became so used to his father's extravagance that he began to take advantage of it. Soon, Charles found his generosity had extended to Ben's friends and their demands. One weekend, Charles found himself paying for everyone when he brought Ben and his friends to the amusement park. This was not necessary since the parents had given their children more than enough money to cover the day's events. Ben's friends thought this was great because they were able to pocket their parents' money. Since Charles never complained, and in fact encouraged this behavior, he found his weekends becoming increasingly costly.

Before he knew it, Charles had excessive credit card debt. Instead of curtailing his spending (which to him wasn't an option), it continued to spiral out of control until he was forced to stop. One night he took his children to an expensive restaurant and all three of his credit cards were declined. Not understanding why this happened, Ben asked his dad what the problem was. Charles finally broke down and admitted his financial problems.

To his amazement, Ben and Virginia started suggesting things they could do that didn't cost money. They said, "Dad it's not important what we do, just that we do it with you." They even admitted that they felt they were always rushing around during their weekends with their father. In trying to give them so much, Charles succeeded in giving them *too* much.

The sudden realization that he didn't have to buy their

love was liberating. At that moment, Charles' insecurity, which was driving his overspending, disappeared. Charles found that after his insecurity went away, so too in time did his financial problems.

Freedom: What are the Odds?

People for whom freedom is a motivating drive see money as a source of adventure and liberation. They use money to try and achieve their dreams. When controlled, the freedom motivation can be wonderful and help people live life to its fullest. When this motivation gets out of control, it can lead to the risky world of gambling.

Gambling can take many forms: playing the lottery, going to Las Vegas, day trading on the Internet, or choosing a job that pays mostly on commission. The commonality among all of these different versions of gambling is that they involve high risk for a potential huge reward. The price to pay for the chance of winning big is that the odds are greatly stacked against you. Why then, do so many people gamble?

For many, the allure of high-risk wagering is the vision of how their life would change if they did win big. The money from that commission would pay for an expensive car. The yearly payout from winning the lottery would negate the need to ever work again. A life of leisure would be the ultimate reward. If these things are not even remote possibilities in your current situation, you might take the chance. If you feel powerless on your own to change your life significantly, you may decide that the risk is worth it.

Another factor is patience. While your current plans might allow you to one day achieve your dreams, you may not want to wait. As you will learn in Chapter 11, saving money early and consistently is the best guarantee of reaching your goals. Unfortunately, the years of dedication that saving

money requires do not allow you to have instant gratification. If you want something now and are not willing to wait, gambling may seem like the perfect solution.

Margot always took chances. She saw money as a way to get herself out of her boring life. She married early, right out of high school, and with her husband Ernie she immediately started a family. Ernie was her high school sweetheart and their life in suburban Chicago proved predictable. She was now twenty-two years old with two young children, and she daydreamed frequently about living a luxurious lifestyle. She reasoned that if she got enough money, she could change her life. Regrettably, this plan was not consistent with a job that had a stable salary. Margot always chose jobs that were based almost entirely on commission. These jobs had the possibility of earning big money, but more often than not they made her no money.

Margot's risky attitude extended to the stock market. When she had money to invest (in those rare cases that a deal did go through), she did so in high-risk stocks. These investments promised that her shares would escalate in value quickly. She was sure that this company in Texas would strike oil any day or this new Internet stock would skyrocket in value, but rarely did she even get back her original investment. Eventually, gambling became an addiction that caused Margot to lose control over her life. Her view of money as a source of "freedom" to allow her choices ultimately led to this addiction.

Her husband Ernie had tried to be supportive, but one day he forced her to see a credit counselor after discovering that she had gambled away all the money they had saved for Christmas presents. He didn't know what he was going to tell the kids when they discovered there weren't any gifts under the tree.

As the counselor went over Margot's expenses, it was easy to discover where the money went. She spent hundreds of dollars monthly on lottery tickets, went weekly to the racetracks (during work hours), and played poker several times a week. Margot's involvement in all these activities was carefully concealed from her husband.

Her gambling was threatening to destroy her marriage. Although rationally Margot knew that the odds of winning in gambling were very slim, she was emotionally compelled to continue. Finally, Margot agreed to allow Ernie to control the money. She also agreed to start attending Gamblers Anonymous meetings. This decision was a difficult one for Margot because she had to admit that her gambling had become addictive. She always assumed she could stop any time she wanted to do so. The fact that she couldn't stop and needed help was a tough admission. Margot succeeded in taking the first step, admitting she had a problem. Now the passage of time will show whether she can stay committed to a gambling-free life.

To improve her chances of giving up gambling, Margot needed to change her attitude about money as a savior from her boring life. Until she stopped believing that money is the only way her life could change, she would continue to be vulnerable. By looking at other ways to spice up her life, like choosing an interesting hobby or joining a social club, she would feel less of a need to gamble.

The attitudes we have can sometimes cause us to fail in our attempts to take control over our finances. If you recognize any of the following characteristics or attitudes in yourself, be on guard against them. Here are some common attitudes that can cause a financial plan to fail:

- Denial—Some people refuse to look at their financial condition in a frank and honest manner. They continue using available credit or borrow from friends to cover their perceived needs and refuse to admit a problem exists.

- Helpless apathy—Some people believe that their current financial difficulties are simply a result of a run of unfortunate circumstances or bad luck. They believe that things will work out with time and that there is no real cause for their financial difficulty.
- Placing blame—Others are convinced that someone else is responsible for bringing on their financial difficulty. This is rarely the case, but even when the blame for the problem does belong to someone else, the responsibility for resolving it may not be.
- Cinderella syndrome—Because some people are secretly waiting for someone to take them away from their wretched situation, they do not really want to deal with money issues.
- Emotional spending—For emotional spenders, buying is attached to a sense of reward for a job well done or consolidation for having suffered something. To these folks, learning to say "no" feels like punishment.
- Diet mentality—Some people think that once they have resolved their financial difficulties, they will be able to spend all they want. Like the dieters who think they can eat whatever they like after they lose twenty pounds, these budgeters will soon be in trouble again.

Do you ever see life this way? Do you have these attitudes? If so, you may have discovered that your financial situation did not improve, because these ways of dealing with problems are eventually self-defeating. Be on guard to recognize and change any of these attitudes in your life.

Power: You Are What You Drive

Using money to create an illusion of power can prove very tempting. You can control the impression that you allow others

to have of you. If you try to project the image of a successful businessman or woman, it is imperative that you project an image of wealth. The type of car you drive, the clothes you wear, the home you live in, and your choice of activities all must fit this image. Sometimes the pressure to create a certain image is self-imposed, but other times you may feel you do not have a choice but to appear to be the kind of person your surroundings dictate. This causes many people to get in way over their heads with payments they can ill afford.

Take the case of Phil. He had purchased a brand new, luxury foreign car that he couldn't afford. At the age of twenty-two, he had recently graduated from college and his first entry-level job only paid him $36,000 a year. The car he just bought was equal to an entire year's salary! When asked what possessed him to purchase a car he couldn't afford, Phil replied that he really hadn't even planned on buying a new car, he had simply wanted to test drive the new model. The hook happened during his test drive.

As Phil was driving, he noticed women honking and waving at him. Being single, Phil enjoyed this attention and noticed that he never got this reaction when he drove his old used car. Phil could feel his self-confidence increasing as he continued his test drive. When he arrived back at the dealership, the salesman remarked how sharp Phil looked behind the wheel. Phil looked in the rear view mirror and agreed.

Before he knew what had happened, Phil had signed the loan papers and driven his new car off the lot. He took a seven-year loan so that he could afford the monthly payments. He confessed later that he felt powerless to stop himself. His recollection was fuzzy; it seemed like a dream. The car in the driveway the next morning assured him that it was not.

Decisions are usually made with both emotional and logical reasoning involved. Sometimes logic is more compelling than emotion in the decision-making process, sometimes emotion is more compelling than logic. How many of your decisions regarding finances were influenced by logic and how many were influenced by emotion? Take a moment to fill in the following chart with major financial purchases you have made in your life. Then next to each purchase, decide whether it was an emotional or logical decision. When you have finished, total up the amount of times you answered "emotional" and "logical." The column with the highest total shows you your inclination to follow your heart or your head:

Purchase	Emotional	Logical
Ex. Brand new car	X	
Ex: Student loan		X
TOTALS		

How many of your money mistakes were emotional decisions compared to logical ones? If the greater percentage were decided emotionally, you may want to refrain from making hasty purchases in the future. You should retreat from the point of purchase and think about it for a while. Comparing prices and analyzing against your budget are ways to involve the logical mind more in the purchasing process.

Phil fell in love with a car that he couldn't quite afford, but had to have anyway. This was an emotional decision. On the other hand, if he had passed up the perfect car in favor of another one, which fit his original budget, his decision would have been a logical one.

As soon as he drove off the lot, his new car immediately became used and promptly lost several thousand dollars in value. Buyer's remorse filled his consciousness as he drove further and further away from the dealership. Phil consoled himself with the sense of "power" he now felt in his hot new car.

Phil put the extra expense out of his mind by concentrating on the beautiful women he was sure that his new car would attract. He imagined meeting the woman of his dreams and living happily ever after. But before Phil had the opportunity to meet this woman of his dreams, his car was repossessed.

Ironically, as Phil was forced to take the bus to work, he met a woman seated next to him one morning. They started talking and ended up making plans to meet for coffee. One thing led to another and Phil is now happily in a relationship with this woman. Phil learned an expensive lesson: "Not everyone judges you by what you drive."

Phil had attempted to use money to bolster his self-esteem. Using money for power can have a darker side, including blackmail and bribery. But using money as any form of control, whether you want to control someone's impression of you or his or her vote in Congress, is likely to lead to a result you will regret. If you relate to money as a source of "power," you will want to avoid this extreme behavior.

Security: Save for a Rainy Day

For some people, money is a source of security. Therefore, they are very careful to maintain a source of savings. Saving is always smart, but should not be taken to the extreme. Neglecting to also spend or share (the other two uses of money) will create an imbalance. If all of your money is diverted to your savings accounts, you may end up being labeled a "penny pincher" or a "tightwad." Are you so against spending money that you would rather live a miserly existence?

The need to feel secure is normal. Spending money wisely will help to achieve this sense of security. However, some people have a heightened fear of losing this security. This apprehension may lead to their hoarding money out of proportion to what the experts deem as sufficient:

Emergency Savings Account
Minimum = Total monthly expenses multiplied by three
Maximum = Total monthly expenses multiplied by six

Willy's mother Marian followed the expression "Save for a rainy day" religiously. Willy was a senior in high school and was used to his mother's penny-pinching ways. She saved all the time and only spent money when it was absolutely essential. Even then, she never paid full price and always took full advantage of coupons and rebates. Marian was ready for a rainy day; in fact she was ready for years of rainy days.

Her obsession with not spending money came from a Depression-era mentality passed down to her by her parents. They had lost everything they had in the Great Depression and were forced to live very frugally in order to survive. Marian never forgot her parents' stories of their struggle and she decided that she was never going to suffer the way they did. In order to make sure this never happened, she created a security blanket by stockpiling the money she and her husband earned. After twenty-five years of hoarding, Marian had a huge stockpile.

This excessive saving did not come without a price. Willy and his brother Dave grew up feeling deprived, always wanting for more. They were ashamed that they were seemingly the poorest family in their neighborhood. They lacked basic necessities like an adequately heated house, food to fill up their stomachs, and clothes without holes. Their car was getting so old it was on the verge of collapse. They prayed that their parents would make more money so that their situation would improve. Over the years, their parents did get promotions or found better paying jobs. For some reason, the situation at home never improved.

When Willy decided to go to college, he was sure that he would qualify for financial aid grants since his family was so poor. To his great surprise, he was turned down because his parents made too much money. Confronting his parents, they explained that they saved their money for a rainy day. Willy responded, "The rainy day has arrived."

His parents were so terrified to part with their money that they refused Willy's request for college assistance. Their great fear of losing their money and deep need for security at all costs ended up costing them their son. Willy ended up borrowing the money for college and has not spoken to his parents in years.

Willy's parents had lost sight of the reason behind saving and were obsessed only with the act of saving itself. By being scared to withdraw any money, they kept their family in unnecessary poverty. They could have easily withdrawn money for important necessities like a reliable car, a college education, and improved living conditions without reducing their savings to an inadequate level. In fact, with their savings they could have sent both of their children to Harvard and still have had a very substantial amount in their retirement account.

Their fear of running out of money and ending up in poverty turned out to be a self-fulfilling prophecy because they lived a poverty-like existence. By confronting this fear, their family could have lived a life without so many deprivations. Their son Willy might still be talking to them, and their hard earned money could have proudly been responsible for part or all of his college education.

If only they had developed a plan to reach their family's goals (which is detailed in the next chapter) they could have been comforted by the knowledge that they had enough money to send their children to college. Unfortunately, Willy's parents never developed a written plan and had no idea of their actual financial situation. If you find yourself hoarding money or acting miserly, having the facts and figures of your financial situation down on paper will open your eyes to the reality and help you set appropriate spending levels.

Words of Wisdom

It is important to learn to realize your tendencies and also be aware of the dangers of carrying any of the money characteristics to the extreme. Never underestimate the power of the psychological impact of money. Money involves many human emotions like greed, envy, compassion, anger, and jealousy. To understand what money means to you and how it governs your decisions allows you to be better equipped to control the power of money instead of letting money control you.

By completing the quizzes and charts from this chapter you should have become more aware of the reasons behind your emotional money decisions. You will have recognized:

- Your primary money drive.
- Any mood patterns when spending money.
- Any self-defeating attitudes toward money.
- Whether your financial decisions are primarily emotional or logical.
- The amount you should have in an emergency savings account.

10

'Til Debt Do Us Part

Prosperity begets friends,
adversity proves them.
—*Anonymous*

One of the most difficult things for a married couple to deal with is their finances. Money problems have frequently been cited as one of the leading causes of marital stress amd divorce. Even couples who stay together often argue about money. Research has shown that money was the most frequently reported issue that couples argue about. They fight over differences in ways to spend it, the need to save, how to invest it, who should pay what, how to divide up the responsibility for money tasks, and many more issues. Almost all marital decisions, in some way, are linked to money, from taking a new job to choosing what model of car to buy to deciding whether or not to have children.

The amount of money that the couple earns is not often the problem, it is how they manage the money they do have. People who spend money unwisely will do so no matter how much they have.

Since many still feel uncomfortable talking about money, it is rarely discussed. Usually the subject is brought up only when a problem exists, and then it becomes not a discussion but an argument. By waiting until the simmering problem explodes into a crisis, it becomes difficult to approach the situation calmly and with a rational mind. This tendency to avoid discussion is why money tends to inflame so many passions and result in so many relationship crises.

Couples find that when they can resolve their financial difficulties and conflicts, their marriage or relationship usually improves. This is not to say that a lack of money problems guarantees a happy marriage, but it definitely results in less strain on the relationship.

This chapter will profile relationship financial problems, such as:

- Having incompatible money habits and goals
- Handling a partner's money addiction
- Believing that money buys love
- Avoiding communication about finances
- Assuming responsibility for joint debts
- Being too poor to divorce

Working as a team should be what relationships are all about. Having a financial direction that is proceeding along the same path, not in opposite directions or intersecting only occasionally, should be the ultimate goal. Unfortunately, many times one partner may be led down a path that is not of their choosing.

For Richer or for Poorer

Savers often end up married to spenders. Even if two partners have a similar money philosophy, one usually will end up as more of a saver and the other as more of a spender. Every couple needs someone who will set limits. Keep in mind that there may be subtle or extreme differences in these roles. For example, if two spenders marry, one may be a more conservative spender while the other may be the "super spender." If two savers marry, one may be the extreme tightwad while the other does not mind spending money as long as their retirement accounts have been funded for the month. However, the coupling of a saver with a spender usually results in the most extreme differences in approaches to money out of all the pairings.

This balancing out effect can be a positive influence on couple's lives. If two savers marry, they may miss out on opportunities in their lives since they are averse to spending money. They may never visit a foreign country or go to the opera. Conversely, if two spenders marry, their tendency to splurge may lead them to bankruptcy court.

The following are some common polarizations that couples may adopt in their attitudes about money:

- Saver vs. Spender (Do you prefer to put extra money in the bank or in the cash register?)
- Ostrich vs. Agonizer (Do you pretend nothing is wrong or do you lose sleep over money problems?)
- Gambler vs. Security Guard (Do you prefer high-risk investments or do you put your money in safe government bonds?)
- Plotter vs. Romantic (Do you plan your financial moves in detail or just dream about that house you have always wanted?)
- Joint Accounts vs. Separate (Do you have the philosophy that "what's mine is yours" or "what's mine is mine"?)

Which category do your parents fall into? What about you own relationships? Do you see a pattern emerging? Usually your financial attitudes will remain the same from one relationship to the next but their degree of intensity will vary depending on your partner.

Susie always thought her husband Sam was wealthy. They met in Paris the summer after Susie graduated from college. Her parents had paid for this trip as a graduation gift to their daughter. She first saw Sam while visiting the Louvre museum. Sam said that he had just popped over for the weekend from New York, where he lived. Susie, age twenty-one, had just accepted an internship in New York City and didn't know anyone there, so she was happy to exchange phone numbers. After she moved to New York City, Sam asked her out on their first date.

While they were dating, Sam wined and dined her. He brought her to fancy, expensive restaurants and every week sent exotic flowers to her office. All the other women she worked with were jealous. Sam always dressed only in designer suits and had a foreign luxury car.

Because Susie had an entry-level salary, she had to live with three other roommates just to make ends meet. She lived on a tight budget, having just started her career. Even though Sam was the same age, she was sure he made much more money than her. She never saw him clipping coupons or shopping at discount stores. He must be making excellent money to be able to afford all these things, she thought.

It never occurred to Susie that appearances could be deceiving. In reality, all of these things were being paid for by incurring debt. One night while out at dinner, Sam's credit card was declined. He then pulled another card out of his wallet to pay, which also was not approved. At this point, Susie glanced at Sam's wallet as he searched for another credit card and she saw that his bulging wallet contained at least twenty different credit cards. Being a conservative spender and owning only one credit card herself, she started to panic. "How many credit cards do you have?" she demanded. Sam responded that he didn't know. Susie then grabbed his wallet and started to count them. She counted twenty-two. "How much do you owe on these cards?" she again demanded. He didn't have the answer to that question either.

Susie then proceeded to go through Sam's credit card statements as they arrived in the mail and added up the damage. By the time she had calculated the total, it was a shocking $40,000. This is a lot of debt for someone who is only twenty-three years old. She discovered his designer suits, dinners out, imported flowers, and even his trip to Paris had all been charged. Sam must have been very dedicated to spending to accumulate that much debt in such a short time. Susie had always admired Sam for his tenacity to get what he wanted. In this case, he must have wanted debt badly.

In fact, it wasn't debt that Sam wanted, but it came along as a consequence to what he really wanted, which was to be rich. He had received his first credit card in college and suddenly found it to be a way to overcome his feelings of being deprived. He had been raised in a very poor family. He was on an academic scholarship at Yale, where the education of most of the students was funded by their parents, or so he assumed. With credit cards, he now had a way to fit in. He could buy expensive clothes, treat his friends to dinner, and join them on weekend excursions.

In spite of his debt, Susie decided to marry Sam. It took the two of them about five years and a dramatic lifestyle change to pay off his debt. Even after they were debt free, Susie continued to harbor a grudge that since her hard earned money was being spent to help reduce Sam's debt, it could not be used for other things like paying off her student loan debt sooner or saving for a house. She resented not having a say over where they allocated their earnings.

This issue of debt being brought into a marriage has been shown to be a primary problem area for newlyweds, according to the Center for Marriage and Family. As couples struggle with everyday financial management in early marriage, the addition of debt that a husband or wife has brought into the marriage adds another level of complexity

It is very important that couples make decisions about financial questions together. Do they combine their money or separate it? If they decide to have children, will someone stay at home or will both work? Below are some common personal goals. Please indicate their importance to you by circling the appropriate number. Add other goals, which are important to you but not listed. Once you finish, have your partner take this test also. You may want to photocopy this page so their answers are not influenced by yours. Remember that a goal must be written down and a plan made to reach it. Otherwise, the goal will remain a dream and not a reality.

Goals	**Importance to me**		
	Low	**Med**	**High**
Maintain present standard of	1	2	3
Improve present standard of living	1	2	3
Have children	1	2	3
Private school education for children	1	2	3
College education for children	1	2	3
Financially support adult children	1	2	3

Goals	**Importance to me**		
	Low	**Med**	**High**
Passing wealth to heirs	1	2	3
Financially support parents or parents-in-law	1	2	3
Financial independence at age sixty-five	1	2	3
Financial independence before age sixty-five, at age ____	1	2	3
Get out of debt	1	2	3
Pay off medical bills	1	2	3
New car	1	2	3

Rent a better home	1	2	3
Buy a house	1	2	3
Vacation house or recreational vehicle	1	2	3
Travel internationally	1	2	3

Other goals:

______________________________	1	2	3
______________________________	1	2	3
______________________________	1	2	3
______________________________	1	2	3
______________________________	1	2	3

If you find that you have incompatible goals, what do you do? Will you compromise or give up a goal? How will you decide to spend extra money like bonuses, inheritances, or an income tax refund? How will you allocate your investments and who will make the decisions?

All these questions and many more will arise within a relationship. Since so many of these questions require difficult answers, it is no wonder that many couples prefer to avoid discussions about money. Unfortunately, not talking about these issues won't make them go away. It is better for the relationship to make decisions together instead of unilaterally or by default through inaction.

Susie felt she had had no choice but to assist in paying off Sam's debt. She resented the fact that Sam's debt burden pushed them back so many years financially. Although they had succeeded in erasing the debt, unfortunately they couldn't succeed in erasing Susie's memory of it. Susie and Sam understood clearly why debt is the primary issue that couples quarrel about.

Each partner brings his or her financial past and present into the marriage. Even though one partner is not responsible for debts incurred prior to marriage by the other, their legacy will impact the couple as a whole. Susie understood why her husband had gotten in debt, but she also understood that even though the debt he had acquired before their marriage was not legally her problem, the reality of his debt load was their problem!

It probably is a good idea to find out your spouse-to-be's credit history before you say, "I do." I suggest a frank pre-marriage discussion about each of your respective financial situations so that no surprises spoil your marital bliss.

So as to never repeat their debt burden again, Susie and Sam have two credit cards now and both are in *Susie's* wallet!

Out of Sight, Out of Mind

Some partners purposely hide purchases or assets from the other. In fact, a 2005 *Redbook*/lawyers.com survey found that nearly one-third of adults who are in a committed relationship say they have been dishonest with their partner about their spending habits. Despite their lack of candor on this issue, 24 percent of those polled said that honesty about finances was more important than honesty about fidelity.

When the data is separated by gender, women are more likely to be the ones with less candor (33 percent for women and 26 percent for men). In fact, one in four women said they lied to their partner about the money they spent on items like clothing or shoes. Many women may feel they can safely "bend" the truth since they have had success in hiding the purchases through their husbands' inattention to their wardrobe details.

Additionally, the poll found that 18 percent of adults admitted to having entirely separate bank accounts. Without

knowledge of each other's finances, it can be easy to maintain a cash stash that their partner does not know about. These nest eggs are sometimes considered "mad money" to be used as the individual saw fit or as a "safety net" if that person needed to get away or separate from their partner.

Keeping money matters secret can cause problems, especially if one partner's actions involve unwise money moves. If the couple is married, one partner's decisions will inevitably affect the other, as Mort tragically found out.

Mort had made up his mind to acquire success both professionally, personally, and materially. He started his career as an investment adviser and at the age of twenty-five he was branch manager of a busy downtown Washington, D.C. bank. Personally he had also experienced success. Mort had married a wonderful young woman, Linda, who had attended one of Mort's investment seminars. She became pregnant shortly after their marriage and was now taking care of their two-year-old full-time.

One day, not feeling well, Mort came home from work early. Linda was not home, so when the phone rang he answered it. He was very surprised to discover it was a bill collector. At first Mort thought they must have the wrong number but he soon realized that indeed they were trying to contact his wife. "It must be a mistake," he thought. "I'm sure she'll have an explanation."

When Linda came home later that afternoon he told her about the call. Instead of confirming his conclusion that it had been a mistake, she started crying. A confession ensued where Linda admitted to having twenty credit cards. Mort was astounded since he never saw the bills or noticed an inordinate amount of purchases. She explained that she had always intercepted the bills since she could retrieve the mail before Mort came home from work. And since she was responsible for paying the household bills, Mort never knew the extent of their debt.

Linda loved to shop and often spent her days pushing their

son in his stroller through the stores at the mall. Mort never saw evidence of her purchases since she was careful to cut off the price tags before he got home. He was so wrapped up in his work that he hadn't noticed.

Linda had been able to keep this spending a secret for so long because she had been making only the minimum payments on the credit cards. The allowance Mort gave her had been enough to make these small payments. But now Linda had acquired so much debt that she couldn't even make the minimum payments and didn't want to alert her husband by asking for more spending money.

Mort decided to take over her debt payments, but did not want to touch their retirement accounts to pay down the debt. He lectured his clients to never touch their retirement accounts and he wasn't about to become a hypocrite. So he chose to continue working even harder and use the extra income to wipe out her liabilities. Three years later, he had finally paid off every penny.

Imagine his horror when he again discovered that Linda had accumulated an additional $40,000 in credit card debt! She simply acquired new credit cards and followed the same pattern as before. Worried that the pattern would just repeat itself, Mort went with his wife to a therapist who diagnosed Linda with an overspending addiction. Credit cards were her drug of choice. She used them to alter her mood of loneliness over never being able to spend time with her husband. Once the core reason was discovered, a solution was easy. Mort needed to cut down his hours at work and spend more time with his wife.

Unfortunately, this was not possible if he was to again pay down her debt. The therapist pointed out that his workaholic lifestyle had contributed to the situation in the first place so to continue this pattern would assure the same results. The only solution that remained was to withdraw money from their retirement accounts to pay off the debt. Mort chose this course of action and had to painfully watch about 50 percent of his money disappear after he was taxed and penalized for taking out this money before he reached the allowed disbursement age of fifty-nine and one-half.

Linda's financial relationship to Mort was analogous to that of a daughter receiving an allowance from her father. There was obviously no money communication beyond doling out the money. There were no discussions as to where it was spent or what was bought. Therefore, it was easy for Linda's debt to spiral out of control without Mort's knowledge.

Hidden stashes and concealed purchases are the symptoms of deeper relationship issues. If money is hidden so that a quick getaway from the relationship is possible, what does that say about the belief in "'Til death do us part?" If purchases are hidden because the other partner might get angry, what does that say about the commitment to trust? The *Redbook* Poll found that 72 percent said that trust was essential to a successful romance.

There is nothing wrong with maintaining separate accounts, as long as there is frequent communication as to the financial activity that is taking place. Couples have many choices to make concerning where they keep their money if they both work:

- Combine it all into one joint account.
- Keep entirely separate accounts.
- Maintain a combination of both joint and separate accounts.

Once these decisions are made, it needs to be determined who will pay what. Do you assign certain bills to each partner? Does one person pay the rent while the other makes the car payment? Do you lump all the money together and pay the bills from the communal total?

An additional consideration is what to do when one partner earns more money. If you earn less but are asked to equally contribute to the household bills, this will leave less money for your own needs. Is this fair? If you decide to pay in proportion to your income contribution, how do you decide which bills you are responsible for? There are no easy answers; each couple needs to figure out these arrangements on their own.

A further complication occurs when the woman earns more. Among married couples, 25 percent of wives earn more than their husbands, according to the U.S. Census Bureau's 2005 data. But for many men and women, they have been socialized to believe that the man should be the primary wage earner. Even though the wage gap has been shrinking and the majority of women are in the workforce, many households would still feel it was a matter of concern if a wife earned more than her husband.

All of these issues are not easy ones to resolve but they are crucial. The following checklist for couples will help to make sure you address these and other important questions.

We have:

- ❑ Discussed our financial attitudes and values
- ❑ Investigated each other's income and employment patterns
- ❑ Discussed each other's credit history
- ❑ Read through each other's health, automobile, and life insurance plans
- ❑ Developed separate time lines for what we hope to accomplish in the next year, three years, longer
- ❑ Put together a budget we both believe in
- ❑ Agreed to distribution of payment responsibilities
- ❑ Made decisions about joint or separate accounts

Without addressing these issues, couples will continue to face financial difficulties.

No Money, No Honey

The notion that money buys love can be a very real perception. If a person has low self-esteem, they may feel that their net worth makes them a more desirable person. While playing the dating game, one's profession is definitely either an asset or a liability for many people. Especially if women are looking for a "provider," they may be drawn to someone who can financially take care of them. Since "How much money one makes" can be a strong factor in choosing a mate for some people, it is easy to make the assumption that this aspect is equally important for everyone.

Frank, a twenty-three-year-old computer engineer, came into the office for his credit counseling session and listed twenty-five credit cards on his application. Frank's income was high since his profession was in such demand. Because he earned so much, he had been able to make the minimum payments on all of his cards, which incidentally had very generous credit limits. Now, three years after he had started to accumulate this debt, Frank finally reached the point where he was so overextended he couldn't manage the payments anymore.

He was an extremely smart man who was living way beyond his means. The counselor discovered when going over his budget that Frank did not spend a lot of money. However, his girlfriend Ruth definitely had no problems spending Frank's money. The counselor suggested an honest discussion with Ruth to ask that she cut down on her spending. Frank refused to even consider the suggestion. When the counselor asked why, he replied, "I'm a computer geek. If I tell my girlfriend to stop spending she'll leave me and I'll never find another girlfriend."

The counselor encouraged Frank to be honest with Ruth. Frank was just assuming that his girlfriend was with him for his money. If she really did love him, money shouldn't matter. Frank should give Ruth an opportunity to prove his fears wrong.

Frank never did muster the courage to share his financial situation with his girlfriend. He was paralyzed into inaction by his fear of her leaving him. The counselor realized her advice had not been heeded when Frank came in for another credit counseling session a year later after filing bankruptcy.

Unable to hide his bankruptcy from Ruth, she ended up finding out what he had been working so hard to hide. Rather than leave him, Ruth was actually sitting beside him in the counseling session. As they went over their budget with the counselor, Ruth offered to cut down or eliminate some of her expenses. She had always spent a lot of money because Frank had never even hinted she should stop. Ruth assumed Frank was one of the internet millionaires and he in no way said anything to dispel that image. Instead of abandoning Frank, she became his advocate and willingly gave back the support he had given her. Unfortunately, it took an act as traumatic as a bankruptcy for Frank to learn the true depth of his girlfriend's love.

It is helpful to remember that each individual has a different style in how they deal with money. By overcoming the inability to communicate about money, much of the bitterness, anger, betrayal, and lack of trust can be eliminated, and money will hopefully not be the reason if you choose to part.

Frank approached money as believing that "Rich means happy." If he was not rich, how could he be happy? Frank's fears were based on his perception of what his girlfriend would do if he curtailed her spending. Studies have shown that over 90 percent of what we worry about never comes to be. If Frank had mustered up the courage to be honest with his girlfriend about their financial situation, he would have found out that having "lots of money" was not that important of a priority for her. Then Frank would have been able to explain his financial limitations and the debt load would not have gotten out of control in the first place.

The Perfect Wedding

Routine discussions about the family's finances are a good way to avoid periodic surprises and to keep each other informed. Although talking about money may be uncomfortable at first, it will become a habit over time. You may also discover that your money arguments will decrease. The more situations that can be resolved before they become major problems, the better. Unfortunately, Jennifer did not see the value of disclosing her financial decisions to her fiancé.

Jennifer started planning her wedding to Cliff as soon as he proposed during his senior and her junior year at Northwestern University. She wanted the wedding to be perfect and wouldn't settle for anything less; it didn't matter how much it cost. She wanted to hire the most expensive band, the best caterer, the most elegant reception hall, a designer wedding dress, and a honeymoon at a five-star resort.

Their parents contributed financially to the wedding, but not on the scale that Jennifer envisioned. Cliff thought Jennifer was being a little extravagant, but he wasn't really aware of the expense since Jennifer was handling all the arrangements. Besides, he didn't want to upset his fiancée, whom he loved deeply, by appearing to be stingy.

The wedding was perfect, just as Jennifer had planned. When they settled back into their apartment after their honeymoon, a stack of mail awaited them. Jennifer was exhausted and went to bed. Cliff stayed up and opened their mail. To his astonishment, the majority of their mail was wedding bills. In fact, after he added up all the bills, the grand total was $50,000!

Jennifer had asked for many of the wedding expenses to be billed to them and put the others on her many credit cards. Cliff was furious, he couldn't believe she could have spent so much money without his approval. They had planned to buy a house, but needed to save up for the down payment first. Now with this wedding debt to pay, their dream of a house would have to be postponed.

The stress of the debt started to affect their relationship. Cliff had to negotiate payment arrangements with many of the vendors, which was humiliating to him. He ended up working overtime to pay for the debt. It seemed to Jennifer that he spent more and more time away from home. In fact, Cliff was so mad at the circumstances caused because of the wedding debt that after only a year their marriage fell apart. The irony was that Jennifer had wanted the perfect wedding so badly that she had failed to consider the most important ingredient of a successful marriage, communication.

Problems occur when communication is lacking. One person's statement may be interpreted in a way that was not the intent:

Statement	Interpretation
It's my money, I'll buy anything I please.	Your views are unimportant.
Don't worry; I'll take care of you.	You can't take care of yourself.
I don't want to talk about it.	It's none of your business.
All I do for you and this is the thanks I get.	You are ungrateful.

Statements like, "I don't want to talk about it," are counterproductive. Since relationships are a partnership, the couple must learn to make financial decisions in concert and not independently. Arguments are sure to arise when unilateral decisions, such as how to spend the income tax refund or the company bonus, are made. If the wife arrives home to discover a motorcycle in the driveway instead of that long promised vacation, there is sure to be trouble.

Even though frank money discussions are uncomfortable, they are necessary. A regular time should be set aside for discussing money. It is recommended to have the facts and figures on paper. This will result in the discussions being shorter, calmer, and more productive. Cliff's discovery of Jennifer's planned spending wouldn't have necessarily meant the marriage would have been called off, but it might have impacted many of their financial decisions. Maybe the wedding would have been scaled down or they wouldn't have taken such an expensive honeymoon. Regardless, they would have tackled their money problems sooner rather than later.

Cliff and Jennifer should have worked out a budget prior to planning for their wedding. The following is a sample wedding budget:

Expenses	**Amount**
Invitations	
Announcements	
Thank you cards	
Formal portraits	
Photographer	
Videography	
Limousines	
Bridal luncheon	
Rehearsal dinner	
Travel for out-of-town guests	
Church/synagogue fees	
Food	
Beverages	
Wedding cake	
Valet parking	
Music/Band	

Expenses	Amount
Wedding dress	
Veil	
Shoes	
Gifts	
Flowers	
Wedding favors	
Hotel accommodations	
Honeymoon	
Wedding consultant	
Other	
TOTAL	

Once completed, you should make a commitment to stay within your spending limitations without exception. The emotions that go along with a wedding are powerful and sometimes motivations like jealousy, inadequacy, or even envy can interfere with rational spending behavior. In Jennifer's case, she grew up in a household that had always struggled financially. Jennifer was determined to leave her poverty behind and start out a new life free of its constraints.

If Jennifer had only learned to accept her feelings of inadequacy as valid but had not allowed them to control her, she wouldn't have had this uncontrollable need to have the "most perfect" wedding. She still could have succeeded in having a memorable wedding but one that was within their capacity to afford. Then Jennifer could have taken away from the wedding its memories and not its debt.

It's Not My Responsibility

Blaming one another and pointing the finger is not a constructive way to resolve differences. Everyone's situation is unique. You need to handle the situation in the way that is best for you, without comparing other's actions.

If your money situation has gotten out of control and talking about it amongst yourselves hasn't happened or hasn't worked, you should consider professional counseling before you do something as drastic as get a divorce. If the relationship does end up in divorce, certain precautions should occur prior to separating.

Since joint debts are both parties' responsibility, it is a good idea to close all joint accounts so that no further debt can be added. Creditors can and will come after any party that they think has the capacity to pay. They will usually go after the person who has the money, regardless of whom the court has assigned the responsibility to pay the debt.

Opal and Paul had tried to work it out. They were in their mid-twenties and had been married for five years. They had been going to a marriage counselor for the past two years, but they could never seem to resolve their problems. Finally, they were full of so much anger that they couldn't stay married any longer. This anger was apparent during their divorce proceedings. They only communicated to each other through their lawyers.

It was an ugly settlement. They fought to the bitter end over the division of their property. They each ended up with roughly half of the assets and half of the debts since they had comparable incomes and no children. All of their credit cards were joint accounts so the judge divided them up and assigned each person half of the debts to repay. From that moment on, Opal no longer felt any sense of responsibility for the debts assigned to Paul. This turned out to be a false sense of security.

Opal went about her new life without Paul and consistently paid her half of the joint debts that had been assigned to her. One year after their divorce, she received a phone call from a creditor saying she owed on a credit card that had been assigned to her ex-husband. Opal told the creditor that this was not her responsibility. Her ex-husband had been assigned that credit card in her divorce settlement and not her.

The creditor explained that she was equally responsible since it was a joint credit card in both of their names. Opal decided to agree to pay it since she didn't want to ruin her credit report. She remembered that the balance was not that high when she divorced and after a year there was probably not much left to repay. To her horror, her ex-husband had charged the credit card up to its $10,000 limit.

Opal received several more of these calls that week from other creditors. It was always the same story. Her ex-husband had apparently charged up the credit cards to the limit with no intention of paying them off. In his bitterness, Paul purposely wanted to hurt Opal knowing that they would go after her for payment after they had given up trying to collect from him. In fact, Paul was currently unemployed. He knew, having once worked in a collection agency, that the creditors would always go for the deepest pocket. If one pocket is empty, they will go after the other. Opal eventually paid Paul's assigned debts, not wanting to hurt her credit since her name was still on the joint account.

Opal did not know she should have closed the joint accounts that had been assigned to Paul. That way, her ex-husband wouldn't have been able to increase the debt owed upon their divorce settlement. Since the accounts remained open, nothing stopped her ex-husband from charging more on the credit cards. If Opal had periodically looked at a copy of her credit report, she would have discovered that the balances were increasing. Sadly, Opal was never advised to do this. Opal learned the hard way that joint accounts are both parties' responsibility and creditors are not legally bound by any decisions made in court.

To recap, the following steps should be taken when joint debts become separated:

1. Realize that you cannot take your name off the account as long as a balance remains, even if the account was assigned by the court to your ex-spouse.
2. Cut up the credit cards. This will prevent further usage.
3. Close the accounts (write a letter to the creditor asking to stop any additional activity on the card). This will show up as "closed at consumer's request" on your credit report.
4. Request a copy of your credit report periodically to check activity on any accounts not under your control.
5. If the creditor comes after you because of your spouse's nonpayment, do not ignore them.
6. Don't forget that ultimately joint accounts are both parties' responsibility.

Too Poor to Divorce

Divorce can lead to financial problems in many instances. In fact, according to the U.S. Census Bureau, less than half of the custodial parents who were due child support received the full amount of their court-ordered child support payments. Mothers were due $26.4 billion and fathers $2.7 billion. This shows that the unsupplemented burden of child and household support falls more often to women with single incomes and can result in a decline in their lifestyle following a divorce. Additionally, men can also suffer if they have large alimony and/or child support payments to make. The reality is that the amount of money that once supported one household must now support two. There are now double the bills in most expense categories.

Prior to considering a divorce, the post divorce financial picture should be calculated. Estimate any anticipated changes to your current budget. Line items like rent or mortgage, utilities, food, and income are examples of some of the monetary amounts that will most likely change as the result of a divorce. Your income may be affected depending on the amount of child support or alimony you receive, your housing costs may change if you decide to move, or your childcare costs may increase if you decide to go back to work. Completing a budget will give you a preview of what future financial situation may await you:

Expenses	**Monthly Amount**
Savings	**$**
Emergency fund	
Investments	
Retirement fund	
Shelter	
Rent or mortgage payment	
Property tax	
Insurance	
Gas and electric	
Water, sewer, and garbage	
Association dues, space rent	
Gardening, pool care, repairs	
Food	
Groceries	
Meals out	
School lunches	
Transportation	
Car payment	

Continued

Expenses	**Monthly Amount**
Gas and oil	
Insurance, license	
Auto repairs	
Parking	
Public transportation	
Health	
Life and health insurance	
Doctor and dentist	
Prescriptions and glasses	
Clothing	
Clothes	
Work clothes and uniforms	
Laundry and dry cleaning	
Other (special events)	
Household	
Telephone, mobile phone	
Cable TV	
Appliance repairs/replacement	
Cleaning supplies/maid service	
Personal Expenses	
Beauty care	
Recreation/entertainment	
Pets	
Gifts, charity	
Hobbies, lessons	

Continued

Expenses	**Monthly Amount**
Miscellaneous	
Newspapers, magazines	
Church tithes	
Cigarettes and alcohol	
Vacation	
Christmas	
Childcare, counseling	
School tuition	
All credit payments	
Total monthly expenses (B)	
Total net monthly income (A)	
Difference: (A–B)	

Once you have finished this projected budget, you need to compare it to the budget you completed in Chapter 2. Put side-by-side, the pre- and post-divorce budgets will clearly show how your financial state of affairs will change if you decide to split up. Sometimes the resultant hardships are determined to be worse than the current situation. This reality may affect your ultimate decision to separate and may encourage you to try and work out the issues in your marriage.

In Kayla's case, she had always paid the bills in the family since she was extremely organized. Her husband, Matt, was focused on the big picture and not into the details. This tendency, she believed, caused him to be careless. One day while paying the credit card bills, she noticed a charge for a trip to Las Vegas (although he claimed to have taken a business trip to Cincinnati), a flower shop, and a lingerie boutique. This was how she learned her husband was having an affair.

For Kayla, there was no such thing as a second chance. She hired a lawyer right away and started the divorce process. Matt begged for her to try and trust him again and not leave him. He assured Kayla that he would change and never cheat on her again. Kayla reconsidered and ended up deciding to stay with Matt, but for reasons that were solely financial.

As she was going through the figures with her lawyer, she came to the horrifying conclusion that they were too poor to divorce. Matt was the sole wage earner (Kayla stayed home with the children) and on his income alone he could adequately support the household. But when required to support two households on his income solely, Kayla discovered she wouldn't receive enough child support from Matt to make ends meet. Not wanting her two children, ages two and four, to decrease their standard of living significantly, Kayla decided to stay with Matt.

Further supporting her decision was the worry that she would have trouble establishing credit since she had no credit in her name. Since all their credit cards were in Matt's name, she lacked a credit history. It is always wise to obtain credit in your own name so that you can become financially independent and not reliant on your spouse's history. This is particularly true if the spouse has a blemished credit history. It may be more of a detriment and may not accurately reflect your timely payment habits.

As the years went on, Kayla learned of other affairs her husband was having. His promise to her to never stray again had turned out to be false. She felt financially trapped and forced to live in the same house with a man whom she distrusted and had begun to despise.

Kayla eventually did move out with her children, but only after her parents provided the money to allow her to support herself as a single mom. This money enabled Kayla to stay at home until her children entered school and she started working full-time.

Words of Wisdom

Relationships take work. Disagreements are inevitably going to occur, especially where money is concerned. Money is something that is dealt with every day in addition to the financial decisions that go along with it. Although money decisions may appear to be very cut and dry and unemotional, they are in fact just the opposite. In order to weather the financial storm that many times accompanies financial difficulties, the lessons learned in this chapter are extremely valuable. A couple should:

- Communicate openly and often about money.
- Decide upon mutual goals and develop a plan to reach them.
- Share their financial past and present prior to beginning a life together.
- Avoid hidden stashes.
- Figure out payment arrangements (who pays what).
- Discuss any major purchases or money expenditures prior to acting on them.
- Remember that joint debts are both parties' responsibility.
- Once a divorce is decided upon, do a financial analysis of their post-divorce situation prior to separating.

11

"I'm Too Young to Start Saving," and Other Excuses

A penny saved is a penny earned.
—*Benjamin Franklin*

The 2007 retirement confidence survey conducted by EBRI found that seven out of ten workers say their assets total less than $10,000. This is not a very encouraging figure when contemplating the ever increasing need for workers to make up the shortfall between their current standard of living and what social security will provide. Experts say that when you retire you will need to replace about 70-85 percent of your pre-retirement income in order to maintain a similar standard of living.

But for many people, social security replaces only a portion of their current income: 50 percent or more for those earning less than $25,000 and 25 percent or less for those earning more than $100,000. Compounding the problem is the fact that one-third of retirees rely on social security for 90 percent or more of their income. With an average payment of around $1,000, it is not hard to see that many retirees' standard of living will plummet.

Despite these sobering statistics, there is always an excuse to not save money. Common excuses are that you're too young, too much in debt, don't make enough money, or just had children. There never seems to be a right time to start. However, you'll find that as each excuse disappears, a new one appears to take its place.

From age eighteen to twenty-five, people say: "Me invest? Are you kidding? I'm just getting my education. You can't expect me to be able to invest now. I'm young and I want to have a good time. If and when I get out of college, I'll start investing."

From age twenty-five to thirty-five, people say: "You don't expect me to invest now, do you? Remember I've only been working a few years. Things will be looking up soon and then I'll be able to invest. Right now I have to dress well in order to make a good impression. Wait until I'm a little older. There's plenty of time."

From age thirty-five to forty-five, people say: "How can I invest now? I'm married and have children to care for. Why, I've never had so many expenses in my life. When the children are a little older, I can start thinking about investing."

From age forty-five to fifty-five, people say: "I wish I could invest now, but I just can't do it. I have two children in college and it's taking every cent and more to keep them there. I've had to go into debt the last few years to meet the college bills. But that won't last forever and then I can start investing."

From age fifty-five to sixty-five, people say: "I know I should be investing now but money is tight. It's not easy for a person my age to better himself/herself. About all I can do is hang on. Why didn't I start to invest twenty years ago? Well, maybe something will turn up."

At age sixty-five and over, people say: "Yes, it's too late to begin saving now. I have Social Security, but who can live on that? If only I had invested when I had the money. You can't invest when you have no income."

Have you ever made any of these excuses yourself? Have

you heard them from your brothers, sisters, parents, or grandparents? The reality is that there is no better time than the present to save. So why do we try so hard to avoid something that is so good for us? Could it be that saving has no immediate benefit compared to spending or sharing your money? Spending has an immediate benefit because you can use your purchase. Your new car, new outfit, new bike, and new dishwasher can be driven, worn, or used. Likewise, when you share, the recipient usually shows you their gratitude by their expression or some other form of thank you. Even anonymous contributions can bring joy and satisfaction. But with saving, it's like watching the grass grow—not very exciting. Your money is sitting somewhere waiting until some future date, which always seems too far away!

Americans seem to have lost their faith in the power of saving. In fact, AARP states that 48 percent of voters think they will have little or no money to retire. These assumptions can be powerful, especially if the sense of hopelessness causes one to reject saving altogether. The difficult but rewarding task is to overcome these mental barriers and believe in the value and necessity of saving. Then you will provide for yourself a secure future that is not reliant on the solvency of Social Security or on whether or not you receive an inheritance.

In this chapter you will learn:

- How to become a millionaire
- The value of compound interest
- Why you need an emergency fund
- The 70-20-10 rule
- The Rule of 72

Let's start by examining why it is in your best interest to start saving now and not later.

Worry about Retirement? I'm Still in High School

The eighteen- through twenty-five-year-old excuse of being "too young" to save money was an excuse that Curtis had perfected. He used to say "Retirement is something only old people have to worry about. I'm only seventeen and a senior in high school and I'm worried right now about how I'm going to pay for the senior prom." That sentiment is common among young adults. The perception is that saving for retirement is not a priority, given the more immediate alternative uses for their money. Curtis didn't see the point in saving; he just lived one day at a time.

Curtis' childhood role models consisted of single parent families, most on welfare. Those in his Baltimore neighborhood with money usually got it through illegal means. Curtis didn't see any other way to get money. He definitely didn't want to live the hand-to-mouth existence that most of his neighbors did.

Curtis had a part-time job at a gas station during high school. The money he earned went to buy clothes, shoes, cigarettes, and fast food. He also went out almost every weekend with his girlfriend or his friends and spent money on entertainment. The things he bought had a short life span. The fast food was gone as soon as he ate it, the cigarettes became ashes, and the entertainment ended as soon as he left the sports arena or the dance club.

One day, Curtis' economics teacher, Mr. Richards, held a class session on the value of saving. The teacher asked Curtis if he could save a dollar a day. Curtis said he probably could. The teacher then showed that in ten years time, if Curtis didn't touch the money and it earned 5 percent interest, Curtis would have $4,720. He could have a substantial down payment for a moderately priced new car in only ten years or he could make an outright purchase of a used one. In the later case, he could actually own the vehicle and not have to make payments on it! For a car, $1.00 a day seemed a small sacrifice to Curtis. If he could save even more, $5.00 a day, he would have $23,600 in ten year's time.

Since Curtis was eighteen years old, his teacher asked him how many twenty-eight- year-olds he knew who owned their own home. Curtis answered, "None." Did Curtis want to own a home one day? "Yes," he replied. Mr. Richards explained he could do it by saving only $5.00 a day. The $23,600 he will have saved over ten years would be a substantial down payment. In fact, Mr. Richards went on to explain that if Curtis stopped smoking and put the $5.00 a day he spent on smoking into a savings account, he would have his down payment for his home and most certainly improve his health in the process.

Curtis' teacher wondered if his lesson on the value of saving had had any impact. The concept of delayed gratification had to compete with both peer and advertising pressure to spend money. One day he saw Curtis with a group of friends who were all smoking—except for Curtis. When Mr. Richards asked him the next day if he had quit, Curtis answered that it was easy to quit. Every time he had the urge to buy a pack of cigarettes, he would take the picture of his dream house out of his wallet. The urge to smoke would go away.

By instilling the saving habit early in life, even the goal of becoming a millionaire by the age of sixty-five can be reached. By starting at the age of twenty and saving $95 per month, you can end up with a million dollars by the age of sixty-five, assuming a 10 percent return on the money (tax deferred). This is also assuming that none of the money will be withdrawn during the waiting period.

This goal also can be reached if you wait until you are older to start saving, but the amount you must contribute monthly increases dramatically the longer you wait. For example, if you wait until you are thirty years old, you will need to save $263 a month. If you wait until you are forty years old, you will need to save $754 a month, and if you wait until you are fifty years old, you will need to save $2,413 a month. This chart also shows how you can reach the $1 million goal by age sixty-five if you prefer to make a one-time investment. You may choose to use an inheritance, bonus from work or equity from the sale of a home towards this one-time investment:

Age	One-Time Investment	Monthly Investment	Annual Investment
20	$13,719	$95	$1,391
25	$22,095	$158	$2,259
30	$35,584	$263	$3,690
35	$57,309	$442	$6,079
40	$92,296	$754	$10,168
45	$148,644	$1,317	$17,460
50	$239,392	$2,413	$31,474
55	$385,543	$4,882	$62,745
60	$620,921	$12,914	$163,797

*Source: Harvard Financial Educators and the Financial Literacy Center.

Do you think it's easier to part with $95 a month or $2,413? The value of starting early can further be summed up by this next example. Fred and Steve are both twenty-two years old. Fred started putting $2,000 a year into an Individual Retirement Account (IRA) for nine years, starting at age twenty-two and ending at age thirty-one. Steve waited nine years and then started putting $2,000 a year into an IRA, at age thirty-one, for thirty-four years until retirement at age sixty-five. Assuming both IRAs earned 9 percent, who has more money at the age of sixty-five?

Fred will. His account will grow to $579,504. Steve's account will only grow to $470,247. How can this be—Fred only invested $18,000, while Steve invested $70,000? The answer is compound interest. While Fred invested less money, he started nine years sooner than Steve did. Steve's money just didn't have enough time to grow.

The following chart illustrates the pattern of Fred's early contributions and then Steve's later contributions:

Age	Early Contri-butions	Year-End Balance	Age	Later Contri-butions	Year-End Balance
26	$2,000	$13,046	26	0	0
27	$2,000	$16,401	27	0	0
28	$2,000	$20,057	28	0	0
29	$2,000	$24,042	29	0	0
30	$2,000	$28,386	30	0	0
31	0	$30,941	31	$2,000	$2,180
32	0	$33,726	32	$2,000	$4,556
33	0	$36,761	33	$2,000	$7,146
34	0	$40,070	34	$2,000	$9,969
35	0	$43,676	35	$2,000	$13,046
36	0	$47,607	36	$2,000	$16,401
37	0	$51,892	37	$2,000	$20,057
38	0	$56,562	38	$2,000	$24,042
39	0	$61,653	39	$2,000	$28,386
40	0	$67,202	40	$2,000	$33,121
41	0	$73,250	41	$2,000	$38,282
42	0	$79,843	42	$2,000	$43,907
43	0	$87,029	43	$2,000	$50,039
44	0	$94,862	44	$2,000	$56,722

Continued

Age	Early Contri-butions	Year-End Balance	Age	Later Contri-butions	Year-End Balance
45	0	$103,400	45	$2,000	$64,007
46	0	$112,706	46	$2,000	$71,948
46	0	$112,706	46	$2,000	$80,603
48	0	$133,907	48	$2,000	$90,037
49	0	$145,959	49	$2,000	$100,320
50	0	$159,095	50	$2,000	$111,529
51	0	$173,414	51	$2,000	$123,747
52	0	$189,021	52	$2,000	$137,064
53	0	$206,033	53	$2,000	$151,580
54	0	$224,576	54	$2,000	$167,402
55	0	$244,788	55	$2,000	$184,648
56	0	$266,819	56	$2,000	$203,446
57	0	$290,833	57	$2,000	$223,936
58	0	$317,008	58	$2,000	$246,270
59	0	$345,539	59	$2,000	$270,614
60	0	$376,638	60	$2,000	$297,149
61	0	$410,535	61	$2,000	$326,072
62	0	$447,483	62	$2,000	$357,598
63	0	$487,757	63	$2,000	$391,962
64	0	$531,655	64	$2,000	$429,419
65	0	$579,504	65	$2,000	$470,247
Total Invested	$18,000		Total Invested	$70,000	
Amount Available at Age 65	$579,504		Amount Available at Age 65	$470,247	

The numbers prove the point that investing early in life can result in a greater accumulation by retirement. The moral to this story is to start saving today and not procrastinate.

Flying Through Life in First Class

For saving to actually occur, it must be made a priority. But for many young adults just starting their careers, there are other more pressing priorities for their money. The first time accumulation of things is especially important. There is the need for furniture, cars, business clothes, and shoes. The cost for these things can add up, making it difficult to find money to save.

Pete and Heather Howard were both in their mid-twenties. Their savings excuse was "You don't expect me to invest now, do you? Remember I've only been working a few years. Things will be looking up soon and then I'll be able to invest. Right now I have to dress well in order to make a good impression. Wait until I'm a little older. There's plenty of time."

Pete and Heather Howard were very concerned about making a good impression. In fact, the Howards would never have been caught dead in coach class on an airline. They only dined at restaurants which made the top ten list in whatever city they happened to be in. Their friends were dazzled by their stories of exotic vacations to far away destinations or spur of the moment weekends jaunts to Paris or London. Their clothes, cars, house, furniture, and everything else that they owned seemed to be top of the line.

Both Pete and Heather had high-paying professional jobs, having graduated from college as a lawyer and an engineer. Even so, their friends who made comparable salaries wondered how the Howards managed to afford this high quality of life while their budgets didn't stretch nearly as far. Their friends came to the conclusion that they must have invested very wisely to have the money to afford all these things. The reality was quite different.

While Pete and Heather's friends invested their money in anticipation of their retirement and also put money aside in an emergency fund, the Howards never saved any of their income.

They habitually spent every dime they made. As their salaries increased, so did their spending. Sometimes their spending increased faster than their salaries, and in those cases their credit cards would help to fill the gap.

Before they knew it, their combined debt had reached $30,000. At an average interest rate of 18 percent, they paid $5,400 a year just in interest on this debt. What if they had invested this money instead? Let's see the difference by using the Rule of 72. The Rule of 72 states, "Any interest rate divided into the number 72 will give you the number of years necessary to double your initial investment." For example:

Example of an investment earning 3 percent (like a savings account)

72 ÷ 3 = 24 years

If your initial investment is $200, it will take twenty-four years to reach $400 and forty-eight years to reach $800 at 3 percent.

Example of an investment earning 6 percent

72 ÷ 6 = 12 years

If your initial investment is $200, it will take twelve years to reach $400; twenty-four years to reach $800; thirty-six years to reach $1,600; and forty-eight years to reach $3,200.

Example of an investment earning 12 percent

72 ÷ 12 = 6 years

If your initial investment is $200, it will take six years to reach $400; twelve years to reach $800; eighteen years to reach $1,600; twenty-four years to reach $3,200; thirty years to reach $6,400; thirty-six years to reach $12,800; forty-two years to reach $25,600; and forty-eight years to reach $51,200.

If the Howards had saved their $5,400 at 10 percent (instead of losing it to interest payments) they would have doubled this

amount in a little more than seven years. If the Howards continue to keep their debt level around $30,000, they will continue to pay $5,400 each year until they are debt free. This time may never come if they keep spending and their debt level never decreases. In seven years time, they will have paid $37,800 in interest compared to earning $10,800 if they had saved the first year's interest.

The value of having your money work for you instead of against you was not lost by Pete's boss, Mr. Andrews. When Pete first joined the firm several years ago, he was a young lawyer right out of college. Mr. Andrews became Pete's mentor and Pete tried to become a clone of the boss he respected so much. In fact, he modeled not only his boss' work habits but his personal ones as well. Mr. Andrews lived a lavish lifestyle. He always went out to eat at expensive restaurants and bought the most expensive suits, watches, and briefcases. Pete envied this lifestyle and became even more bound and determined to become just like his boss.

Pete was very sad when Mr. Andrews finally announced his retirement. By the time Mr. and Mrs. Andrews had reached retirement age, they had a very full scrapbook of memories from their life's adventures, but a very empty bank account. Faced with a severely decreased income from social security, their standard of living plummeted drastically from the standard to which they were accustomed. This was a serious shock to them. After a lifetime of being able to do almost anything they wanted without having to budget, the reality of living on a fixed income at their age proved very sobering.

By living only in the present with no thought for the future, the Andrewses found that the future had arrived, but they weren't prepared for it. If they had only realized that their lavish lifestyle had only been made possible by Mr. Andrews' high salary and that social security income could not hope to compete. The Andrewses also followed the savings excuse for their age:"Yes, it's too late to begin saving now. We have social security but who can live on that? If only I had invested when I had the money. You can't invest when you have no income."

With no retirement income available to them other than social security, their only hope to increase their income to the levels to which they had become accustomed was for Mr. Andrews to go back to work. To them, it was worth it in order to maintain their standard of living. Delaying retirement was their solution for now, but retirement can't be delayed forever. Eventually one's age and continued capacity to work will catch up to them.

Although Americans dream of early retirement, most have accumulated little in the way of savings and have done even less planning to make that retirement happen. In fact only 11 percent of workers under thirty-five years of age indicate that they are participating in their company's 401(k), according to the AICPA 2007 poll.

Although Pete was very happy to have his old boss back at work, the reason for his return scared him. Upon returning, Mr. Andrews had a heart-to-heart talk with Pete and said that he was worried he was following the same path that had led to his financial predicament. He encouraged Pete to save while he still had the time so that he wouldn't be forced to continue to work once he reached Mr. Andrew's age.

We Didn't Expect...

There will always be unexpected expenses, "life events" that seem to pop up at the most inopportune times. Sometimes these unplanned expenditures happen at the same time or one right after another. When they occur, the result is an additional burden to your budget. Although ideally your monthly budget should always have money set aside for these expenses, more times than not, this money is not allocated.

When "life events" occur, money that could have been saved is now spent. The secret is to learn how to balance the inevitable life events with the need to save. The following story illustrates this struggle.

Tatum's father was a bank executive who was reminded daily of the virtues of saving money. He did not want this valuable lesson to escape his daughter so he lectured Tatum constantly about this topic. She remembers her father's first savings lesson when he gave her a piggy bank while she was a first grader.

Tatum had tried all her life to fill up the piggy bank, but it always seemed to stay empty. Now nineteen, Tatum's piggy bank had been replaced by a savings account in her father's bank. This account also remained virtually empty. It wasn't that Tatum did not have a savings plan, it just seemed that something always occurred to cause her plan to be delayed. "I didn't expect" became her overused phrase to explain why she couldn't possibly start saving now.

As a graduation present from high school, Tatum's parents gave her a used car. Although Tatum did not have monthly loan payments because the car had been a gift, she still ended up paying other car-related expenses. First it was the air conditioning that stopped working and needed to be repaired. Then came the new set of tires to take the place of the threadbare ones. Finally, the brakes became so worn that they needed to be replaced before an accident occurred. All of these unanticipated car expenses put a strain on Tatum's limited finances.

Eager to assert her adulthood, Tatum chose to move into an apartment with her friend Jenny. When they moved into their new, unfurnished home, they found that to their surprise, "unfurnished" meant that the rooms were empty. They needed to make large purchases to fill up the rooms. Tatum made a trip to a furniture store, which gave her an instant credit limit of

$10,000. Since Tatum was starting from scratch, she had a lot to buy. This high credit limit came in handy as she purchased a bedroom set, desk, kitchen utensils, and a living room sofa. She now had an extra expense line in her budget reserved for "furniture payments."

Once the apartment was under control, Tatum thought she could finally start saving. But she had not counted on her roommate Jenny causing the next delay. It turned out that Jenny had bulimia. This illness resulted in her eating large quantities of food that she would purge shortly afterwards.

In fact, before Tatum noticed Jenny's illness, she had always wondered how the food she bought at the supermarket disappeared so quickly. After discovering Jenny's bulimia, she found herself frequenting the supermarket daily to replace the food Jenny had consumed. This was becoming rather expensive in addition to straining their relationship.

Even though Jenny ate most of Tatum's food, Jenny's food expenditures still exceeded the amount she allotted for rent. When she did not have enough rent money, she would just avoid paying Tatum. This presented a problem for Tatum since she did not make enough money to cover both of their rent portions. In desperation, she called Jenny's parents and told them what was going on. Once Jenny found out that her parents knew about her eating disorder, she was furious with Tatum and moved out.

Although Tatum felt relieved that she no longer had to deal with Jenny's problem, she realized that she now had a new one to take its place. How was she supposed to afford her apartment on her own? She solved her immediate problem by relying on her credit cards to pay the rent until she found a new roommate. By the time she found one, she had accumulated a substantial debt. Every dollar went to pay down the debt, which left none to be saved.

Tatum needed to get into the habit of paying herself first. When savings is last in the expense line, invariably there is no money left by the time the end of the line is reached. There will always be obstacles to saving your money; therefore you must commit an amount of your income to saving before you start spending.

Most young adults like Tatum do not realize that saving money can actually pay! The following table illustrates the value over time of $1,000 invested annually (only $84 a month):

Interest Earned	5 Years	10 Years	15 Years	20 Years
5%	$5,526	$12,578	$21,579	$33,066
6%	$5,637	$13,181	$23,276	$36,786
7%	$5,751	$13,816	$25,129	$40,995
8%	$5,867	$14,487	$27,152	$45,762
9%	$5,985	$15,193	$29,361	$51,160
10%	$6,105	$15,937	$31,772	$57,275
11%	$6,228	$16,722	$34,405	$64,203
12%	$6,353	$17,549	$37,280	$72,052

Investing $10,000 in a one-time lump sum also pays off:

Interest Earned	5 Years	10 Years	15 Years	20 Years
5%	$12,763	$16,289	$20,789	$26,533
6%	$13,382	$17,908	$23,966	$32,071
7%	$14,026	$19,672	$27,590	$38,697
8%	$14,693	$21,589	$31,722	$46,610
9%	$15,386	$23,674	$36,425	$56,044
10%	$16,105	$25,937	$41,772	$67,275
11%	$16,851	$28,394	$47,772	$80,623
12%	$17,623	$31,058	$54,736	$96,463

*Source: National Endowment for Financial Education.

It may have taken a lot of hard work to accumulate that $10,000 lump sum you initially deposited. However, the hard work doesn't end after you make your deposit. As the chart shows, $10,000 that earns 12 percent interest will add up to $96,463 after twenty years. You have done nothing but make the initial deposit; your money itself does the rest of the work.

When Tatum turned twenty-one, her father gave her an unexpected birthday gift, a savings account. He had been contributing a portion of his salary to this account since Tatum was born. In fact he had been depositing $1,000 per year for twenty years. Averaging 6 percent interest, Tatum's account was now worth almost $37,000. This gift was Tatum's savior from her debt burden. After paying off what she owed, she promised herself she would follow her father's example. Winston Churchill once said, "Saving is a very fine thing. Especially if your parents have done it for you."

Americans have saved (percentage wise) in the low single digits for the last decade while other Western industrialized countries have savings rates in the double digits. For the 2006 year, the average personal savings rate in our country was a dismal negative 1 percent according to the Department of Commerce (experts recommend 10 percent). This means that Americans have started to spend more than they save, adding to their ever-increasing debt level. Unless this trend is reversed, adequate savings cushions will never be realized.

Every Little Bit Adds Up

Many young adults do not bother to save because they feel the small amount they would be able to set aside is too little to make any meaningful difference. The reality is that even saving a couple of dollars a day can make a difference and add up to a substantial amount by retirement. Remember the example shared with Curtis at the beginning of this chapter—if a twenty-year-old can save $95 a month he can become a millionaire by the age of sixty-five (at 10 percent interest). This monthly amount equals approximately $3 a day.

There are many "painless" ways to save. Here are some ideas for finding that $95 a month that will turn you into a millionaire:

- Every time your family sends you a cash gift, put some of it into your savings before you spend the money.
- Check out prices for sports equipment online and in secondhand stores, rather than buying it new in a department or sports store.
- Shop for your clothes at thrift stores.
- Buy your furniture at garage sales or ask your relatives and friends if they have furniture they plan on replacing.
- Sell items you don't use any longer.
- Call around and compare car insurance rates. Switch companies if you find one with a better rate.
- Start a side business. Do you have a talent or hobby you can turn into a moneymaker?
- Do not drive alone. Carpool or use public transportation.

In the case of Pierre, age twenty, he discovered that even saving change made a difference. Since men's wallets seldom have a place to put coins, men tend to put change in their pockets, in their car, or leave it around the house. It was the latter that bothered his roommate Jillian the most. Pierre's change was always lying around. She found it everywhere—the bedroom, the kitchen, the living room, and even the bathroom.

Jillian decided to take this change and put it into an empty glass container. Pretty soon, the container was full, so she transferred the change to a larger bottled water container. When this filled up, she started filling up another water container. After a year of putting Pierre's change daily into the water containers, she had completely filled up four large water containers that she kept stored in the garage.

One day, Pierre came home from work with the news that the Internet company he worked for had finally gone out of business. He knew that they had not shown a profit for the past two years, but he just assumed they would find another venture capitalist to continue the funding. When the funding never materialized, Pierre wished he had begun to save his money years ago. He knew working for a start-up was risky, but he never took any precautions.

Luckily for Pierre, his roommate was a financial planner. The first thing Jillian had Pierre do was create a complete budget of all his expenditures in relation to Pierre's new income from his unemployment compensation. It is more realistic to budget with actual income you can count on rather than projecting income from a new job, since the length of the job search is unknown. They found Pierre was going to be $400 a month short. Jillian then proceeded to identify expenses that he could eliminate or reduce like his mobile phone, sports club monthly fee (he never went), cable television, expensive dinners out, and other "wants" in his budget. After doing this, he was only $100 short.

Pierre had heard that it took an average of one month to find a job for each $10,000 of annual earnings. So he anticipated he would need approximately five months to be able to find a job with a comparable salary ($50,000) to his last position. The dilemma remained to find the $500 he needed (the $100 monthly shortage multiplied by five) to be able to cover all his monthly expenditures. By completing a net worth sheet (see Chapter 1), he would be able to identify assets that he could possibly sell to cover this shortage.

After completing the net worth form, they discovered that

Pierre had a positive net worth, but that all his assets were untouchable. He had equity in his car but didn't want to sell it. He rationalized it would not make any sense to do so since he would have to buy a replacement car to get to his new job. He tried to obtain a second mortgage on his condominium, but couldn't qualify since he was unemployed. His other assets were a savings and checking account with balances almost at zero.

Jillian remembered the water containers in the garage. Pierre was skeptical as to how much money they contained. He was not too hopeful that the little amount of change would amount to anything. Jillian decided to take the containers to the bank anyway to have the coins counted. When she returned home, to Pierre's astonishment, she presented him with $500! They were amazed that the change that he hardly missed could have amounted to that sum in just a year's time.

Pierre found a job in three months. As soon as he started working, he opened a savings account. He now realized that even small amounts saved can add up. He also understood it was important to save accessible money for those life events that can and do come up. A retirement fund is a safety net for the future, but it is just as important to have a safety net for the present. Remember that by putting money into a retirement account only, this money cannot usually be withdrawn without substantial penalty before age fifty-nine and one-half. By setting aside an emergency fund (equal to at least three months of your total living expenses), this fund will serve as an excellent savings safety net.

Accessible savings are needed not only for emergencies, but also for both short- and long-term goals. The 70-20-10 Rule shows how you can successfully divide your money into amounts saved for retirement, emergencies, and goals. To follow the 70-20-10 Rule, divide your net income in the following manner:

- Spend 70 percent for living expenses such as rent/mortgage, food, clothing, and gasoline.
- Spend no more than 20 percent for debt payments like car payment, credit cards, and student loans, but exclude first mortgage.
- Save 10 percent:
  - Save 5 percent for specific goals—vacation, car, school tuition, and computer. At the same time you should build up and then maintain an emergency fund with three to six months of living expenses in the account. This is not for impulse spending. Keep it for unexpected expenses like car repairs, lay-offs, and medical expenses.
  - Invest a minimum of 5 percent for the long term. These funds are earmarked for your retirement—IRA, 401(k), or 403(b).

Realize that when you exceed these percentages in any category, it means a reduction in the other areas. If your living expenses are high, you won't be able to save as much. Similarly, if your debt level is too high, you won't be able to contribute as much to your savings, investments, or both. If you want to put more money into your savings, all you have to do is decrease your living expenses, decrease your debt, or do both.

If you get into the habit of paying yourself first, this is the most effective way to save money. In fact, money never seen cannot be missed. If your company can automatically deposit a percentage of your paycheck into a retirement account, the money never actually comes into your possession for you to spend. Other tips to make saving easier include:

- Let the person in your household who is the best at saving control the finances.

- Put your credit card in your freezer and thaw out only for emergencies (it's hard to go shopping at the mall with a frozen card). Tip: microwaving the card will only melt it.
- Buy savings bonds (you can't redeem them until they mature—usually several years waiting time).
- Put your money in a six-month or one-year certificate of deposit (CD) so that you can't touch it.

Use whatever method works the best for you. My preferred method was the credit card in the freezer. It worked for me, although my friend who discovered my credit cards while looking for ice cream thought I was a little odd!

Words of Wisdom

Most people agree that saving is a good thing; they just say that it's impossible because of their financial situation. In reality, money that comes in has three places it can go—savings, living expenses, or debt payments. The choice is up to you. It just depends on your priorities.

If you follow the guidance in this chapter, you can make saving money the highest priority. Just remember the follow lessons:

- Pay yourself first.
- The earlier you start, the better.
- Do not make excuses.
- Even little amounts saved will add up.
- You, too, can become a millionaire.

12

Easy Come, Easy Go

The first rule of becoming wealthy is not to lose money. The second rule is not to forget the first rule.

—*Warren Buffet*

Many people who receive large sums of money all at once end up losing it within a short period of time. This scenario has been repeated many times over the years by people who have received inheritances, won the lottery, signed a huge sports contract, or had a hit in the entertainment business. For many people, the tendency is to see a windfall as unlimited. You think you couldn't possibly spend it all. Now is the opportunity to buy that new car to replace the old, to move into a one-bedroom apartment and out of that cramped studio, to get a whole new wardrobe, or to visit those exotic places you've always dreamed of.

Oftentimes a sudden influx of money causes confusion to people who are unaccustomed to dealing with such large amounts. For example, the same story often repeats itself for celebrities who have new-found wealth and can't cope with their riches. We read of their now chaotic lives that contrast strongly with their grounded and focused lives before their wealth.

What people do not tend to realize is that even large sums of money can go rather quickly if one lives extravagantly.

Celebrities such as Toni Braxton and MC Hammer sold millions of albums, but were unable to hold onto this wealth and ended up filing for bankruptcy protection. To continue living a luxurious lifestyle usually requires a continuous resupply of money to replace the money that has been spent. This is where the problem arises. Many people only receive a one-time windfall. When the money is gone, it's gone.

It becomes very difficult to adjust back to a modest lifestyle after having had a taste of the lifestyle of the rich and famous. Would you be content going back to driving a Hyundai after you had driven a Porsche? Would you be content leaving an apartment with an ocean view to go back to a view of an alley? Would you be content staying at home and renting videos after having flown off to Paris for the weekend? Most people find it hard to scale back so instead they continue to live their enhanced lifestyle and finance it through artificial means, like borrowing.

This chapter will teach you how to hold onto money that is unexpectedly received. It will concentrate on lump sums of money instead of constant streams of anticipated money, like your regular paycheck. If you are fortunate enough to receive a "windfall," you need to learn how to leverage this largesse so that it works for you instead of just making a pit stop in your savings account.

You will learn from the mistakes of other windfall recipients:

- Indulging in spending sprees
- Not creating a financial plan
- Investing without doing adequate research
- Not diversifying places your money is invested
- Spending to the maximum
- Engaging in risky ventures

As this first story demonstrates, the mistake of "indulging in spending sprees" is hard to resist.

Squandering a Windfall

The tendency to spend money is a common denominator among people who have received extra money, regardless of how they obtained it. Whether the money was received through an inheritance, a signing bonus, or a sports contract, the end result is that you have more money than you are accustomed to possessing. This new wealth may feel more like a gift than money you have earned or to which you are entitled.

This perception affects how you ultimately handle your money. If you feel you did not earn the money, you will part with it more easily. Money slaved for is not so easily given up. Unfortunately, most money that comes quickly can go just as quickly.

A good friend of mine, Ken, has often said, "Everyone should blow at least one windfall." He should know. In the two years after he received a fairly sizable inheritance while a senior in college, he bought and sold a vacation condo (on which he lost money), bought several thousand dollars worth of Christmas decorations on a spree, bought and sold a classic car which regularly needed repairs that his normal income could not afford, and systematically overspent the rest.

When the money ran out but the bills remained, Ken started acquiring debt to finance his expenses. At first, cash advances on his credit cards and loans were successful in eliminating the shortfall, but eventually Ken's borrowing reached a limit. When his spending and borrowing spree ended, Ken found himself with about the same amount of debt, if not more, than before he received his inheritance.

Compounding the problem was the fact that he had acquired spending habits that were very hard to curtail! Ken became used to living a life of luxury. The realization that his good fortune would end proved very painful. To downscale and have to give things up would be difficult for Ken to do. He knew how his friends, also recent college graduates, were struggling financially. Now Ken had no choice but to join them in their "budget" lives.

Looking back on this time in his life, it is still hard for Ken to believe that his inheritance has disappeared. He received $80,000 at the age of twenty-two. By the time he turned twenty-four his inheritance was gone. How could such a large sum of money have disappeared so quickly? He suddenly realized why "windfall" was such an appropriate word. The wind comes and goes without a trace, just like his inheritance did.

Whether rich from the lottery, an inheritance, a bonus from work, or settling some type of legal dispute, people often go on a spending spree with no regard for their long-term costs. Commonly, such people end up a few months or years down the road with a lot of toys (depreciating assets) and a standard of living that cannot be maintained.

Some of the most common things major lottery winners have done are:

1. Put money in the bank (earning low or zero interest)
2. Made bill/loan payments
3. Shared with relatives
4. Purchased a car
5. Purchased appliances/furnishings
6. Renovated home
7. Took vacation(s)
8. Made mortgage payments
9. Made charitable donations
10. Invested in stocks

If you are going to choose No. 1 and let your money just sit, you should at least put it in a place where the interest earned is working for you. By investing your money in a low- or zero-interest earning account (as the majority of lottery winners do), it is the same as putting the money under your mattress.

What's the right way to handle this windfall? In order to avoid becoming a statistic and ending up with a lot of toys but no real increase in net worth, a financial plan needs to be designed to allocate your money. Take time to create this plan and get input from everyone in the family. Families tend to spend more time discussing the weather (something we can't change) than we do discussing our financial situation (something we can change).

Your financial plan should be developed with your input and the assistance of a qualified financial planner. Once the plan is decided upon, it is a good idea to continue to have a professional monitor your account and give you continual advice. When choosing a financial planner, make sure you also trust this person.

Problems can result if you entrust your finances to someone who is not looking after your best interests, or, in the worst-case scenario, is stealing from you. Child star Gary Coleman, one of the highest paid television child actors of his era, sued his adoptive parents for mishandling his funds. He claimed they had misappropriated money from commissions, salaries, fees, and his pension fund. The case was not settled until 1993, with Coleman being awarded 1.3 million dollars from his parents. Coleman said that this money was quickly devoured by lawyer's fees and poor investments. Therefore, it is important to find a financial planner you can trust and whose interest in your finances is impartial.

Once you are comfortable with your choice of a financial

planner, you then need to craft a plan. You need to determine your priorities, whether they involve retirement, college education, home ownership (not just the cost of buying a home, but owning a home), clothing, furniture, electronics, or cars. The goal is to fund each of the determined priorities and then let the magic of compound interest take care of funding the rest. Fill in the following chart to discover your priorities:

Order of Importance	Spending Priorities
1.	
2.	
3.	
4.	
5.	
6.	
7.	

Whatever you determine to be your main funding areas, you should try and stick to the plan. When you deviate from your set route, you can easily become distracted and find it hard to get back on track. This chart should be posted in a common location, such as a refrigerator or bathroom mirror, where you will constantly be reminded of your priorities. The more you can actually observe your goal, the greater your chance of succeeding.

If my friend, Ken, had followed this advice he could have visited a financial planner instead of acting rashly. Together, they could have worked out a plan to deal with Ken's newfound wealth. Without a plan, the danger of spending large sums of money quickly is ever present. A smart plan would have allocated some money for Ken's priorities and some for an emergency savings account. The plan would have put the majority of his inheritance in investment funds specifically designated for his retirement. This would have ensured that Ken would not run out of money before he retired. Since no plan existed in Ken's case, he ended up running out of money about thirty years before he had planned to retire!

Eighteenth Birthday Present

Upon receipt of a windfall, it is advisable not to make any decisions that may be risky and result in you losing this sum. We have seen that in Ken's case he lost his windfall by not controlling his spending habits. Equally dangerous is investing the entire amount in risky areas. Putting your money under your mattress is one example of a risky location. What would you do if there were a fire or a burglary? Although most people would agree that a mattress is not the safest place to leave your money, other locations that are not as obvious may be just as risky.

Since it may be difficult to determine if some locations are unsafe, it is best to avoid putting all of your money in one place. A smart move is to diversify your investments so that you spread the risk. If an unwise choice causes you to lose your money in one place, at least you have not lost it all. Sadly, Tim did not understand this concept of not "putting all your eggs in one basket."

Upon the birth of his son Tim, Alan started investing a portion of his salary every payday. These funds were held in a custodial stock account for his son to receive as a birthday present when he turned eighteen years old. To Tim, this gift of stock was just a certificate of paper, but to his father this gift was evidence of his twenty-five years of employment with his company. Since these shares were the result of his many years of toiling, they eventually amounted to a significant sum of money. The stocks increased in value over time and rose with the stock market. By the time Tim was eighteen, the stocks were valued at $400,000.

When parents or grandparents save or invest money on your (their children's) behalf, they have usually sacrificed a portion of their earnings for your benefit. This money could have been used to pay for their own wants and needs, but they made a conscious decision to share part of it with you. Although this money is usually readily accepted, it is usually not truly appreciated. Don't forget the earlier lesson that money received that is not earned is money that does not hold as much value.

Tim received these shares of stock upon his eighteenth birthday. Unfortunately, he found there was no owner's manual accompanying this gift of stock. Since Tim was of legal age and the stocks were in his name, he had complete control over them. With access to all this money, Tim decided to drop out of college (which he didn't see as necessary) and start his own business. He was anxious to become even richer and his newfound wealth gave him a sense of bravado. Tim ended up purchasing a fast food franchise whose down payment depleted almost all of the value of his stocks.

With little expertise in running a business (other than a business class he took in high school) and very little money in reserve, Tim had problems from the beginning. At the outset, Tim had not perceived college to be worthwhile, but now he wondered if he had made a mistake. Tim was wishing he had had the benefit of taking classes in accounting, economics, advertising, and entrepreneurship.

A novice businessman, Tim made numerous uninformed decisions. For instance, he didn't realize that it could take years for a small business to turn a profit. As a result, Tim failed to plan for expected losses.

Less than a year later, the money that his dad had worked so hard to save for Tim's future was completely gone. Tim's business both opened and closed its doors in the same year. Eighteen years of consistent saving had been an important commitment for Tim's father, but he did not mind making the sacrifice. This money was to have provided Tim with a security blanket to last throughout his life.

Even though Tim had turned the age to be legally considered an adult, he was unable to make wise adult business decisions. Tim's father should have been more proactive in aiding his son to make sensible decisions. Instead, Tim's father believed that experience was the best teacher. Unfortunately, experience can be an expensive teacher.

The concept of diversification is a strategy designed to help reduce risk. Distributing your money among different investments is a less volatile approach than one that is concentrated in a single type of investment (like Tim's business venture). To assess your risk tolerance, you need to determine how much or how little safety is necessary for you. The following chart will help you to figure out your attitude toward risk. Each category lists descriptors that explain the different levels:

Conservative	Safety of principal is the main concern. Risk must be kept to an absolute minimum. Asset: 55% bonds; 20% stocks; 25% cash
Conservative to moderate	Safety of principal is most important, but a secondary goal is growth of capital. Some risk is acceptable where growth opportunities exist. Asset: 45% bonds; 40% stocks; 15% cash
Moderate	Safety of principal and growth of capitalare of equal importance. A smallamount of risk is acceptable. Assets: 30% bonds; 60% stocks; 10% cash
Moderate to aggressive	Growth of capital is the main concern, but safety of principal is also important. A moderate amount of risk is acceptable. Assets: 20% bonds; 75% stocks; 5% cash
Aggressive	Growth of capital is the main concern. Reasonably high risk is acceptable. Assets: 95% stocks; 5% cash

If Tim had figured out his risk tolerance prior to deciding to invest almost all of his money into a business venture, he probably would have determined that he was "aggressive." He was willing to accept a high level of risk in return for potentially large profits. Unfortunately, Tim's profits never materialized.

The Big One

The human tendency to spend more when more is available can be dangerous when "more" is not just a raise in salary but a huge bonus. By always living to the maximum extent of our income, we not only make saving impossible, but we also establish a behavioral pattern that is difficult to change. The only way to prevent such behavior is to restrict access to your own money. If it cannot be touched, it cannot be spent.

Patty was a sophomore in college and had just turned twenty. Her grandmother raised her after both of Patty's parents died in a car accident when she was six. Although Patty's grandmother did not have the money to fund her college tuition, she did indirectly pay for her room and board. When her grandmother decided to move into an assisted living facility, she deeded the house to Patty instead of selling it. The house was near her college campus, a big advantage to Patty.

Patty's house was located in Northridge California in an area that experienced earthquakes on a regular basis. Living in California, the expression "the big one" refers not to a hefty hamburger but to the fear of a large-scale earthquake that will one day wreak widespread destruction. In fear of this day, most homeowners make sure they have earthquake policies on their homes to prepare for this imminent disaster.

Disasters, like earthquakes, are life events that no one ever wants to experience. We prefer to stay in denial and think that disasters happen to other people and not to us. This attitude is irrational, especially if you live in an earthquake or hurricane prone area. Since there are no certainties in life, coverage is smart "insurance" against these life events.

When an earthquake struck, Patty was glad her grandmother had wisely paid her earthquake premiums. She had been visiting a friend in San Diego during the earthquake and when she returned, her house was almost completely destroyed. Some of her neighbors were luckier; they had suffered minor structural damage that could be repaired. Patty did not have this option.

Her insurance company made the assessment that her house was unfit to live in. Patty watched as her house was demolished. She received from her insurance company a check in the amount of $200,000 to cover the value of the home. Patty's grandmother had been lucky to buy her house thirty years ago before, and its value had increased substantially. Her house had always been her greatest asset and now it was reflected by the check in Patty's hands.

Patty's decision not to rebuild was based on the fear of another earthquake occurring. She decided to move to Las Vegas and transfer to a local university there. Patty purchased another house, but was pleasantly surprised to discover it cost much less than houses in and around Los Angeles. After she made a down payment, she still had a significant sum left over.

During the course of discovering her new city, Patty also came across its many shopping malls. Patty didn't worry when she went on her regular shopping sprees because there was plenty of money from her insurance settlement. Her lifelong pattern of spending as much as she had was being repeated, but on a much grander scale. If she wanted a new mountain bike, hot tub, or expensive vacation, she would purchase one. She never really kept track of how much money she spent. As long as the ATM machine dispensed money, everything was fine. That is, until one day when the machine wouldn't give her any more.

Patty was sure her bank had made an error on her account. It wasn't possible to have gone through $120,000 (her insurance settlement minus the $80,000 down payment on her new house) in less than six months. When she met with a bank representative to go over her account, Patty was amazed to discover that she had in fact spent all the money in her savings account.

If Patty had learned to live according to a budget, she would have set limits each month on what she could spend in each category such as food, clothing, or entertainment. Without a budget, Patty spent money whenever and however she wished.

Living by a budget would have set a limit on her spending. When she reached it, she would have had to stop. The urge to spend needs to be contained if you want to succeed in cutting down on your expenditures. The following quiz should be taken before deciding to make any major purchases:

1. Do you really need this item?
2. Is the price reasonable enough to justify buying it?
3. Is this the best time (season) to buy this item?
4. If this is a bargain, is it a current model?
5. If "on sale," is the price a true sales price?
6. Can a less expensive item be substituted?
7. Are you sure there are no major disadvantages?
8. Will this item truly satisfy an inner need?
9. Have you checked and researched the item?
10. Do you know the retailer's reputation?
11. Does this retailer offer any special services with the item?

Add up the number of times that you answered yes. If you answered yes only one to five times, don't waste your money. You might as well just hand your wallet directly to the sales clerk. If you answered yes more than six times, go ahead and buy the product. You'll probably never find a deal as good as this one.

If you have failed the test but are still fighting the urge to spend, consider these suggestions:

- Set up a buddy system with a friend who you can call when you have the urge to spend.
- Do not take more money with you when you leave the house than you will need for the day.
- Leave your credit and debit cards at home.
- Make a shopping list and stick to the items on it. Do not be tempted to buy items not on the list.
- Use the envelope method for certain expenses. When the envelope is empty, no more money can be spent in that category. For example, if the entertainment envelope is empty, do not borrow from the food envelope.

Once Patti learned to restrain her spending, she made sure that she followed one other smart money strategy, obtaining insurance. Insurance for all areas of our lives is something that should be considered a "need" instead of an "exception" in our expense budgets. However, a 2006 study by NAIC found that 20 percent of young adults that currently have automobile insurance say they would consider letting their insurance lapse as a way of saving money. In addition, 14 percent said they would consider letting their health insurance lapse. By maintaining insurance "just in case," we will be assured that any loses in our lives will be compensated. Usually these losses come with a hefty price tag, as Patti can testify.

Hoping for Quick Gains

When a windfall is received, it may appear to be "easy money." If you expended little or no effort to receive the money, you may be tempted to double or triple your initial bounty. However, a short cut to making money is not usually guaranteed. More times than not, the promise of high percentage yields turns out to be only that, a promise and not a certainty.

Trine, at the age of nineteen, chose to drop out of college. She had only finished her first year in a computer science program but already the offers were coming in. She felt she could not pass up the promise of riches and stock options for a diploma. Trine figured that if she waited three more years to get her diploma, she might miss out on some of the opportunities that were available right now. The current job market was robust, but it could stall by the time she graduated. Her parents were upset, but Trine would not listen to their pleas to stay in school.

After only one year of working for an Internet start-up, Trine felt vindicated that she had made the right decision. A huge corporation bought her company and its stock price rose sharply. Trine decided to cash in her stock options and retire at the age of twenty. She figured that with $500,000 in the bank, she would never have to work again.

Her original contentment with her nest egg slowly led to discontent. Having access to all this money caused Trine to become greedy. She wanted more. Besides, she had always been told that you need to have money to make money. She now had money and she planned to use it to make much more.

She had become fascinated by stories she heard of people becoming millionaires from investing in private equity opportunities and hedge funds that skyrocketed in value. She figured that she could invest her nest egg in a fund of this type and reap the same rewards without having to work. Now that she had retired, she had lots of free time, so exploring this new opportunity seemed like the next natural step.

After much research online, Trine decided to invest in a private equity fund that was trying to turn around an unprofitable airline. Private equity funds usually target struggling companies and then install new management to try and make them profitable. These funds usually have substantial entry costs, with most private equity funds requiring a significant initial investment (usually upwards of $100,000). Trine didn't have a problem contributing the entry fee. In fact, she decided to invest half of her $500,000.

Trine had been warned that there was a risk associated with private equity investments and that you can lose all your money if the private-equity fund is unable to turn around the failing company. However, Trine preferred the high risk. She knew the only way to make a lot of money quickly was to risk losing a lot. She still had $250,000 in the bank, so she wasn't worried about the risk. If she made a bad investment decision, she was sure she could recoup her losses with future luckier investments.

At first, her investment proved profitable. She made a 30 percent return on her investment in the first six months. She wondered why she had worked eighty-hour weeks that first year at the Internet start-up when it was so easy to make money this way. Unfortunately, her luck never repeated itself. Trine's attraction to high-risk investments took its toll.

Before she knew it, she was taking more money out of the bank to add to her private equity investment. She thought it seemed ridiculous to keep the rest of her nest egg in the bank earning a low interest rate when she could dump it all into the private equity fund.

One day, she checked on her investment and learned that its value had plunged. Apparently the airline was now in bankruptcy with little hope of recovering. Before she knew it, her total investment was practically worthless.

If Trine had been honest with herself, she would have acknowledged that her initial research on the internet into private equity funds did not adequately prepare her as an investment expert. To become certified, a financial planner must study and pass a difficult exam. After that it takes years of experience and continual studying to begin to be qualified as an expert.

If you decide to make your own investment trades over the Internet, the following suggestions are ways for you to prepare yourself:

- Subscribe to a money magazine like *Young Money* (www.youngmoney.com) or *Better Investing*.
- Check out money websites like MSN Money (money-central.msn.com) and The Motley Fool (www.fool.com).
- Order materials that teach investing basics (click on "resource clearinghouse" at www.jumpstart.org).
- Enroll in finance classes offered in your high school or college.
- Attend money management programs offered by your church, your job, or your local community agency.
- Buy personal finance books that teach the basics of investing.

Trine chose risky investment funds as her next "business venture" without much research. Her decision to enter the world of hedge funds and private equity had been prompted by several newspaper articles that she had read which chronicled huge profits by several traders. After having read these articles, her decision was made. However, if she had done research on the risks and profitability of these types of investments, Trine may have chosen a different path.

Words of Wisdom

As we have seen, receiving any large sum of money is usually a mixed blessing, not the proverbial pot of gold at the end of the rainbow. Large or small, the use of any unusual income should be carefully analyzed so that you do not end up broke. And of course, for very significant sums, a professional advisor should be consulted.

The influx of money can occur because you lost a loved one, received an insurance claim from a natural disaster, or because of some other tragedy. Therefore, there are always heightened emotions and sometimes unclear thinking that surround this newfound money. The best way to avoid making any rash decisions, which could turn out to be disastrous, is to do nothing for thirty to sixty days. Pretend the money is not even there until you can think clearly and plan rationally. A carefully crafted budget and a plan are absolutely critical.

At the same time, most people are not prepared to suddenly receive a large sum of money and they do not handle it well. In many cases, more harm than good will result if the recipient is ill advised or not advised at all. This possibility should be acknowledged by the person thinking about gifting a large sum of money. For example, putting inheritances in a trust fund that restricts withdrawals is a way to ensure the money lasts for an extended period.

This chapter has given you some suggestions as to how you can hold onto your windfalls. You should remember to:

- Avoid spending sprees.
- Identify a trusted, qualified financial advisor.
- Develop a long-term financial plan.
- Do research.
- Do not put all your eggs in one basket.
- Resist spending the maximum that is available.
- Steer clear of risky investments.

13

Wall Street Panic

Money makes money and the money
that money makes
makes more money.

—Poor Richard's Almanac

The stock market crash of 1929, which triggered the Great Depression, made many people who lived through it fearful of investing in the market ever again. Many were good savers, but they chose to put their money in safe savings accounts or bank certificates of deposit instead of the stock market, since banks became virtually risk-free (FDIC protected up to $100,000). These savers' money grew at a slower rate, but they never had to worry about losing it.

Unfortunately, the rate at which their money was growing was outpaced by the increase in the cost of living. The irony is that in trying to avoid risk, this group of conservative savers actually put their money in jeopardy. Because the banks did not provide a high interest rate, their money did not grow while the cost of living skyrocketed.

Young adults need to be prepared for a similar growth in the cost of living expenses. Look at the anticipated increase in prices of everyday objects thirty years from now:

	Today	In 30 Years
The cost of a new car	$17,000	$41,000
The cost of a vacation for two	$1,400	$3,400
The cost of blue jeans	$35	$85
The cost of a new condo	$120,000	$291,000
The cost of two movie tickets	$18	$45

Young adults today do not remember the Great Depression, but when it comes to investing, the same hesitation to play the stock market exists. Whether the reason is fear, lack of funds, or ignorance of the need to invest, only about 29 percent of Americans surveyed in 2004 were investing in an Individual Retirement Account (IRA). Additionally, only 42 percent of Americans who are eligible to invest in an employment based retirement plan, like a 401(K), are actually doing so. If the employer provides a "match" to your contribution, not investing is like throwing away free money.

If your first job includes benefits, one of the questions you will be asked by your employer is "How much do you want to contribute to your 401(k) or similar retirement fund?" If you have a choice in investment options, you also may be asked, "Which funds do you want to contribute to?" If you find these questions confusing, you may elect not to invest at all just because you don't know how to answer the questions.

Social Security used to provide adequately for a comfortable retirement, but according to the EBRI 2007 Retirement Confidence Survey, most retirees now receive their income from four main sources:

1. Their own savings and investments — 42 percent
2. Employment — 2 percent
3. Workplace retirement benefits — 27 percent
4. Social Security benefits — 40 percent

Since Social Security provides only a portion of replacement income and its future may be in question, it makes sense for Americans to start taking more control over their own retirement income.

Investing is not a hobby, nor is it gambling. It requires research in order to make informed decisions and the patience to not panic when the market faces a correction. Although investing requires effort, it is effort that can be well rewarded. Even if you consider yourself to have little knowledge about investing, you don't have to stay in the dark.

This chapter will cover the following investment issues:

- Fear of the market
- Need for a long-term perspective
- Emotional investing
- High-risk investments
- Recognizing con artists
- Gambling online
- Popular Internet stocks
- Selling a loser
- The value of an investment professional

Paralyzed by Indecision

For some investors, the pain and loss associated with negative stock market experiences actually drive them away from the market. Losing money can be a traumatic experience. Most people expect growth when they make investments, and when they are dealt a loss instead it becomes an experience no one wants to repeat. Even though there is no reason to believe subsequent investing experiences will prove as negative as the first, it is hard to maintain a rational attitude when the memory of that first loss becomes so painful.

Martha had her initial experience with the stock market

not by choice, but as part of her company's benefits package. Upon graduation from a community college at the age of twenty, she took a job with a telecommunications firm. In addition to her salary, she regularly received shares of the company stock. For years she watched the value of her stock increase. Even though Martha's salary was lower than her comparable position at other companies, she never complained because she counted her stock value as part of her salary.

When the company went through reorganization and the stock value fell, she was assured that the company would reemerge stronger than ever. Unfortunately, the reorganization her firm referred to was a Chapter 11 bankruptcy. Shortly after filing bankruptcy, the company had a massive layoff and Martha lost her job. Her stock was now virtually worthless.

Even though Martha is now reemployed at a strong, stable company, she is still paralyzed to enter the stock market. She refused a stock options package when she was hired. Other employees who were hired around the same time as Martha have seen their stock value increase by 200 percent. Martha knows she is missing out, but she cannot get over her fear of investing. Consequently, she has opted to leave her money in a low interest savings account.

She is not alone. As of 2004, Americans had $259 billion in checkable deposits, $4.3 trillion in savings deposits and $903 billion in bank money market accounts, according to the Federal Reserve. However, many checking accounts don't pay any interest at all. And for those accounts that pay interest, it is often at a low rate. Rates vary greatly depending on the financial institution but the current average interest rate on a passbook savings account is a mere 2-4 percent, and bank money market accounts pay on average only 4-5 percent.

This chart by Bank Rate Monitor shows what would happen to a deposit of $10,000 over ten years. Based on an average annual return per product:

Savings Product	Average Interest Rate	Growth of $10,000
Interest checking account	1.36%	$11,446
Bank money market	2.40%	$12,677
One-year certificate of deposit	4.36%	$15,323
Mutual fund money market	4.30%	$15,235
Top-paying money market	5.00%	$16.289
Ave. stock market mutual fund	11.1%	$28,651

Based on her negative experience, Martha's apprehension of investing is understandable and is best confronted by a very conservative approach. Since she is fearful of losing money, she should invest in very low-risk funds. Good choices for her would be government bonds, which have a guaranteed fixed interest rate. After her confidence is restored, she can include some riskier funds in her portfolio. The following is a sample of different investment options and their characteristics:

1. Bonds—certificates of debt; represents a loan to a corporation or agency; issued by corporations or government agencies that promise payment of interest on specific dates, with payment of the original investment amount at maturity.
2. Certificate of Deposit (CD)—savings certificates in a specific amount of money for a specific amount of time with a specific rate of interest; one main feature is convenience; you select a maturity date to fit your needs.
3. Collectibles—may be coins, stamps, artwork, baseball cards, or any of a number of other items that can be bought, held, and sold, depending on supply and demand.
4. Commodities—life's basics, such as wheat and metals that can be purchased in contract form to speculate on

future world demands, or to hedge against present investments.

5. Insured Savings Account—available through banks, credit unions, and other financial institutions; insured by a government agency (FDIC) up to $100,000 per account; considered safe and convenient; easy to open.
6. Mutual Funds—diversified investment alternative; for individual investors to pool dollars that are professionally managed, to meet various investment objectives.
7. Stocks—investment that represents a share of ownership in a company; value of the stock may increase or decrease, based on the success, or perceived success, of the corporation.
8. Treasury Issues—bills, notes, or bonds, in denominations of $1,000 to $1 million; mature from thirty days to more than five years after their issue by the Treasury Department.
9. U.S. Savings Bonds—available through many financial institutions and payroll deduction plans; provide an opportunity to invest in the U.S. government by buying a bond with a set maturity date at a price below face value.

The worst thing Martha can do is nothing. She is frozen by the unpredictability of the stock market. The fact remains that none of us have a crystal ball. We can't guess which funds will perform well and which will not. The only sure forecast is that not investing will guarantee that you miss out on huge potential gains.

Chasing the Hot Dot

Many people believe that making money in the stock market is all about "buying low and selling high" within a very short

period of time. Everyone has overheard a conversation where someone claimed they made a fortune by jumping on a tip they picked up at the golf course. However, people do not brag about how many times they lost a fortune by doing just that.

Acting like a trader instead of an investor is a mistake. What is the difference? A trader is someone who tries to make money on short-term buys and sales by taking advantage of fast changes in the market. An investor, on the other hand, views the short-term fluctuations in the market as irrelevant, and follows a high-quality buy and hold policy. Nick got into trouble by acting as a trader instead of following a strategy of long-term investments.

Nick had turned twenty-two in the fall of 1991. He realized he had accumulated several certificate of deposits (CD) at various banks. Whenever he received a birthday or Christmas gift of money, he would deposit it in a CD. Upon graduation from college, Nick received numerous cash gifts, which he also promptly added to his CDs. He was getting tired of seeing his CD rates drop when it seemed like the mutual funds he kept hearing so much about were performing much better. He had watched his six-month CD rates go from almost 10 percent in 1989 to barely 8 percent in 1990, and now the banks were dropping to less than 6 percent. It was time to do something.

In October, several of his CDs matured and Nick decided to invest his money elsewhere. He started by buying several of the most popular money magazines and checked the results of the best performing mutual fund poll for the previous year. The returns (increases in value) listed were impressive. Certainly these funds were winners; their managers must be geniuses. He proceeded to invest a quarter of his CDs (at least he was not going to make the mistake of putting all his eggs in one basket) in a biotech fund that had just begun operating the year before.

By the end of 1992, the biotech sector had lost about 20 percent for the year. This is not uncommon. Often, when one sector of the market goes through a period of very strong gains, it is followed by some period of sub-par performance. Nick decided to cut his losses on that fund, so he took all of the money from the biotech mutual fund and another quarter of his CDs out of the bank (since the six-month rate was now below 5 percent). Nick then divided this money between the best two funds for 1992, which happened to be high-yield bonds and a mutual fund that invested primarily in NASDAQ stocks.

The year of 1993 went pretty well, and Nick was feeling good about how savvy he had been with his investment decisions. Both funds earned about 15 percent that year. He had been hearing a lot about investing in Asia, so he decided to put another quarter of his CDs in an Asia fund. He decided not to change his earlier investments for another year.

At the end of 1994, Nick's NASDAQ fund lost 2 percent, his high-yield fund barely moved, and his new Asia fund, that grew 70 percent the year before, had done absolutely nothing since he bought it. He was tired of all the stress his financial investments had caused him. CD rates had been gradually climbing all year, so Nick finally just gave in and transferred all his money back to CDs, locking it in for two years so he could earn more than 6 percent interest.

Of course, the rest is history. The next four years brought an unprecedented string of yearly stock market gains in excess of 20 percent. Nick's NASDAQ fund alone gained over 40 percent the year after he was out. Even the biotech fund he had originally invested in was up over 60 percent in 1995, which would have made up for several years of poor performance.

Because we live in a society where success and accomplishments are in a short time frame, when something isn't going exactly the way we want it to, we feel the need to do something or fix it somehow. Just keep in mind that sometimes the best thing to do is nothing.

The temptation among many investors is to get in quick, then get out quick, taking profits or cutting losses at a moment's notice. But by focusing only on the short-term, many investors like Nick lose sight of the big picture. Performance over the long-term instead of short-term gains or losses should be the motivation behind investing. The stock market has outperformed all other savings vehicles over every ten-year time frame. In fact, the S&P 500 has increased an average of 12 percent a year over the last eighty years. The chart below shows the average rate of returns for various intestments over an eighty-year time period from 1926-2006:

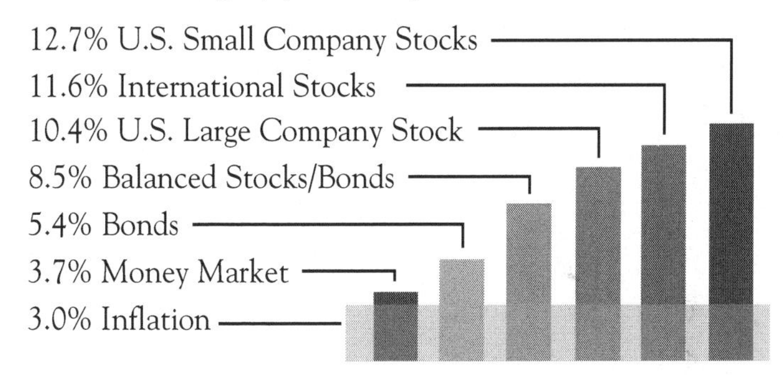

Nick's tendency to switch stocks every time they slid in performance ended up costing him dearly. If he had held on instead of saying, "Let me get out while I can," Nick would have profited when the value of the funds went through the roof.

Successful mutual fund and stock investing has one necessary ingredient that seems to be lacking in many people's psyche, patience. An oft-quoted saying that bears repeating is, "It is time in the market, not timing the market that will most likely produce the greatest profits in investing in the stock market."

Anyone that has started a business can tell you that the greatest chance of failure occurs within the first five years. Yet how many investors expect their investments to profit within that time frame? The average mutual fund investor only sticks with their decision for two to three years. As a result, they do not even come close to matching the returns that many mutual funds advertise as their average annual return.

Averages can be very misleading, especially in niche markets, aggressive growth funds, or international funds. Huge swings in a stock can average out over time to a value that does not even come close to approximating the stock's real value at any single moment.

The longer you own an investment, the closer you will get to the real average return on that investment. To reach realistic goals, you have to hang on to a good mutual fund for at least five years, preferably ten! This is not to say you shouldn't diversify and buy and hold a few different types of mutual funds. Just don't sell a mutual fund that had a good long term track record (when you bought it) because another fund is doing better, or because performance seems to be lacking.

If you've done your homework, and the fund has a ten-year performance record that you were happy with when you started your investment, then do yourself a favor and hang on to it for at least five years. Most likely, you will eventually look back at the one to three year mark when you considered dumping it as a time when you probably should have bought more stock.

When investing money, emotions tend to obscure the wisdom of buying low and selling high. When the market corrects itself by dropping, the tendency is to sell when in fact it should be the time to buy. Think of a correction as an opportunity to purchase stock in companies at a significantly lower price (a sale) instead of as a time to jump ship. Rarely does the ship sink; it's just encountering rough seas with lots of waves. Interestingly, the State Street Investor Confidence Index for August 2007 found that despite the recent sub-prime mortgage crisis, investors' enthusiasm has not been dampened. This may seem paradoxical but it should be remembered that for every seller, there is a buyer. Those viewing downturns as a buying opportunity can accumulate assets at relatively attractive price levels.

This example is a clear indication that many consumers are taking a long-term approach to investing and resisting doom and gloom prophesies that can lead to emotional decision making.

It's Only a Buck, How Low Can It Go?

Beware of any investments that promise incredible gains. No one can offer such assurance. Although it is tempting to want to believe someone's pledge of huge profits, in reality, if their promise were true, it would be common knowledge. Everyone would want to be getting a piece of the action.

Greed is a strong motivator and one that con artists rely upon. Before you make any decisions which involve spending money, make sure your rational mind, and not your emotional one, is making the decision. Remember that not everyone you come in contact with in business is an honest person. Be wary of any transaction that appears too good to be true. If you remain skeptical and ask lots of questions, you hopefully won't end up like Aaron.

Aaron was a freshman in college and at the age of nineteen was living on his own for the first time. Aaron was reading his mail one night after dinner, throwing away another credit card application from the midst of his junk mail, when the phone rang. He was expecting a friend to call to set up a basketball game on Saturday. The caller turned out not to be his friend, but a wolf in sheep's clothing.

Aaron was caught completely off-guard while the man on the phone excitedly rambled on for almost three minutes about an unbelievable opportunity for certain selected "lucky" individuals to get in on the ground floor of an offshore oil field venture that was about to "take off." Aaron couldn't get a word in edgewise. When Aaron discovered that the man was selling the stock for only $1.25, he calculated that it would only have to increase to $2.50 for Aaron to double his money. The caller practically assured Aaron the stock has "nowhere to go but up."

Aaron got so caught up in the moment and the caller's persuasive abilities that he pulled out the credit card application he had just thrown away. Since Aaron didn't have the cash the caller needed, he decided he would take out a $3,000 cash advance against this new credit card. After he made an easy thousand or two, he would then payoff the advance and close out the account.

This turned out to be a very bad idea. By the time he got his first performance statement, the oil field stock was worth only $2,400. Aaron angrily called the "broker" phone solicitor who had another great idea. He said the stock was now at an even better price. If Aaron liked it at $1.25 he should love it at $1.00! So Aaron sent in another $1,000 from a cash advance to his credit card and waited for the next monthly performance statement.

He couldn't believe his eyes! The value was only $2,800 from his total investment of $4,000! He had lost $1,200 on something that sounded like easy money. The horror was not over yet. Aaron called the penny stockbroker and told him to dump his shares. He couldn't afford to lose any more money and keep paying credit card interest on something that was not going up in value.

The cold-caller's upbeat tune suddenly changed and now for some reason there were no buyers who wanted his stock. In addition, he had more bad news that the drilling that had looked so promising had come up dry, new plans were moving slowly, and so on. "But the value on my statement says my account is worth $2,800, are you saying I can't get that if we sold today?" asked Aaron incredulously. The broker replied, "Actually, the value printed on the statement was eighty-two cents per share, but we would have a really hard time finding a buyer for 3,400 shares of this stock right now. It might take a week or so to sell it all off and by selling so much at once, it could really drive the price down!"

About two weeks later Aaron got a check for the total value of what was left, $2,380. This was not enough to pay off his credit card cash advances of $4,000 plus the added interest. Although it sounds like a nightmare, Aaron should have felt lucky he got any of his money back at all!

Being open to new opportunities is not unwise. However, the source of these new opportunities should be scrutinized thoroughly. Was the source an unknown person over the phone, a tip from a client about a start-up venture, or advice from a financial message board on the Internet? The motivation behind the referrals might be very self-serving. For example, the Internet message board might be attempting to influence a stock's price. Anonymous message posters can be placed as a way to run up a stock's price. In Aaron's case, he should have followed the golden rule: don't ever buy stock or other investments from someone you don't know and trust.

If you insist on taking a gamble, make sure you have a strong enough portfolio to allow you to take a high-risk investment every once in a while. It is never recommended to use any of your retirement money for a high-risk investment, and you should definitely limit the investment to no more than 10 percent of your discretionary funds. But don't ever borrow money on a credit card for something that seems like a get-rich-quick opportunity. The best advice for someone like Nick—if something sounds too good to be true, it probably is!

A con artist is difficult to detect by appearance or tone of voice alone. But you can often spot him or her by their words or expressions:

Cash Only	Why is cash necessary for a proposed transaction? Why not another form of payment like a check or credit card?
Secret Plans	Why are you being asked not to tell anyone?
Get Rich Quick	Any scheme should be carefully investigated.
Something for Nothing	A retired swindler once said that any time you are promised something for nothing, you usually get nothing.
Contest	Make sure they aren't a "come-on" to draw you into a money-losing scheme.
Haste	Be wary of any pressure that you must act immediately or lose out.
Today Only	If something is worthwhile today, it's likely to be available tomorrow.
Too Good to be True	Such a scheme is probably not good or true.
Last Chance	If it's a chance worth taking, why is it offered on such short notice?
Leftover Material	Leftover materials might also be stolen or defective.

Whenever you hear any of these expressions, you should act cautiously. A good con artist is usually a master of conversation. They can make you believe almost anything. Since it is easy to get sucked into their schemes, your best defense is to pay attention to clues. In addition, you should never act in haste. Speedy decisions are often regretted.

The Stock Market Is One Big Casino

The advent of on-line trading accompanied the increase in overall activities that became possible due to the Internet. In 1997 there were 4.1 million online trading accounts; in 2003, there were an estimated ten million. Since young adults have grown up in the technology age, it is no surprise that they comprise the highest percentage of on-line traders. Why do they do it? Twenty-six percent said for the "fun/challenge" of it.

Percentage of traders, by age, who traded online in 2005:
Age 18–40 (19%)
Age 41–61 (15%)
Age 61 and older (10%)
Source: Forrester Research

Many of the young adults that trade on-line have placed orders from schools, mostly universities.

The lure of making money with little effort other than a click of the mouse is tremendously appealing to many young adults. Combined with this thrill is the need for immediate gratification. Investing should be a long-term proposition, but many young adults are more concerned with making money now. Slow steady increases in their portfolio are not acceptable when they could have bigger returns instead. Unfortunately, the route to quick profits is usually through high-risk speculation.

Daniel had been an occasional gambler in college sports matches while he was at Ohio State University. Daniel had even won a few big purses. He gambled mostly for amusement. After graduation, Daniel married and began to concentrate on building a life with Penny. Away from his friends at school, he never bet on sports again.

However, during a period when he was at home recovering from a motorcycle accident, he discovered a new form of gambling—the stock market. A friend introduced him to day trading and told him he could make lots of money with little effort. Since Daniel's income had precipitously dropped after he began to receive disability payments, he thought he could use the extra money.

The advent of online trading in the information age allowed Daniel to buy and sell stocks on his own without ever leaving home. He didn't worry that he did not have a professional financial advisor to guide him. Besides, his day trading firm's premise was that "educated investors don't need brokers." Daniel enjoyed the challenge. He was also drawn to the familiar excitement and anticipation that his gambling days had first allowed him to experience.

As soon as the New York Stock Exchange opened, he placed his first bet, hoping that the shares of stock would go up in value by the end of the day. Daniel's profits in day trading depended solely on the small movements in stock prices before he cashed out at the end of the day. If the stock went up, he made money. If it went down, he lost.

His first attempt earned him several thousand dollars and Daniel excitedly started daydreaming about not going back to his regular day job even after he recovered. Subsequent trades were just as profitable and Daniel quit his job. At first, his wife Penny was happy to have him at home since he had always worked long hours and she rarely saw him. In time, his trading became addictive, and Penny again rarely saw him. Once trading consumed him, he ignored Penny. Daniel would lock himself in his office and spend his time trading or thinking about trading. On the rare occasions that Daniel would leave his office, he would be glued to the financial shows on television.

Emboldened by his winnings, Daniel started placing larger trades more frequently. Typically he would exceed hundreds of online trades a day, getting in and out of various stocks and usually ending the day by selling all of the shares. Unfortunately, his streak did not last.

Daniel started moving through the traditional phases in the addiction process. The first stage was a winning phase, where he was winning more often than losing. Excitement predominated and any worries that he had disappeared. Then Daniel moved into the losing phase. He started losing more often than he won. He would leverage his stock purchase by borrowing money to buy and sell stocks. Finally, he moved into the desperation phase. Playing the market became an obsession. His life centered on getting even and paying off debts. His wife no longer wanted to be with him since he was so unpleasant. In desperation, Penny even got rid of his computer so he couldn't make any more trades online. That didn't work. Daniel just started to make trades over the phone.

When time came to pay taxes, he found he needed to account for each separate transaction. Since he traded daily, this involved an enormous amount of paperwork. He had to hire an accountant to help him sort out the mess. He ended up paying his accountant all of the profits he had earned from his first year of day trading!

Penny was fed up with his destructive behavior and decided to leave him. Only when she left did Daniel finally wake up to the consequences of his behavior. Daniel had allowed himself to become mesmerized by his ability to trade stocks in real time on the Internet. With the constant access to the market that online trading affords, Daniel found it addictive. His day trading addiction became no different than that of an alcoholic in the stress it placed on his family.

Daniel took the first step to recovery by going to a Gamblers Anonymous meeting. He has been attending for several years now and has returned to his day job as a construction supervisor. Any investment decisions are now made through his company's retirement fund manager.

Not everyone will become addicted if they engage in online trading. But short of addiction, many can find themselves trading so often that they wish they could stop or at least slow down. Watching your stock portfolio every day is unnecessary and can result in making bad moves. If a falling stock price scares you, you might be tempted to sell with a few keystrokes on your computer. Without the benefit of having a broker, there is no one to talk you out of making a bad move. Turning the computer off or vowing not to check your account every day is another way to cut down on excessive trading.

With more and more people taking charge of their own finances, more mistakes than ever are being made. Charles Schwab, the largest online broker, estimates that 50 percent of their new customers are considered to be unseasoned and inexperienced. Whether it's a lack of doing sufficient research (e.g., the company's track record, the tax consequences) or being confused by conflicting analyses, many investors just hope and pray they have made the right choice. For most, the reality is not what they hoped and prayed for. In fact, it is estimated that only one out of ten day traders make more money than they lose. At the bare minimum, newer investors should become knowledgeable by familiarizing themselves with common stock market terms:

- AMEX—the American Stock Exchange, which is one of the organized stock markets in New York City.
- Annual Report—the annual statement published by a corporation after the close of the fiscal year. The annual report includes the balance sheet and profit and loss statements of the proceeding and current years.
- Asked (or Offer) Price—the price that sellers are willing to accept for a particular stock at a given time.
- At the Market—an order to buy and sell a stock at the best price currently available.
- Auction Market—the type of market found in organized stock exchanges. As in an auction, stocks are sold to the person willing to pay the highest price and purchased from the person willing to sell for the lowest price.

- Bear Market—a stock market with falling prices over an extended period of time.
- Benefits of Trade—the advantages obtained by buyers and sellers when they trade a stock.
- Bid Price—the price that buyers are willing to pay for a particular stock at a given time.
- Blue Chip—a reference to a certain type of company or its stock. A blue chip company is nationally known, highly esteemed, and noted for the quality and wide acceptance of its products and services as well as for its consistent record of making profits and paying dividends. The term comes from poker, where the blue chip is the most valuable.
- Broker—an individual or business that specializes in bringing together buyers and sellers of stocks.
- Bull Market—a stock market with rising prices over an extended period of time.
- Close Price—the final, or last traded, price of a stock at the end of the trading day.
- Commission—the fee a broker and/or stockbroker collects for helping people buy and sell a stock.
- Contrarianism—the theory that small investors are usually wrong and that it is advantageous to pursue strategies opposite to the popular investing trend.
- Diversification—the spreading of investments across a number of assets in order to eliminate some, but not all, of the risk.
- Dow Jones Industrial—the average of thirty well-known "blue chip" stocks. This average is the best-known stock index.
- Floor Broker—a member of a brokerage house who completes a customer's buy or sell order on the floor of a stock exchange.

- Growth Stock—a stock whose return to investors comes from increases in share price. Growth stock might pay few or no dividends because much of its earnings are used to keep the company growing.
- Hedge fund—a private fund charging a performance fee and typically open only to a very limited range of qualified investors.
- Income Stock—a stock that has a consistent record of paying high dividends.
- Investment Banker—a business that gives a corporation advice on how to raise money and also sells new issues of stocks and bonds.
- Limit Order—an order to buy or sell a stock at a certain (or better) price. A buyer's limit order for $20 would be completed only if each share can be bought for $20 or less.
- Listed Stock—stocks that have been approved and listed for trading by one of the organized stock exchanges. These stocks must meet specific financial and other requirements to qualify. Unlisted stocks are those that trade over the counter (OTC) and do not need to meet certain standards.
- Market-Maker—a stock trader who agrees to buy and sell in a company's stock. The trader uses his firm's money to purchase stock so he has shares available for people to buy. A market-maker also must agree to purchase stock back when investors want to sell. Market-makers buy and sell NASDAQ and OTC stocks. Smaller companies usually have only a few market-makers while large companies have dozens.
- NASDAQ—the NASDAQ Stock Market is an electronic marketplace where buyers and sellers get together via computer. More than 5,000 companies are listed on NASDAQ's computerized market. NASDAQ is not an

exchange because it doesn't have a central floor.

- Net Change—a change in value over time.
- New-Issues Market—a market in which a corporation sells new stock to raise money for a start-up or expansion. This market is often called the primary stock market.
- NYSE—the New York Stock Exchange, which is one of the organized stock markets in New York City.
- Over the Counter (OTC)—a way of trading stock other than trading on an exchange. Over the counter quotations are supplied by the National Association of Securities Dealers Automated Quotations (NASDAQ) system. OTC stocks are usually small, and not frequently traded.
- Pink Sheet Market—another name for the OTC market. The "pink sheets" are lists of OTC stocks and the prices at which dealers are offering to buy and sell them. These lists are printed on pink paper and distributed early every morning to the trading community.
- Primary Markets—those markets in which stocks are offered for sale the first time.
- Private equity—a broad term that commonly refers to any type of non-public ownership equity securities that are not listed on a public exchange.
- Quotes—the highest price bid by a buyer and the lowest price asked by a seller for a stock at a given time. Quotes are usually expressed in dollars and fractions of a dollar. For example, a share of Apple Computer was quoted at 27¾, which meant $27.75.
- Round Lot—one hundred shares of a stock. Stocks are generally traded this way.
- Secondary Markets—those markets in which stocks can be bought and sold once they are approved for public sale.
- Specialist—a broker on an exchange who trades in certain stocks at a specific location on the trading floor.

Each specialist has an assigned location where all trading of particular stocks occur. Specialists quote the current prices of stocks traded at their posts and they complete limit orders.

- Stockbroker—a broker who accepts orders to buy and sell stock and then transfer those orders to other people who complete them.
- Stock Exchange—one of the organized stock markets with a centralized trading floor. In this market, auction-type trading allows traders to sell stocks to the highest bidder or buy stocks from the lowest supplier. These markets consist of the New York Stock Exchange and the American Stock Exchange, both of which are located in New York City. Also included are the regional stock exchanges found outside of New York City. These are the Boston, Cincinnati, Intermountain (Salt Lake City), Midwest (Chicago), Pacific (Los Angeles and San Francisco), Philadelphia (Philadelphia and Miami), and Spokane stock exchanges.
- Stock Market—a market in which the public trades stocks that someone already owns. This market allows people to buy and sell stocks quickly and easily. Examples are the New York Stock Exchange and the American Stock Exchange (this market is often called the secondary stock market).

In addition to knowing the vocabulary of the stock market, you also need to learn how to read common stock quotes. Abbreviations are commonly used and your familiarity with their meaning will help you to understand your funds' performances. These quotes will assist you in tracking the movement of your funds. Are they increasing in value or moving in the other direction?

Reading Common Stock Quotes

High-52 week	Low-52 week	Stock	Div.	Yld. %	P-E Ratio	Sales in 100s	High	Low	Close	Net Change
24⅜	16	AAR	.56	2.3	16	274	24¾	24⅛	24⅜	+⅜
19⅛	10⅛	AGS			14	175	18½	17¼	17¼	-1⅛
14	9⅞	AMCA				1	9½	11½	11½	
50	32½	AMR			7	8,618	42¼	41	41	1-⅜
24½	18⅝	AMR pf	2.18	8.9		6	24⅜	24	24⅜	
25⅞	23	ANR pf	2.67	11.2		1	23¾	23¾	23¾	
11⅞	7⅝	APL			5	27	10⅝	10½	10½	-⅛
15⅜	9	ARX			14	66	15¼	15	15	-⅛
55¾	32¾	ASA	2.00	5.7		436	35½	34⅝	35¼	-¼

High & Low 52 week	Highest and lowest price paid for one share during the past year.
Stock	Abbreviated name of the corporation.
Div.	The annual dividend paid per share of stock; "pf" denotes a preferred stock.
Yld. %	Yield percentage, which is found by dividing the dollar amount of the dividend by the closing price of the stock. The result is multiplied by one hundred to produce the actual yield percentage. Dividend yield is a measure of the flow of income produced by an investment in a particular stock.
P-E Ratio	Price to earnings ratio, the ratio of the latest closing price of the stock to the latest available annual earnings per share of the firm. Earnings per share can be calculated by dividing the closing price on the day being reported by the P-E ratio.

Continued

Sales in 100s	Number of shares traded during the day, expressed in hundreds of shares. The entry must be multiplied by one hundred to arrive at the actual volume of transactions.
High	The highest selling price of one share of stock for the day being reported.
Low	The lowest selling price of one share of stock for the day being reported.
Close	The price of the last share of stock sold on the day being reported.
Net Chg.	Difference between the closing price of the stock on the day being reported and the closing price on the previous trading day. A plus sign indicates the closing price for the day being reported is higher than for the previous day. A minus sign indicates the closing price is less than the price for the previous day.

Armed with knowledge about investing principles, online investors can make more informed decisions. Having control over your own accounts is a serious responsibility. You owe it to yourself to become as educated as possible and make investment decisions that you will not come to regret later.

The Internet Millionaires

The skyrocketing rise in the value of certain Internet and tech stocks has almost become folklore. Stories abound of people who invested on the ground floor or as employees of a fledgling Internet company and are now millionaires. The value of Internet stocks seems to be like a rocket launched into space. While they can soar very quickly, every now and then the rocket comes crashing down to earth.

Roger had been fascinated with the stock market ever since he played the Stock Market Game in his high school economics

class. He eagerly started investing on his own as soon as he could legally do so at the age of eighteen. Now twenty years old, Roger had grown his savings from part-time jobs into nearly $10,000 by making smart investment decisions. Roger had read countless stories of how people had literally become rich overnight after investing in Internet stocks. He was skeptical until one of his friends actually did so himself. This news turned Roger into a believer and he became obsessed with finding the right Internet stock and the precise moment to invest.

One weekend he heard a tip on the radio about a forthcoming Internet stock offering for a hot new company. The stock would open at $30 a share so he left directions with his broker to buy three hundred shares as soon as the market opened Monday. Roger's broker followed his directions exactly. There was only one problem; the stock jumped up to $90 a share by the time he filled the order.

Roger had planned on investing $9,000, not $27,000. He was still in shock over how he was going to find the money to cover his purchase when he received the additional bad news that the stock closed the day at $40 a share. In one day, Roger had lost $15,000. This amount might have been small potatoes for a wealthy investor, but Roger was not wealthy. By analyzing the day's events, his actions would ensure that he never would be one!

Often, investors rely too heavily on timing. Roger had not done much investing, and saw this opportunity as a chance to score big. If he got in on the ground floor, he would just ride the wave up and make a lot of money. Unfortunately, Roger's wave came crashing down. Just getting in at the beginning of a stock doesn't assure an investor that the stock will rise. Similarly, jumping into the stock market during a sell-off in the market doesn't mean that the market will bounce back with a vengeance. It might even drop lower! Roger learned the hard way that individual stocks can be volatile. He would have been safer investing in mutual funds and diversifying his investments.

To avoid making investing mistakes like Roger did, the following guidelines of "don'ts" for investors should be committed to memory:

- Don't make any investments that you do not adequately understand or that make you uncomfortable.
- Don't expect too much too soon—be patient.
- Don't be married to a stock because you are reluctant to take losses. Learn to accept mistakes and reallocate the remaining funds.
- Don't be too greedy for capital gains. Just because a stock has gone up does not mean that it will do so indefinitely.
- Don't overreach for income. Relatively high dividend yields may indicate considerable risk.
- Don't trade in and out of individual stocks too often. Brokerage fees, taxes, and other expenses can reduce or eliminate profits.
- Don't let worries about short-term market fluctuations erode your long-term plan and confidence.

In attempting to get the highest return on your investments, what factors ensure the best performance: selection, timing, or allocation? Is it more important what you select, when you select, or how the selection is divvied up? Since we can't control the markets or time, the surest bet to solid performance is allocation. But what is the correct formula to follow for allocating investments? The answer is that it depends on your age and the degree of risk you are willing to take. As a general rule, the younger you are, the more aggressive plan you can consider (see page 181).

Like an aspiring actor, an aspiring investor must work hard and pay dues. The most important thing to remember regarding performance is that you can't hope to receive a standing ovation if your stage fright prevents you from performing in the first place. If you're not investing, start now. Since we can't control timing, there is never a bad time to start investing and there is no excuse for not starting. Once the performance starts, you can't quit. If you keep the performance basic, you'll never forget your lines. Finally, don't let one bad review cause you to drop out altogether! This advice combined with the guidance of a professional can be the best determinants to success in Wall Street.

Abandoning the Sinking Ship

Although it is wise investment strategy to have a long-term perspective, there are times when losses should be taken in order to avoid even greater losses. If it is obvious that certain investments are not going to recover or are on a steady decline, you will need to take action. Even with the best research and advice prior to making an investment decision, there will be instances when performance will prove unacceptable. Realizing you have made a mistake can be a very wise money move.

Timothy was successful in everything he ever tried. He was president of his high school class, won a football scholarship to college, graduated with a law degree, and now, at the age of twenty-four, worked for a successful law firm. He began to believe everything he touched would turn to gold. With overwhelming confidence, Timothy entered the stock market.

He understood the philosophy of keeping an investment for the long term, but after two solid years of consistent losses on one of the stocks in his portfolio, his broker advised him to sell. Timothy resisted and assured himself that the stock was just undervalued and the price of his stocks would increase. In fact, he actually bought more shares of stock and convinced himself that he had made a wise decision. One year later, the stock was worth 20 percent less. Timothy's broker again advised Timothy to sell, but Timothy wouldn't admit that he might have made a mistake and picked a lousy stock. He ended up holding onto the stock until it was basically worthless. He never did sell his stock. It is now worth two cents a share.

People have a tremendous aversion to taking losses. In Timothy's case, he felt that his ego was on the line. He wouldn't ever sell until he broke even with the original price of the stock. Only then would he feel comfortable selling, knowing that he had not suffered a loss. We hate losing money even more than we like getting it. We tend to hold on to a lousy stock not because we think the value will go up but because we can't deal with the fact that the stock was a bad choice.

By waiting for the stock to rebound, we end up losing valuable time. Every year that we are not investing wisely is a year when we are not adding to our retirement fund. It is crucial to fund our retirement accounts to their maximum. With inadequate funding, we risk running out of money before we die. Considering the fact that Americans are living longer with an average life span into the eighties, it is highly probable that our funds will be depleted too soon. The following chart illustrates the years it will take to run out of money if you withdraw it at a certain percentage rate. Notice how higher expected rates of return (interest earned on your account) will add more years to your funds' lifespan. Your funds' longevity also will be affected by how much you withdraw. The higher the withdrawal percentage, the faster you will go through your money:

Years until All Funds Are Depleted

Expected Rate of Return											
With-drawal Rate	5% APR	6% APR	7% APR	8% APR	9% APR	10% APR	11% APR	12% APR	13% APR	14% APR	15% APR
6%	37	*	*	*	*	*	*	*	*	*	*
7%	25	33	*	*	*	*	*	*	*	*	*
8%	20	23	30	*	*	*	*	*	*	*	*
9%	16	18	22	29	*	*	*	*	*	*	*
10%	14	15	17	20	27	*	*	*	*	*	*
11%	12	14	15	17	20	25	*	*	*	*	*
12%	11	12	13	14	16	19	24	*	*	*	*
13%	10	11	11	12	14	15	18	23	*	*	*
14%	9	10	10	11	12	13	15	17	22	*	*
15%	8	9	9	10	11	11	13	14	16	21	*
16%	8	8	8	9	10	10	11	12	14	16	20
17%	7	8	8	8	9	9	10	11	12	13	15
18%	7	7	7	8	8	8	9	10	10	11	13
19%	6	7	7	7	8	8	8	9	9	10	11
20%	6	6	6	7	7	7	8	8	9	9	10

* Funds will never be depleted at this combination of return and withdrawal.

Timothy could have cut his losses by realizing that the performance of this particular stock was probably not going to recover. There is a difference between selling too quickly when the stock takes a slight dip and holding on to a stock which is in a nose-dive. Since it is often difficult to tell the difference, the advice of a trusted, experienced financial advisor's assessment (like Aaron's) should be followed.

What is the value of good advice versus the cost of investment mistakes? Many people want to be the CEO of their own investment company, but they don't have the time, don't have the expertise, or are too emotional to manage their own money. Would you represent yourself in court? Fix your own plumbing? Give yourself medical advice? For specialized advice, we normally go to a specialist.

If there are so many advantages to working with a specialist, why then do so many people choose to invest their own money without seeking advice? A common answer is to save on commission charges. Remember though, the purpose of investing is to make money. Ask yourself the question, "Does the commission fee offset the performance of an identified high-quality fund and the lessening of mistakes when made by a professional?" Or another question, "What is it worth to you to achieve your goals?" Depending on your answer to these questions, it may make sense to have a professional investing your money. This is especially true if you tend to react emotionally in regards to your money.

Words of Wisdom

Investing is probably the most complicated and confusing of all the money management skills discussed in this book. However, the skill of investing wisely is arguably one of the most important. Without investing at all or investing naively, you will be certain to have financial goals that are never reached and a retirement that is not funded adequately. With such high stakes, you should seriously consider adopting the lessons in this chapter:

- Get over your fear of investing.
- Realize that every experience does not have to be a negative one.
- Understand your various investment options.
- Do not chase the latest "hot" stock.
- Do not panic and sell when the market goes through fluctuations.

- Maintain a buy and hold strategy.
- Diversify.
- Research before making investment decisions.
- Beware of con artists and "sure things."
- Avoid online gambling.
- Acquaint yourself with stock market terms and stock quote tables.
- Act cautiously when considering risky hedge funds or start-up company stocks.
- Do not react to tips without doing research.
- If you have made a mistake, admit it.
- Consult a financial professional.

These lessons will help you to avoid making unwise investment moves. It may even protect you from experiencing the trauma of a bankruptcy.

14

Bankruptcy—Is There an Easy Way Out?

There is no such thing as a free lunch.
In the end, you pay for everything.

Personal (non-business) bankruptcies, which had been increasing steadily throughout the 1980s and '90s, peaked in 2005 at slightly over 2 million filers. This number was an all time high. Although the numbers of filers went down dramatically in 2006 to a little under 600,000, most experts think this is because most people who had been contemplating bankruptcy quickly ran to file in 2005 before the new, more restrictive bankruptcy law came into effect.

The recently enacted Bankruptcy Reform Law was intended to cut down on consumers who engaged in overspending behavior and then promptly filed bankruptcy to get their debt forgiven. The new law includes provisions that consumers be fully informed about the bankruptcy process, alternatives to bankruptcy and the potential consequences of filing a bankruptcy. The new law also requires debtors, prior to receiving a bankruptcy discharge, to complete a financial management instructional course. The hope is that this type of education will cut down on future financial problems and avoid repeat bankruptcies.

The bankruptcy rate among twenty-five to thirty-four-year-olds increased between 1991 and 2001 with that age group having the second highest rate of bankruptcy (just after those aged thirty-five to forty-four). And with personal savings at inadequate or nonexistent levels, there is no safety net for these young people. Without sufficient savings, more and more young people look to credit as a source of money when the going gets tough. This adds to their existing debts, and in many cases push them over the edge—landing in bankruptcy court.

This chapter will summarize the actions that several young adults took which led them to file for bankruptcy. Their mistakes included:

- Using credit as an additional source of income
- Not turning to others for help
- Not exploring other options
- Failing to budget an irregular income
- Trying to escape obligations
- Not realizing the power of a credit report

Deadbeat Dad

Credit never should be used as an additional source of income. Never forget that credit is not your money. When you come to rely on credit to pay your bills, you are following a pattern that adds to your debt level. The day will come when the debt level will surpass your ability to pay. When this happens, you might find yourself so deeply in debt that you feel bankruptcy is the only recourse.

Martha never believed that her divorce would end up taking such a huge financial toll on her life. She married Rob during her senior year in college. They planned to wait until they graduated, but they needed to share expenses for financial reasons. Since their parents would never allow them to live together if they were not husband and wife, they tied the knot.

Now two years out of college, their financial situation had gotten worse along with their marriage. They had student loans to repay, in addition to their ever-present credit card debt and car payments. Martha and Rob were barely able to pay all their bills when they decided to divorce. Martha worried that the divorce would result in a drastic reduction in her income since she made much less money than Rob did. Martha first worked as an aide for a first grade class. But when the judge calculated the alimony payments she would be entitled to receive, she relaxed. These payments supplementing the income from her job would be sufficient to cover her expenses. Unfortunately, Martha's peace of mind only lasted one month.

The first alimony check did not arrive on the scheduled day. In a panic, she called her ex-husband who assured her that it was coming, he had just forgotten to put it in the mail. She called him again when days passed without the payment arriving, but this time the phone had been disconnected. Since Rob worked out of his home, she went over there to confront him in person about the payment.

To her shock, when she arrived, his apartment had been vacated. The landlord told Martha that Rob said he would call her with his forwarding address after he had relocated. She promised she would call Martha as soon as he contacted her. Martha never heard from the landlord again.

With no address for Rob, the district attorney's office could not find him to force payment. Without a known job, his wages couldn't be garnished. The district attorney's office said they were understaffed and therefore could not supply the resources to locate Rob. It was up to Martha, who, of course, had no skills as a private investigator and didn't have the money to hire one.

With unpaid bills continuing to pile up and no alimony in sight, Martha decided to take a part-time job at home during the evening to supplement the income from her full-time job.

This extra money helped, but it wasn't enough to pay for anything other than the necessities in her budget. When her car needed repairs or she had to go to the doctor, Martha paid for these expenses with her credit cards. When her credit cards reached the limit, she just got more cards.

Since she paid only the minimum payment when the credit card bills arrived, she was able to accumulate a lot of debt without having problems meeting her monthly obligations. In time, however, she had twenty credit cards in her possession with a total outstanding balance of $35,000. Her monthly payments for her credit cards were now $1,400. At first she was able to make these payments by obtaining more credit cards and paying her credit cards' bills with cash advances, but soon her outstanding debt load prevented her from qualifying for more credit cards.

Confronted with an ex-husband who had not yet resurfaced, exhaustion from working all day and night, and an inability to borrow any more money, Martha felt she had no choice but to file bankruptcy. It seemed the only way to end her problems. She saw an ad in the newspaper for an attorney that only charged $500. It seemed a small price to pay to relieve her of all her debts.

Many people have other options available besides bankruptcy, and should explore these options thoroughly. But others find they have no choice but to file a bankruptcy. A bankruptcy should be an action of last resort. Remember, ten years is a long time for a negative to remain on a credit report. Approximately 80 percent of people who file a bankruptcy choose Chapter 7, which essentially writes off all your unsecured debts (credit cards and revolving credit lines) with certain exceptions. Chapter 7 does not eliminate debts due to taxes, child support, alimony, student loans, court fines or judgments for fraud, personal injury, property damage, or other claims and penalties.

Less common is a Chapter 13 bankruptcy. This involves repayment of your debts according to your ability to pay. You may end up paying ten cents per every dollar you owe. In recent years the preference has been to get more consumers to file a Chapter 13 so that money is returned to the creditors instead of having to be written off as bad debt.

It was only after arriving in court that Martha discovered that not all her debts would be forgiven through filing a Chapter 7. Martha's student loans and money she owed to the IRS for taxes would not disappear by filing bankruptcy. She was comforted that she could at least get rid of her credit card payments. Anyway, she didn't want her credit cards anymore; they had just gotten her into trouble.

What Martha hadn't realized was that she had become dependent on her credit cards as an extra source of income. Before long, she felt she needed "just one." Fortunately, her bankruptcy made qualifying for a credit card difficult and costly. Those credit cards that she could receive usually charged her a higher interest rate because of her negative credit history.

Dissuaded from using credit again as an additional source of income and tired of struggling financially on her own, Martha decided to quit her job and go on welfare. Once she started to receive assistance from the government, they now had an incentive to look for her ex-husband. Amazingly, they tracked him down after three months and began to garnish his wages.

Martha wisely did not turn to bankruptcy right away when things got tough. But when expenses came up that she couldn't afford, Martha should not have turned to credit cards before considering other options like family, government, or charity assistance. Martha said that she had too much pride to turn to others for help. But in the end, she did exactly that by accepting welfare.

Martha could have probably qualified for food stamps, donated clothing, transportation subsidies, and other assistance programs based on her low income. In addition, there are numerous nonprofit organizations that assist in locating absent spouses. Once he or she is located, this information can then be given to the district attorney's office to collect alimony or back child support. Through the garnishment of wages, levying of bank account funds, or seizing of income tax refunds, the delinquency can be made current.

The trauma of going through a divorce is stressful enough without the additional emotional upheaval of a bankruptcy. If there would have been any alternative to filing bankruptcy, Martha should have considered any and all of the options available to her. Starting over after a divorce is a new beginning, but a bankruptcy is not. The illusion is that you are free of debt, but the reality is that its repercussions are felt for a long time after.

A Lucky Break in Hollywood

It is difficult to budget on an irregular income. When money comes sporadically, it is hard to know how much you can spend monthly. When the money is "not" there, you watch every penny you spend and live frugally. The problem usually results when the money "is" there. Then your tendency is to spend, spend, and spend. Your excitement of finally receiving money blunts your survival instinct.

Quinton wanted to be a screenwriter in Hollywood. He was only twenty-one, but had been working for three years since high school to make this dream a reality. First, he worked on finishing a script and then on finding a filmmaker who would buy it. While he was waiting for his lucky break, he worked as a waiter alongside others like himself. He worked with aspiring singers, comedians, and actors. They all shared the same frugal lifestyle, waiting for the day when their hardship would pay off. For Quinton, it took three years.

Quinton sold his first screenplay for what seemed like a fortune to him. He promptly moved from his cheap studio apartment into an upscale place in a high-rent neighborhood. He traded in his old car for a brand new luxury model. He dined in expensive restaurants every night and treated his friends. And of course, he quit his job waiting tables.

This new rich lifestyle that Quinton adopted soon became addictive. Quinton loved being able to spend money without first analyzing his budget to see if he could afford it. The money he received from his screenplay was equal to what most of his friends took years at a steady job to earn. Because Quinton had stopped living on a budget, he managed to spend it all in just a year. It is amazing how fast money goes when you spend it with abandon.

After the money was gone, Quinton was in denial about the fact that he was broke. He enjoyed his lavish lifestyle and was not about to give it up. He rationalized to himself that he deserved it after having to live on such a meager income for so long. Unfortunately, continuous spending without an income to offset it always comes to an end. When Quinton's credit ran out, he was $90,000 in debt.

He completed work on his new screenplay, but soon discovered that he couldn't sell it because no one liked it. With no foreseeable income stream, Quinton had no means to pay his outstanding credit card debts. He decided the only way out was to file for bankruptcy.

All too often, people panic and do not realize there are other alternatives. The reduction of your debt payments is sometimes the answer. You can try negotiating on your own with the creditors to work out a more manageable payment plan. Start by sending them a proposal package. This package consists of everything you can provide to the creditors to enlist their support and cooperation during the delinquency period. Normally, you will want to send them three things:

1. A hardship letter (see Chapter 1)
2. A copy of your budget (see Chapter 2)
3. Any other supporting documentation they may need

If you don't have any luck on your own, consider seeing a specialist. It's usually worth the visit to meet with a nonprofit credit counseling agency (see Appendix) who can give you an unbiased opinion as to whether you can avoid bankruptcy. Usually this visit is free of charge or costs a nominal fee.

If after analyzing and making adjustments to your budget the credit counselor feels you have the capacity to pay off your debts, they will negotiate with your creditors for you. They may succeed in getting your payments down to a level you can handle. This reduction is possible because many creditors cooperate by reducing or eliminating finance charges. Ultimately, it is in the creditors' best interest to work with you because they get nothing if you file for bankruptcy.

One prerequisite to starting a repayment plan with a credit counseling agency is that they will require you to close your current credit accounts. Some offices cut up your credit cards on the spot. This experience can prove quite traumatic, but necessary, if you are used to relying on your credit cards as money. If you are serious about getting out of debt, you can't keep adding to your debt.

In Quinton's case, he did not visit a credit counselor before filing bankruptcy. He filed before the new Bankruptcy Reform Law went into effect that would have required a conversation with an approved credit counseling agency. After swallowing his pride, Quinton returned to being a waiter. He lost his new car, moved back into his old neighborhood, and started eating again at the free Happy Hour buffets. Quinton is currently working on another screenplay, a sequel to his first. Hopefully, he'll have better luck selling his next movie.

Learning how to budget on an income which does not come regularly can prove difficult. Quinton worked in an industry in which money is earned sporadically. When Quinton received the windfall from his screenplay, he should have tried to keep his lifestyle at the same level instead of adjusting upward to a more lavish lifestyle. The mistake he made was to treat his screenplay profits as a reliable continual income. Quinton should have spent this money carefully, since he had no idea when another windfall would take its place.

It's easy to think that a large sum of money in the bank will last forever but without deposits to counteract the withdrawals, even large sums of money will disappear quickly. The more lavish the lifestyle, the quicker the money disappears. If Quinton had chosen to invest his windfall instead of spending it, bankruptcy would never have occurred.

Living Underground

Bankruptcy can be used as a way to avoid obligations. There are no more phone calls from creditors. Ending the relentless legal notices is reason enough for many to choose bankruptcy. Unfortunately, a bankruptcy is not the panacea that cures all. There are some obligations that you cannot run away from no matter how hard you try.

Franklin knew they were after him. The "they" was the district attorney's office for nonpayment of child support. Franklin had not planned on becoming a father at eighteen. Just before he found out his girlfriend was pregnant, he had decided to break off their relationship. However, upon learning of the pregnancy, he worked to maintain an agreeable relationship, although it was purely a financial one since they lived separate lives.

At first, Franklin was able to pay child support while he worked full-time. He only stopped paying after he began to attend school in order to become a chiropractor. Franklin felt some guilt over not paying, but he convinced himself that it was unfair to expect a poor student to be responsible for child support. He was finishing up his chiropractic training and could barely survive on student loans.

After he graduated, he discovered that he was prohibited from getting a chiropractor's license because of his outstanding child support payments. Again, Franklin complained. How was he supposed to make a living without a professional license? His only choice was to become a masseuse.

Unfortunately, he earned much less as a masseuse than he would have made as a chiropractor. In addition, Franklin had high monthly payments for his student loans. Franklin did not feel responsible for paying his student loans back because he never became a chiropractor. Since his education had not led to a job, his loans had been for nothing. Therefore, why should he pay them?

He decided to file for bankruptcy. He chose to save money through a "do-it-yourself" bankruptcy. Franklin went down to the court and picked up the bankruptcy forms that he filled in himself without legal counsel. He found it a liberating experience. No longer would he have the burden of these massive loans. This peace of mind lasted only until he discovered that student loans were not dischargeable in a bankruptcy. In fact, neither were his child support obligations.

Nonpayment of these non-dischargeable debts can lead to extreme measures of collection, including garnishing of wages, levying (seizing) funds in a bank account, seizing income tax refunds, and the inability to obtain or maintain certain professional licenses (in some states this includes drivers' licenses).

These measures may appear severe, but 2003 data from the

U.S. Census Bureau has shown that for the 1.7 million custodial parents who do not receive child support, their annual income was only $23,400. This puts them only slightly above the 2004 poverty level of $18,850 for a family of four.

Franklin couldn't believe that his two largest debt obligations would always follow him. His bankruptcy only served to eliminate several of his smaller credit card debts. Now he had a bankruptcy, which would appear on his credit report for ten years, and no relief from his child support and student loan obligations. Following his pattern of always evading his responsibilities, Franklin decided to leave the country. His self-imposed exile left his money troubles behind him, but so too did he leave his child, friends, and country.

The only way for this story to have a happy ending (unless exile in a foreign land is considered a happy ending), would be for Franklin to take responsibility for his actions. Without admitting and accepting responsibility, Franklin would continue to run away from his obligations until he got caught. His pattern of owing money through student loans, child support, and credit card bills had become a habit. So too had his pattern of not paying his debts.

Franklin had convinced himself that he wasn't obligated to pay off these debts so he tried to ignore them. When he couldn't ignore them anymore, he tried to use the same legal system to his advantage by filing bankruptcy. Unfortunately, this remedy did not eliminate all his debts, as he had believed it would.

Additionally, for those who view bankruptcy as a tool they can utilize repeatedly whenever the going gets tough, a provision in the Bankruptcy Reform Law states that after filing a bankruptcy, the person cannot file a subsequent bankruptcy for eight years. So during this time period, bankruptcy is not an option if they get into financial hot water again.

For Franklin, facing up to his obligations would have required a sacrifice in his lifestyle but it was no comparison to the sacrifice in his self-worth and freedom of movement by running away. He could evade responsibility as long as he remained in hiding and never returned to the United States. Maybe in time, Franklin would realize the ultimate sacrifice he had made.

Ten Years Is a Long Time

The reason so many people choose to file a bankruptcy is that they want to have a fresh start. In reality, after the debts are gone, the memory lingers on your credit report for up to ten years. This fact is significant since your credit report is widely accessed. Not only do lenders pull your credit report, but so too do potential employers, life insurance companies, and landlords. Your credit report will be the basis for many decisions that will be made: your approval for a loan; your admittance to an apartment unit; or your getting a job. Your decision to file a bankruptcy should be influenced by the fact that credit reports are so powerful.

Julie received her first credit card when she was eighteen years old. She worked part-time at the mall. The department store she worked for offered employees a 10 percent discount on their purchases. However, they were required to buy them with the store's credit card. Julie added seven other credit cards to her collection by the time she graduated.

She used credit to buy anything and everything she wanted; she never denied herself. Before it seemed possible, she was $20,000 in debt and, having just graduated, was only making $24,000 at an entry-level job. Her credit card debt had become more than she could handle, so she decided to file bankruptcy. Among the most common reasons for resorting to a bankruptcy is "over-extended credit."

As she walked out of bankruptcy court, Julie felt relieved that the $20,000 in debts were finally behind her and her future had become a clean slate. All these months of worrying were for nothing. It definitely was worth the $1,000 she had paid to the bankruptcy lawyer. Julie was surprised how easy it was and that she didn't feel the guilt she had thought she would.

In the past, there used to be a measure of shame attached with filing bankruptcy. You hid the fact from your relatives, your friends, and your neighbors. In Japan, it is so shameful that many people have committed suicide after filing bankruptcy. Nowadays, bankruptcy has become more commonplace, and some people even regard it as a valid financial tool.

Julie had no regrets until she started running into situations where her credit report was being accessed. The first time occurred when she went shopping for a new car. She had agreed on the purchase price with the car salesman and the only thing that stood between her new car and taking the bus was her credit report. Unfortunately, her credit report showed her bankruptcy. This disqualified the deal and she was referred to another car dealer, who would be able to approve clients like Julie.

This dealer did offer Julie a loan on a new car, with an interest rate of 31 percent. Julie lived in a state where there is no usury law, which sets a limit on how high an interest rate can go. The lender justified this rate since she was a high-risk client, having filed bankruptcy. Julie passed on the offer and decided that the bus wasn't so bad after all.

Although you might agree that a high-risk customer should be penalized by having to pay a higher interest rate, you might not realize that the average customer is also paying a penalty. The average credit card interest rate is 18 percent. This rate has steadily increased over the years, in large part because of the increase in bankruptcies. As companies are forced to write off more accounts, the average consumer ends up recouping the company's losses by paying higher and higher rates of interest.

Just when Julie was getting adjusted to riding the bus and thought the inconvenience was minor compared to getting rid of her debts, she was laid off from her job. To her surprise, almost every company where she went for an interview requested to see her credit report. She could have refused, but they would have wondered what she was trying to conceal. Even though she believed she was a strong candidate for these jobs, she ended up not being offered a position by any of the companies. Julie had a feeling that the bankruptcy was behind their decisions.

Her lawyer had never told Julie that her Chapter 7 bankruptcy would appear on her credit report for ten years. She had assumed that it would remain for seven years like other negatives. She also didn't realize how powerful her credit report was and how often it would be accessed. Had she known these things, she might have thought twice before filing bankruptcy.

Time can serve to clean up your credit report. Making payments on time and never missing a payment can help to strengthen a credit report. Even though a Chapter 7 bankruptcy cannot be legally removed from your credit report before ten years, your actions after your bankruptcy are influential in the decision of whether to grant you credit again. If you have a flawless credit record for several years following a bankruptcy, a creditor may interpret this as a sign that you have learned your lesson. If you continue to act like a responsible money manager, the positives will soon outweigh the negatives and you can be considered a good credit risk again. Be careful that when that day comes, history doesn't repeat itself. Use your fresh start wisely and avoid making the same mistakes twice.

When Julie was contemplating filing for bankruptcy, either option Julie had to choose from presented its own negatives. To avoid bankruptcy, she would have had to scale down her lifestyle considerably in order to pay off her debts. She might have been forced to get an extra job. This alternative was undesirable since it involved giving things up or working more. On the other hand, if she chose bankruptcy, this decision would have left a negative legacy for ten years. There was no easy way out; it was just a matter of choice.

In the end, both routes would have resulted in the debts going away. The difference was in the memory of her decision. Which choice would she have been better able to live with: the decision to take responsibility and pay off her debts or the decision to avoid them and have the creditors write off the loss?

Words of Wisdom

Those who argue that people who file bankruptcy have learned a painful lesson and will not repeat it will be dismayed by the reality. In fact, the few studies done so far, according to the American Bankruptcy Institute, show that repeat filings vary widely by court district and type of filing, ranging from a low of 1 percent to more than 20 percent. These statistics are not surprising since without a change in habits, there can be no guarantee of a change in results. A bankruptcy can be like having someone else take an exam for you. You may end up passing the class, but did you learn anything?

Since the repercussions of filing a bankruptcy can be severe and long lasting, it only makes sense to explore other options prior to filing bankruptcy. If a bankruptcy is inevitable, make sure you learn from this experience and analyze the circumstances that led to this occurrence. The only thing worse than making a mistake is not learning from your mistake and repeating it again.

If you follow the lessons in this chapter, you will never be a bankruptcy statistic:

- Do not rely on credit as income.
- Stay within a safe level of debt (see Chapter 3).
- Ask others for help.
- Try to work out revised payment arrangements.
- Visit a nonprofit credit counselor.
- Remember that certain debts are exempted from bankruptcy.
- Stick to your budget when you receive extra money.
- Understand that a bankruptcy will appear on your credit report.
- Consider all other options before deciding to file.

Someone recently said, "There was a time when a fool and his money were soon parted, but now it happens to everybody!" I certainly do not believe that we are all fools. I truly believe that given the choice, most of us would rather amass money than have it slip away. The way to do this is through education. Although it's never too late to start learning, the power of preventative education cannot be underestimated.

Education is so important since today's young adults face a bewildering world where they will bear primary responsibility for funding their own retirement, and where terms like 401(k) plans, mutual funds, IRAs, and co-branded credit cards are part of everyday language. As technology grows, so will the selection of sophisticated, high-tech financial products and services for consumers.

To expect young adults to get through this financial maze without training is to invite disaster. Just as we wouldn't expect someone to know how to build a house just by giving him or her a saw, a hammer, and some wood, we shouldn't expect someone to know how to manage his or her finances just by receiving a mortgage and a credit card.

To help you reach financial wellness has been one of the goals of this book. Wellness not only means eliminating financial problems, but also accumulating wealth. However, a final word of caution is in order before this books ends: the obsession with the accumulation of money can be disastrous. Marriages have been wrecked, illnesses manifested, and corruption run rampant as the result of the pursuit of money. It is helpful to follow the wisdom of playwright Henrik Ibsen who said, "Money may be the husk of many things, but not the kernel. It brings you food, but not appetite; medicine, but not health; acquaintances, but not friends; servants, but not loyalty; days of joy, but not peace or happiness."

Appendix

Information Resources

American Bankers Association Education Foundation
www.aba.com/ABAEF

Your one-stop route for information and advice on banking and personal finance.

American Financial Services Association (AFSA) Education Foundation
www.afsaef.org

Education materials available to help you understand the credit process, where to go for help if credit problems occur, and to realize the benefits of responsible money management.

Annual Credit Report
www.annualcreditreport.com

This central site allows you to request a free credit file disclosure, commonly called a credit report, once every 12 months from each of the nationwide consumer credit reporting companies: Equifax, Experian and TransUnion

Bureau of Labor Statistics
www.bls.gov

Lists of hot jobs.
Salaries by profession.

Citi Cards
www.citicards.com

mtvU™ Platinum Select® Visa® Card for College Students
Earn ThankYou℠ Points for a good GPA, paying bills on time, buying books, music and more

College Parents of America
www.collegeparents.org

Membership organization for parents of college students.
Offers a one-stop shop for vital information and guidance leading to and through college.

Credit Counseling Agencies

Nonprofit agencies committed to assisting individuals with credit and other financial problems:

National Foundation for Credit Counseling
www.nfcc.org
800-388-2227

Association of Independent Consumer Credit Counseling Agencies
www.aiccca.org
866-703-8787

Money Management International
www.moneymanagement.org
866-889-9347

Employee Benefit Research Institute
www.choosetosave.org

A variety of free savings tools and brochures focused on topics such as Saving for Your Family's Future, Just

Starting Out, The Magic of Compounding, Maximizing Your Company Savings Plan, Why Open an IRA, It's Never Too Late to Save, and much more.

Federal Citizen Information Center
www.pueblo.gsa.gov
1-888-878-3256

Publishes a catalog of free consumer information materials.

Federal Trade Commission
www.ftc.gov

Check out the section on identity theft. You can report an incident to the FTC.

Jump$tart Coalition for Personal Financial Literacy
www.jumpstart.org

Database of financial literacy curriculum for students (K–college)—click on "clearinghouse."

List of youth and money websites—click on "resources" then "websites."

Morningstar
www.morningstar.com

Stock analysts' "picks and pans," research and financial data on funds, articles and market commentary, and more.

National Association of Investors Corporation (NAIC)
www.better-investing.org

A membership organization which provides investing knowledge and practical investing experience delivered through local investment clubs, regional chapters, web-based learning programs and an active online community

Sallie Mae
www.salliemae.com

Provides funds for federally guaranteed student loans. Offers parents, students, and educators comprehensive information on the financial aid process.

The Stock Market Game™
www.smgww.org

Sponsors the Stock Market Game™ (SMG) which gives students the chance to invest a hypothetical $100,000 in an on-line portfolio

Visa U.S.A.
www.visabuxx.com

Provides a prepaid card called Visa Buxx for teens. This debit card is a tool to teach financial responsibility.

Young Money
www.youngmoney.com

A leading national money, business and lifestyle magazine written primarily by student journalists. Young Money specifically focuses on money management, entrepreneurship, careers, investing, technology, travel, entertainment and automotive topics.

Index

N

O

P

Q

R

S

T

U

V

W

Y

About the Author

Photo by Paula Vlodkowsky

Dara Duguay, Director of Citi's Office of Financial Education, has been involved with the issue of financial literacy for over twenty years.

Ms. Duguay is the former Executive Director of the non-profit Jump$tart Coalition for Personal Financial Literacy in Washington, DC. Prior to her work at Jump$tart, she served as the Director of Education at the Consumer Credit Counseling Service (CCCS) of Los Angeles and was a professor at the University of Phoenix (1996–1997) and California State University (1993–1997). She is also the author of *The Citi Commonsense Money Guide for Real People* and *Don't Spend Your Raise: And 59 Other Money Rules You Can't Afford to Break.*

Ms. Duguay is considered a national expert on personal finance. Her media experience includes interviews in major U.S. print publications including the *New York Times*, *Associated Press*, *USA Today*, *Money Magazine*, *Parenting Magazine*, *Investors Business Daily*, *Child Magazine*, and *Better Homes and Gardens*, among others. In addition, she regularly appears as a guest on many national television and radio networks including National Public Radio, FOX News Channel, CNN, Bloomberg, and MSNBC. Ms. Duguay currently records a monthly segment called "Financial Fitness" on the Clear Channel radio network in

Washington, DC. She also is a featured columnist in a quarterly magazine distributed to the U.S. Military called *Military Money*.

An accomplished public speaker, Ms. Duguay has spoken at hundreds of major conferences, including the recent G8 summit in Moscow on financial literacy, the European Commission's summit on financial capacity, the OECD annual meeting, the National Association of State Treasurers, the Society of American Business Editors and Writers, and the American Bankers Association.

Among her many accomplishments, Ms. Duguay has received the Medal of Merit from the U.S. Treasury's Savings Bond Volunteer Committee (1999–2002), was appointed to the National Assessment of Educational Progress (NAEP) Economics Steering Committee, and has served in a consultant role to companies such as JP Morgan Chase, American Express, and Capital One.

Ms. Duguay received her BA in Communications from the University of Michigan and her MA in International Relations from Schiller University in Paris, France.